High Performance Images
Shrink, Load, and Deliver Images for Speed

Colin Bendell, Tim Kadlec, Yoav Weiss, Guy Podjarny,
Nick Doyle, and Mike McCall

Beijing · Boston · Farnham · Sebastopol · Tokyo

High Performance Images

by Colin Bendell, Tim Kadlec, Yoav Weiss, Guy Podjarny, Nick Doyle, and Mike McCall

Published by O'Reilly Media, Inc., 1005 Gravenstein Highway North, Sebastopol, CA 95472.

O'Reilly books may be purchased for educational, business, or sales promotional use. Online editions are also available for most titles (*http://safaribooksonline.com*). For more information, contact our corporate/institutional sales department: 800-998-9938 or corporate@oreilly.com.

Editor: Brian Anderson
Production Editor: Shiny Kalapurakkel
Copyeditor: Rachel Monaghan
Proofreader: Charles Roumeliotis

Indexer: Judy McConville
Interior Designer: David Futato
Cover Designer: Karen Montgomery
Illustrator: Rebecca Demarest

August 2016:   First Edition

Revision History for the First Edition

2016-08-25:   First Release
2016-10-31:   Second Release

See *http://oreilly.com/catalog/errata.csp?isbn=9781491925805* for release details.

978-1-491-92580-5

[LSI]

Table of Contents

Preface. . . . . **xi**

1. The Case for Performance. **1**
    What About Mobile Apps?   4
    Speed Matters   5
    Do Images Impact the Speed of Websites?   7
    Lingering Challenges   8

Part I.   Image Files and Formats

2. The Theory Behind Digital Images. **11**
    Digital Image Basics   12
        Sampling   12
        Image Data Representation   12
        Color Spaces   13
        Additive Versus Substractive   14
        Color Profiles   20
        Alpha Channel   21
        Frequency Domain   22
    Image Formats   22
        Why Image-Specific Compression?   23
        Raster Versus Vector   23
        Lossy Versus Lossless Formats   23
        Lossy Versus Lossless Compression   24
        Prediction   24
        Entropy Encoding   24
        Relationship with Video Formats   25
    Comparing Images   25
        PSNR and MSE   26

SSIM 26
Butteraugli 27
Summary 27

3. Lossless Image Formats. 29

GIF (It's Pronounced "GIF") 29
Block by Block 30
Animation 32
Transparency with GIF 33
LZW, or the Rise and Fall of the GIF 34
The PNG File Format 34
Understanding the Mechanics of the PNG Format 35
PNG Signature 35
Chunks 35
Filters 38
Interlacing 39
Image Formats 43
Transparency with PNG 44
There Can Be Only One! 45
Summary 45

4. JPEG. 47

History 47
The JPEG Format 48
Containers 48
Markers 48
Color Transformations 50
Subsampling 51
Entropy Coding 53
DCT 56
Progressive JPEGs 66
Unsupported Modes 69
JPEG Optimizations 70
Lossy 70
Lossless 70
MozJPEG 71
Summary 72

5. Browser-Specific Formats. 73

WebP 74
WebP Browser Support 74
WebP Details 75

WebP Tools   77
JPEG XR   77
   JPEG XR Browser Support   77
   JPEG XR Details   78
   JPEG XR Tools   79
JPEG 2000   79
   JPEG 2000 Browser Support   79
   JPEG 2000 Details   80
   JPEG 2000 Tools   82
Summary   82

6. SVG and Vector Images. **83**
The Trouble with Raster Formats   83
What Is a Vector Image?   84
SVG Fundamentals   85
   The Grid   86
   Understanding the Canvas   86
   viewBox   87
Getting into Shape   90
   Grouping Shapes Together   92
   Filters   97
SVG Optimizations   102
   Enabling GZip or Brotli   102
   Reducing Complexity   103
   Converting Text to Outlines   104
Automating Optimization Through Tooling   105
   Installing the SVGO Node Tool   106
   SVGOMG: The Better to See You With, My Dear 107
   Pick Your Flavor   108
Summary   108

Part II.   Image Loading

7. Browser Image Loading. **111**
Referencing Images   111
   <img> tag   112
   CSS background-image   113
When Are Images Downloaded?   116
   Building the Document Object Model   116
   The Preloader   117
   Networking Constraints and Prioritization 119

      HTTP/2 Prioritization   121
      CSSOM and Background Image Download   122
      Service Workers and Image Decoding   123
    Summary   124

8. Lazy Loading. **125**
    The Digital Fold   127
    Wasteful Image Downloads   127
    Why Aren't Browsers Dealing with This?   128
    Loading Images with JavaScript   128
      Deferred Loading   129
      Lazy Loading/Images On Demand   130
      IntersectionObserver   131
    When Are Images Loaded?   132
      The Preloader and Images   133
    Lazy Loading Variations   136
      Browsers Without JS   136
      Low-Quality Image Placeholders   137
      Critical Images   140
    Summary   141

9. Image Processing. **143**
    Decoding   143
      Measuring   144
      How Slow Can You Go?   150
      Memory Footprint   150
    GPU Decoding   152
      Triggering GPU Decoding   155
    Summary   155

10. Image Consolidation (for Network and Cache Efficiencies). **157**
    The Problem   158
      TCP Connections and Parallel Requests   158
      Small Objects Impact the Connection Pool   160
      Efficient Use of the Connection   161
      Impact on Browser Cache: Metadata and Small Images   162
      Small Objects Observed   164
      Logographic Pages   164
    Raster Consolidation   166
      CSS Spriting   166
      Data URIs   172
    Vector Image Consolidation   178

Icon Fonts   178
SVG Sprites   185
Summary   190

11. Responsive Images.. 193
How RWD Started   193
Early Hacks   194
Use Cases   195
Fixed-Dimensions Images   195
Variable-Dimensions Images   196
Art Direction   198
Art Direction Versus Resolution Switching   200
Image Formats   201
Avoiding "Download and Hide"   201
Use Cases Are Not Mutually Exclusive   201
Standard Responsive Images   203
srcset x Descriptor   203
srcset w Descriptor   204
<picture>   209
Serving Different Image Formats   213
Practical Advice   214
To Picturefill or Not to Picturefill, That Is the Question   214
Intrinsic Dimensions   215
Selection Algorithms   215
srcset Resource Selection May Change   216
Feature Detection   216
currentSrc   217
Client Hints   217
Are Responsive Images "Done"?   217
Background Images   217
Height Descriptors   218
Responsive Image File Formats   219
Progressive JPEG   219
JPEG 2000   220
Responsive Image Container   220
FLIF   220
Summary   220

12. Client Hints... 221
Overview   222
Step 1: Initiate the Client Hints Exchange   223
Step 2: Opt-in and Subsequent Requests   223

    Step 3: Informed Response   224
  Client Hint Components   224
    Viewport-Width   224
    Device Pixel Ratio   225
    Width   226
    Downlink   227
    Save-Data   228
    Accept-CH   229
    Content-DPR   229
  Mobile Apps   233
  Legacy Support and Device Characteristics   235
    Fallback: "Precise Mode" with Device Characteristics + Cookies   236
    Fallback: Good-Enough Approach   237
    Selecting the Right Image Width   238
  Summary   240

13. Image Delivery. **241**
  Image Dimensions   241
  Image Format Selection: Accept, WebP, JPEG 2000, and JPEG XR   244
  Image Quality   247
    Quality and Image Byte Size   247
    Quality Index and SSIM   249
    Selecting SSIM and Quality Use Cases   253
    Creating Consensus on Quality Index   254
    Quality Index Conclusion   255
  Achieving Cache Offload: Vary and Cache-Control   256
    Informing the Client with Vary   256
    Middle Boxes, Proxies with Cache-Control (and TLS)   257
    CDNs and Vary and Cache-Control   258
    Near Future: Key   260
  Single URL Versus Multiple URLs   260
  File Storage, Backup, and Disaster Recovery   261
    Size on Disk   262
    Cost of Metadata   263
  Domain Sharding and HTTP2   264
    How Do I Avoid Cache Busting and Redownloading?   267
    How Many Shards Should I Use?   267
    What Should I Do for HTTP/2?   267
    Best Practices   270
  Secure Image Delivery   270
    Secure Transport of Images   270
    Secure Transformation of Images   271

Secure Transformation: Architecture   273
Summary   275

14. **Operationalizing Your Image Workflow**................................... **277**
Some Use Cases   277
The e-Commerce Site   277
The Social Media Site   278
The News Site   279
Business Logic and Watermarking   280
Hello, Images   281
Getting Started with a Derivative Image Workflow   282
ImageMagick   282
A Simple Derivative Image Workflow Using Bash   290
An Image Build System   293
A Build System Checklist   296
High Volume, High Performance Images   297
A Dynamic Image Server   297

15. **Summary**.. **301**
So...What Do I Do Again?   302
Optimize for the Mobile Experience   302
Optimize for the Different "Users"   302
Creating Consensus   304

A. **Raster Image Formats**... **305**

B. **Common Tools**.. **307**

C. **Evolution of <img>**... **311**

Index... **323**

Preface

Colin Bendell

Images are are one of the best ways to communicate. So it's understandable that you might feel hoodwinked when you pick up a book filled with words discussing images. Rest assured, you will not be let down. Images are everywhere on the Web—from user-generated content to product advertisement to journalism to security. The creation, design, layout, processing, and delivery of images are no longer the exclusive domain of creative teams. Images on the Web are everyone's concern.

This book focuses on the essentials of what you need to deliver high performance images on the Internet. This is a very broad topic and covers many domains: color theory, image formats, storage and management, operations delivery, browser and application behavior, responsive web, and many topics in between. With this knowledge we hope that you can glean useful tips, tricks, and practical theory that will help you grow your business as you deliver high performance images.

Who Should Read This Book

We are software developers and wrote this book with developers in mind. Regardless of your role, if you find yourself responsible for any part of the life cycle of images, this book will be useful for you. It is intended to go both broad and deep, to give you background and context while also providing practical advice that will benefit your business.

What This Book Isn't

There are a great number of subjects that this book will not cover. Specifically, it will avoid topics in the creative process and image editing. It is not about graphic design, image editing tools, or the ways to optimize scratch memory and disk usage. In fact, this book will likely be a disappointment if you are looking for any discussion around RAW formats or video editing. Perhaps that is an opportunity for another book.

Navigating This Book

There is a lot of ground to cover in the area of high performance images. Images are a complex topic, so we have organized the chapters into two major parts: foundations and loading. In the foundation chapters (Part I), we cover image theory and how that applies to the different image formats. Each chapter is designed to stand on its own, so with a little background knowledge you can easily jump from one section to another. In the Loading chapters (Part II), we cover the impacts of these formats on the browser, the device, and the network.

Why We Wrote This Book

Thinking about images always reminds me of a fishing trip where I met the most cantankerous marlin in the freshwater lakes of Northern Canada. The fish was so big that it took nearly 45 minutes of wrestling to bring it aboard my canoe. At times, I wondered if I was going to be dragged to the depths of the lake. It was a whopping 1.5 m long and weighed 35 kg!

Pictures! Or it never happened.

If I were you, I'd be skeptical of my claims. To be honest, even I don't believe what I just wrote. I've never been fishing in my life! Not only that, but marlin live in the warmer Pacific Ocean, not the spring-fed lakes from the Atlantic Ocean. You are probably more likely to find a 35 kg beaver than a fish that size.

Images are at the core of storytelling, journalism, and advertising. We are good at retelling stories, but they can easily change from person to person. Remember the childhood game of "Telephone," where one kid whispers a phrase to the next person around a circle? The phrase "high performance images" would undoubtedly be transformed to "baby fart fart" in a circle of eight-year-old boys. But if we include a photograph, then the story gains fidelity and is less likely to change. Images add credibility to our stories.

The challenge is always in creating and communicating imagery. The fishing story created an image in your mind using 369 characters. Gzipped, that's 292 bytes for a mental image like the example in Figure P-1. But that image was just words and thus not reliable like the photo in Figure P-2.

Figure P-1. 292 bytes to create an image in your mind's eye

Figure P-2. In contrast, the photograph is 2.4 MB, which reveals my fraud (not me, not Canada, somewhere warm)

Words can conjure images fast but are very prone to corruption and low fidelity. Unless you know something about marlins, the geography of Northern Canada, or my angling expertise, you can't really grasp how "fishy" my story sounds. To get that detail you have to ask questions, questions that take time to send. To develop a high quality image in your mind, you need more time (see Figure P-3).

If only there were a more efficient way to communicate images—a way to communicate with high performance, if you will.

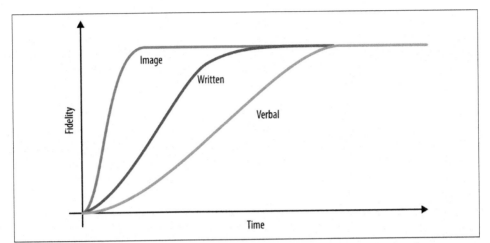

Figure P-3. How much time it takes to communicate image fidelity: graphical, written, and verbal[1]

Historically, creating images and graphics was hard. Cave paintings require specialized mixtures of substances and are prone to fading and washing away. You certainly wouldn't want to waste your efforts creating a cave painting of a cat playing a piano! Over the last century, photography has certainly made images cheaper and less laborious to produce. Yet, with each advance in image creation, we have increased the challenge of transmission. Just think of the complexity of adding images to a book prior to modern software. Printing an image involved creating plates that were inked separately for each color used and then pressed one at a time on the same page—very inefficient!

With ubiquitous smartphones equipped with high-quality cameras, we can take high-resolution images in mere milliseconds. And yet, despite this ease, it is still challenging to send and receive photos. The problem is that—despite the facts that our screen displays are high resolution and have high pixel density ratios; our websites and applications have richer content; our cameras are capable of taking high-quality photographs; and our image libraries have grown—it feels as though our ISPs and mobile networks cannot keep up with the insatiable user demands for data.

This transmission challenge affects not only photos, but also the interfaces for our applications and websites. These too are increasingly using graphics and images to aid users in completing their work more efficiently and more effectively. Yet, if we

---

1 Bailey, R.W. and Bailey, L.M. (1999), Reading speeds using RSVP, User Interface Update (400 words per minute) (*http://www.humanfactors1.com/downloads/feb99.asp*); and Omoigui, N., He, L., Gupta A., Grudin, J. and Sanocki, E. (1999), Time-compression: Systems concerns, usage, and benefits, CHI 99 Conference Proceedings, 136-143 (210 words per minute).

cannot transmit these graphical interfaces efficiently or render them on the screens with high performance, then we are no better off than if we were trying to do a Gopher search on an old VIC-20. While any reference to dark age computing warms the depths of my heart, I want to believe our technology has enabled us to be more effective in our jobs and advanced our ability to transmit images.

This is where we start: no more fish tales. We begin with the question of how we communicate and present images and graphics to a user with high performance. This book is about high performance images, but it is also a story about rasters and vectors, icons, graphics, and bitmaps. It is the story of an evolving communication medium. It is also the story of journalism, free speech, and commerce. Without high performance images, how would we share cultural memes like the blue and white (or was that gold and black?) dress (*http://bit.ly/2bmGpcd*) or share the unsettling reality of the Arab Spring? We need high performance images.

Acknowledgments

Thanks to Pat Meenan and Eric Lawrence for providing detailed feedback throughout the writing of this book. And special thanks to Yaara Weiss for providing the foxy fox illustrations in Chapter 11.

Conventions Used in This Book

The following typographical conventions are used in this book:

Italic
    Indicates new terms, URLs, email addresses, filenames, and file extensions.

`Constant width`
    Used for program listings, as well as within paragraphs to refer to program elements such as variable or function names, databases, data types, environment variables, statements, and keywords.

`Constant width bold`
    Shows commands or other text that should be typed literally by the user.

`Constant width italic`
    Shows text that should be replaced with user-supplied values or by values determined by context.

 This element signifies a tip or suggestion.

This element signifies a general note.

 This element indicates a warning or caution.

Using Code Examples

This book is here to help you get your job done. In general, if example code is offered with this book, you may use it in your programs and documentation. You do not need to contact us for permission unless you're reproducing a significant portion of the code. For example, writing a program that uses several chunks of code from this book does not require permission. Selling or distributing a CD-ROM of examples from O'Reilly books does require permission. Answering a question by citing this book and quoting example code does not require permission. Incorporating a significant amount of example code from this book into your product's documentation does require permission.

We appreciate, but do not require, attribution. An attribution usually includes the title, author, publisher, and ISBN. For example: "*High Performance Images* by Colin Bendell, Tim Kadlec, Yoav Weiss, Guy Podjarny, Nick Doyle, and Mike McCall (O'Reilly). Copyright 2016 Akamai Technologies, 978-1-4919-3826-3."

If you feel your use of code examples falls outside fair use or the permission given above, feel free to contact us at *permissions@oreilly.com*.

Safari® Books Online

 Safari Books Online is an on-demand digital library that delivers expert content in both book and video form from the world's leading authors in technology and business.

Technology professionals, software developers, web designers, and business and creative professionals use Safari Books Online as their primary resource for research, problem solving, learning, and certification training.

Safari Books Online offers a range of plans and pricing for enterprise, government, education, and individuals.

Members have access to thousands of books, training videos, and prepublication manuscripts in one fully searchable database from publishers like O'Reilly Media, Prentice Hall Professional, Addison-Wesley Professional, Microsoft Press, Sams, Que, Peachpit Press, Focal Press, Cisco Press, John Wiley & Sons, Syngress, Morgan Kaufmann, IBM Redbooks, Packt, Adobe Press, FT Press, Apress, Manning, New Riders, McGraw-Hill, Jones & Bartlett, Course Technology, and hundreds more. For more information about Safari Books Online, please visit us online.

How to Contact Us

Please address comments and questions concerning this book to the publisher:

O'Reilly Media, Inc.
1005 Gravenstein Highway North
Sebastopol, CA 95472
800-998-9938 (in the United States or Canada)
707-829-0515 (international or local)
707-829-0104 (fax)

We have a web page for this book, where we list errata, examples, and any additional information. You can access this page at *http://shop.oreilly.com/product/0636920039730.do*.

To comment or ask technical questions about this book, send email to *bookquestions@oreilly.com*.

For more information about our books, courses, conferences, and news, see our website at *http://www.oreilly.com*.

Find us on Facebook: *http://facebook.com/oreilly*

Follow us on Twitter: *http://twitter.com/oreillymedia*

Watch us on YouTube: *http://www.youtube.com/oreillymedia*

CHAPTER 1

The Case for Performance

Colin Bendell

Images are awesome. Which website would you prefer to navigate: a text-only site or one that has a crisp layout and rich, visually appealing content to inform your purchases? Like most people, you probably agree that the rich visual experience is much preferred, but with one condition: that it doesn't get in your way and interfere with whatever activity you are doing.

Numerous studies have concluded what we all know instinctively: that more and higher-quality images lead to higher user engagement (*http://bit.ly/2axyk4N*) and greater conversions (*http://bit.ly/2axygSK*):

- Forrester Research has noted a 75% increase in user expectations for rich content and images on websites and applications: users demand images!

- eBay notes in their seller center that listings with larger images (>800 px) are 5% more likely to sell (*http://ebay.to/2aVxJtF*).

- Facebook observes 105% more comments (*http://bit.ly/2aLjnsP*) on posts with photos over those without.

- Eye-tracking studies done by Nielsen Norman Group also conclude that users will engage most of their time with relevant images when given the chance.

   Users pay close attention to photos and other images that contain relevant information but ignore fluffy pictures used to "jazz up" web pages.[1]

   —Jakob Nielson

---

1 *http://www.nngroup.com/articles/photos-as-web-content/*

Adding graphics and photos in your web or native applications is easy. There are bountiful tools that help you edit photos and design graphics. It is even easier to embed these images in your websites and have full confidence that these images will display just as you intended.

The volume of images being served to end users is growing at an astonishing rate. At the time of writing, Akamai serves over 1,500,000,000,000 (1.5 trillion) images each day to the people on this planet—not including the use of favicon.ico. More incredible is that both the quantity and size of these images are increasing at an astonishing rate. If you sit still and stare at your smartphone I'm sure you will almost be able to see the images grow before your eyes.

Arguably the number of humans on the Internet has also increased at a staggering rate. In the same time that we have added over 600 million people (*http://bit.ly/2b5yD2T*) to the Internet and over 1 billion smartphones (*http://bit.ly/2awYWwV*), the collective web has also doubled the volume of images on an average web page (Figure 1-1). In just three years, according to HTTP Archive (*http://httparchive.org*), the *average* image has grown from 14 KB to 24 KB (Figure 1-2). That's a whopping 1.4 MB per web page (*http://httparchive.org/interesting.php*). This average assumes that users visit sites with the same distribution as HTTP Archive's index. The reality is that users visit sites with more images more frequently (particularly social media sites). This means that an average visited website likely has a much higher volume of images.

Only font growth outpaced image growth, both driven by superior layout and design. Curiously, many of the most common fonts used are icon fonts—images in disguise.

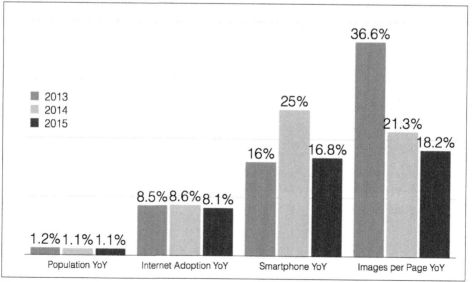

Figure 1-1. Growth rate year-over-year

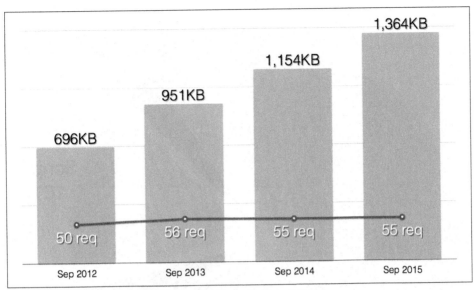

Figure 1-2. Images have doubled in size from 2012 to 2015

Not surprisingly, images make up 63% of the average web page download bytes (Figure 1-3). Interestingly this hasn't changed much as a percentage over time.

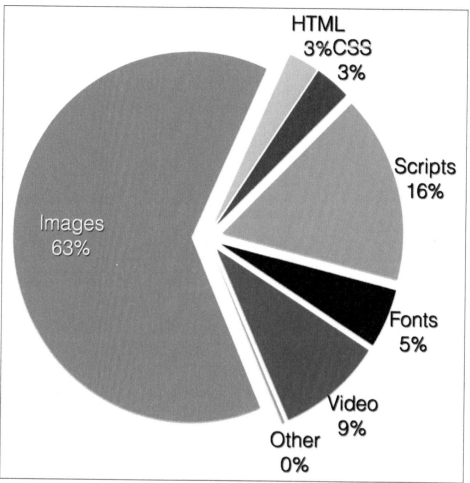

Figure 1-3. HttpArchive.org web page composition (2015)

What About Mobile Apps?

So far we've talked about the impact of images on web pages, but what about mobile and native applications? On the surface, mobile apps, like those on Android and iOS, appear different. Yet they suffer from the same challenges as the browser and web pages.

Apps can differ from websites: apps pre-position their images by containing them in a packaged archive like an *.ipa* or *.apk*. On the other hand, the image formats and image loaders that modern smartphones use are standing on the shoulders of the same technology that browsers have evolved to use. Even apps that don't load over the network are concerned about how quickly they can load and display on the device.

Many apps, like unit converters or offline games, are not network aware. Yet there are many other apps, including news, shopping, and social media apps, that do depend on network access for rich content like images. In fact, since most of these apps don't have to send JavaScript and CSS like their web page counterparts, the number of images as a percentage of traffic is just as much a concern. Consider a recent profiling of the CNN application. In an average session (reading headlines and one article), you see a similar breakdown in content types (Figure 1-4).

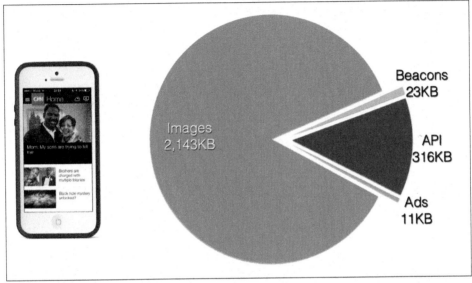

Figure 1-4. Content breakdown on the CNN mobile app

Speed Matters

It can't be said enough: speed matters! Numerous studies have shown the impact of web page performance on your business. Faster websites increase user engagement and revenue and can even drive down COGS (cost of goods sold). Conveniently, WPOstats.com maintains an up-to-date repository of these studies and experiments (Figure 1-5). The bottom line is that the faster your web page is, the more money you'll make.

Figure 1-5. *Case studies and experiments demonstrating the impact of web performance optimization (WPO) on user experience and business metrics*

Fortunately, modern web browsers use preloaders to rapidly discover and download images (though at a lower priority compared to more important resources). Additionally, image loading doesn't block the rendering and interaction of a web page. Similar techniques are available for native apps as well.

The average Internet connection is ever increasing in bandwidth and decreasing in latency. This is good news for loading web pages! The downside is that it isn't growing as fast as images or user demand. Even more challenging is that a growing percentage of web traffic happens over cellular connections. Consider that cellular is ultimately a shared medium. There is only so much spectrum and you share it with the people around you on the same tower. Even as each generation of cellular technology emerges, the new bandwidth discovered quickly erodes as more people utilize the new technology. OpenSignal conducted a study in 2014 of the average LTE connection in the UK. As you would expect, early adopters of LTE started happy, but within a year were probably grumpy because every tween was eating away at their precious bandwidth capacity.

Do Images Impact the Speed of Websites?

Despite browser optimizations to load images in the background, network performance can impact not just the loading of the images proper, but also the loading of the web page itself. If we removed all images from the top 1,000 websites, these sites would load 30% faster on average over 3G (Figure 1-6). I sure hope those images weren't important to selling the product. Clearly we don't want to turn off images and return to the days of the Lynx browser.

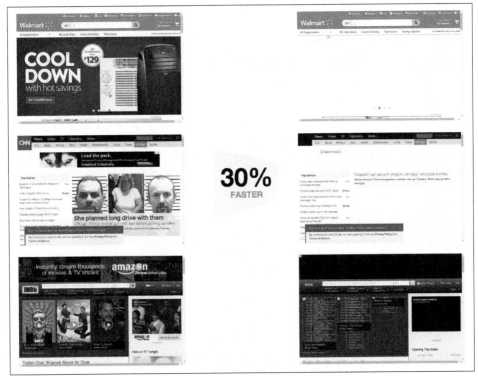

Figure 1-6. Websites without images load 30% faster on average over 3G

Beautiful images and rich interfaces add value; they are clearly not going away. Fortunately, there are many techniques and methods to improve performance of this rich content. Before we dive into the options, it is important to understand the scope of the problem we are charged with solving. To do this, we need to step into our way-back machine.

Lingering Challenges

The following chapters will explore how to balance the highest-quality image with performance—specifically, how to select the right image size for the device and for the network. This is no simple task. We have many formats to choose from with different techniques to optimize for high performance. Complicating this further are the network conditions. How do we factor in latency or low bandwidth when deciding what to serve a user to give the best experience? And what about our Infrastructure and Operations teams, who have to deal with the complexity of the many images now stored, processed, and included in their disaster recovery plan? There are many factors to balance to deliver high-quality images.

Image Files and Formats

Colin Bendell

This first part of this book focuses on the core knowledge you need before we dive into image loading in the second part. It includes discussions on color theory, image types, formats, and image capabilities. Unfortunately, there isn't a single solution for digitally encoding images. Understanding these complexities and the many image use cases is important before we address image loading. Depending on your familiarity with these subjects, you might be tempted to skip over some chapters and jump straight to Part II. That's fine. These chapters are intended to be used as a reference and to help you navigate the complexities of bringing high-quality images to your users.

CHAPTER 2

The Theory Behind Digital Images

Yoav Weiss

Images are an essential part of human history. Film-based photography has made the creation of images easy—it captures a moment in time by allowing light to go through a lens and hit film, where an array of minuscule grains of silver-based compound change their brightness as a response to light intensity.

With the advent of computers, soon came the digitization of photos, initially through the scanning of printed images to digital formats, and then through digital camera prototypes.

Eventually, commercial digital cameras started showing up alongside film-based ones, ultimately replacing them in the public's eye (and hand). Camera phones also contributed, with most of us now walking around with high-resolution digital cameras in our pockets.

A digital camera is very similar to a film-based one, except instead of silver grains it has a matrix of light sensors to capture light beams. These photosensors then send electronic signals representing the various colors captured to the camera's processor, which stores the final image in memory as a bitmap—a matrix of pixels—before (usually) converting it to a more compact image format. This kind of image is referred to as a *photographic image*, or more commonly, a *photo*.

But that's not the only way to produce digital images. Humans wielding computers can create images without capturing any light by manipulating graphic creation software, taking screenshots, or many other means. We usually refer to such images as *computer-generated images*, or *CGI*.

This chapter will discuss digital images and the theoretical foundations behind them.

Digital Image Basics

In order to properly understand digital images and the various formats throughout this book, you'll need to have some familiarity with the basic concepts and vocabulary.

We will discuss sampling, colors, entropy coding, and the different types of image compression and formats. If this sounds daunting, fear not. This is essential vocabulary that we need in order to dig deeper and understand how the different image formats work.

Sampling

We learned earlier that digital photographic images are created by capturing light and transforming it into a matrix of pixels. The size of the pixel matrix is what we refer to when discussing the image's dimensions—the number of different pixels that compose it, with each pixel representing the color and brightness of a point in two-dimensional space that is the image.

If we look at light before it is captured, it is a continuous, analog signal. In contrast, a captured image of that light is a discrete, digital signal (see Figure 2-1). The process of converting the analog signal to a digital one involves sampling, when the values of the analog signal are sampled in regular frequency, producing a discrete set of values.

Our sampling rate is a tradeoff between fidelity to the original analog signal and the amount of data we need to store and submit. Sampling plays a significant role in reducing the amount of data digital images contain, enabling their compression. We'll expand on that later on.

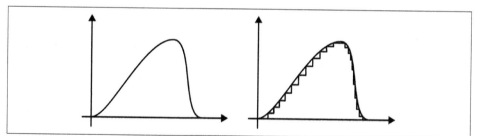

Figure 2-1. To the left, a continous signal; to the right, a sampled discrete signal

Image Data Representation

The simplest way to represent an image is by using a *bitmap*—a matrix as large as the image's width and height, where each cell in the matrix represents a single pixel and can contain its color for a color image or just its brightness for a grayscale image (see

Figure 2-2). Images that are represented using a bitmap (or a variant of a bitmap) are often referred to as *raster images*.

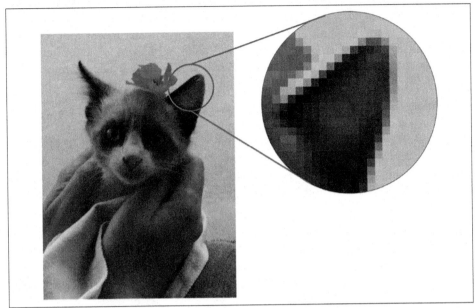

Figure 2-2. Each part of the image is composed of discrete pixels, each with its own color

But how do we digitally represent a color? To answer that we need to get familiar with the following topics.

Color Spaces

We've seen that a bitmap is a matrix of pixels, and each pixel represents a color. But how do we represent a color using a numeric value?

In order to dive into that, we'll need to take a short detour to review color theory basics. Our eyes are built similarly to the digital camera we discussed earlier, where the role of photosensitive electronic cells is performed by light-sensitive pigmented biological cells called *rods* and *cones*. Rods operate in very low light volumes and are essential for vision in very dim lighting, but play almost no part in color vision. Cones, on the other hand, operate only when light volumes are sufficient, and are responsible for color vision.

Humans have three different types of cones, each responsible for detecting a different light spectrum, and therefore, for seeing a different color. These three different colors are considered primary colors: red, green, and blue. Our eyes use the colors the cones detect (and the colors they don't detect) to create the rest of the color spectrum that we see.

Additive Versus Substractive

There are two types of color creation: additive and subtractive. Additive colors are colors that are created by a light source, such as a screen. When a computer needs a screen's pixel to represent a different color, it *adds* the primary color required to the colors emitted by that pixel. So, the "starting" color is black (absence of light) and other colors are added until we reach the full spectrum of light, which is white.

Conversely, printed material, paintings, and non-light-emitting physical objects get their colors through a subtractive process. When light from an external source hits these materials, only some light wavelengths are reflected back from the material and hit our eyes, creating colors. Therefore, for physical materials, we often use other primary subtractive colors, which are then mixed to create the full range of colors. In that model, the "starting" color is white (the printed page), and each color we add *subtracts* light from that, until we reach black when all color is subtracted (see Figure 2-3).

As you can see, there are multiple ways to re-create a sufficient color range from the values of multiple colors. These various ways are called *color spaces*. Let's explore some of the common ones.

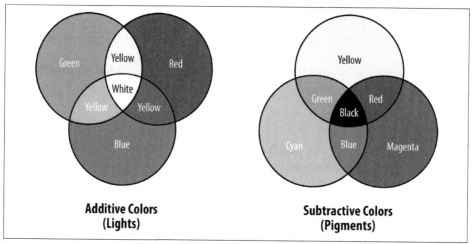

Figure 2-3. Additive colors created by light versus substractive colors created by pigments (image taken from Wikipedia (http://bit.ly/2aOUNt9))

RGB (red, green, and blue)

RGB is one of the most popular color spaces (or color space families). The main reason for that is that screens, which are additive by nature (they emit light, rather than reflect light from an external light source), use these three primary pixel colors to create the range of visible colors.

The most commonly used RGB color space is sRGB, which is the standard color space for the W3C (World Wide Web Consortium), among other organizations. In many cases, it is assumed to be the color space used for RGB unless otherwise specified. Its *gamut* (the range of colors that it can represent, or how saturated the colors that it represents can be) is more limited than other RGB color spaces, but it is considered a baseline that all current color screens can produce (see Figure 2-4).

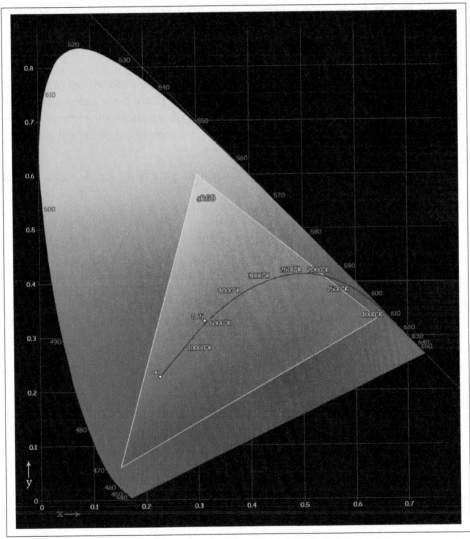

Figure 2-4. The sRGB gamut (image taken from http://bit.ly/2aOUNt9)

CMYK (cyan, magenta, yellow, and key)

CMYK is a subtractive color space most commonly used for printing. The "key" component is simply black. Instead of having three components for each pixel as RGB color spaces do, it has four components. The reasons for that are print-related practicalities. While in theory we could achieve the black color in the subtractive model by combining cyan, magenta, and yellow, in practice the outcome black is not "black enough," long to dry, and too expensive. Since black printing is quite common, that resulted in a black component being added to the color space.

YCbCr

YCbCr is actually not a color space on its own, but more of a model that can be used to represent gamma-corrected RGB color spaces. The Y stands for gamma-corrected luminance (the brightness of the sum of all colors), Cb stands for the chroma component of the blue color, and Cr stands for the chroma component of the red color (see Figure 2-6).

RGB color spaces can be converted to YCbCr through a fairly simple mathematical formula, shown in Figure 2-5.

$$
\begin{aligned}
Y' &= \quad 0 + (0.299 \quad \cdot R'_D) + (0.587 \quad \cdot G'_D) + (0.114 \quad \cdot B'_D) \\
C_B &= 128 - (0.168736 \quad \cdot R'_D) - (0.331264 \quad \cdot G'_D) + (0.5 \quad \cdot B'_D) \\
C_R &= 128 + (0.5 \quad \cdot R'_D) - (0.418688 \quad \cdot G'_D) - (0.081312 \quad \cdot B'_D)
\end{aligned}
$$

Figure 2-5. Formula to convert from RGB to YCbCr

One advantage of the YCbCr model over RGB is that it enables us to easily separate the brightness parts of the image data from the color ones. The human eye is more sensitive to brightness changes than it is to color ones, and the YCbCr color model enables us to harness that to our advantage when compressing images. We will touch on that in depth later in the book.

Figure 2-6. French countryside in winter, top to bottom, left to right: full image, Y component, Cb component, and Cr component

YCgCo

YCgCo is conceptually very similar to YCbCr, only with different colors. *Y* still stands for gamma-corrected luminance, but *Cg* stands for the green chroma component, and *Co* stands for the orange chroma component (see Figure 2-7).

YCgCo has a couple of advantages over YCbCr. The RGB⇔YCgCo transformations (shown in Figure 2-8) are mathematically (and computationally) simpler than RGB⇔YCbCr. On top of that, YCbCr transformation may lose some data in practice due to rounding errors, whereas the YCgCo transformations do not, since they are "friendlier" to floating-point fractional arithmetic.

Figure 2-7. French countryside in winter, top to bottom, left to right: full image, Y component, Cg component, and Co component

$$\begin{bmatrix} Y \\ Cg \\ Co \end{bmatrix} = \begin{bmatrix} 1/4 & 1/2 & 1/4 \\ -1/4 & 1/2 & -1/4 \\ 1/2 & 0 & -1/2 \end{bmatrix} \cdot \begin{bmatrix} R \\ G \\ B \end{bmatrix}$$

Figure 2-8. Formula to convert from RGB to YCgCo (note the use of powers of 1/2, which makes this transformation easy to compute and float-friendly)

There are many other color spaces and models, but going over all of them is beyond the scope of this book. The aforementioned color models are all we need to know in order to further discuss images on the Web.

Bit depth

Now that we've reviewed different color spaces, which can have a different number of components (three for RGB, four for CMYK), let's address how precise each of the components should be.

Color spaces are a continous space, but in practice, we want to be able to define coordinates in that space. The unit measuring the precision of these coordinates for each component is called *bit depth*—it's the number of bits that you dedicate to each of your color components.

What should that bit depth be? Like everything in computer science, the correct answer is "it depends."

For most applications, 8 bits per component is sufficient to represent the colors in a precise enough manner. In other cases, especially for high-fidelity photography, more bits per component may be used in order to maintain color fidelity as close to the original as possible.

One more interesting characteristic of human vision is that its sensitivity to light changes is not linear across the range of various colors. Our eyes are significantly more sensitive when light intensity is low (so in darker environments) than they are when light intensity is high. That means that humans notice changes in darker colors far more than they notice changes in lighter colors. To better grasp that, think about how lighting a candle in complete darkness makes a huge difference in our ability to see what's around us, while lighting the same candle (emitting the same amount of photons) outside on a sunny day makes almost no difference at all.

Cameras capture light differently. The intensity of light that they capture is linear to the amount of photons they get in the color range that they capture. So, light intensity changes will result in corresponding brightness changes, regardless of the initial brightness.

That means that if we represent all color data as captured by our cameras using the same number of bits per pixel, our representation is likely to have too many bits per pixel for the brighter colors and too few for the darker ones. What we really want is to have the maximum amount of meaningful, visibly unique values that represent each pixel, for bright as well as dark colors.

A process called *gamma correction* is designed to bridge that gap between linear color spaces and "perceptually linear" ones, making sure that light changes of the same magnitude are equally noticeable by humans, regardless of initial brightness (see Figure 2-9).

Figure 2-9. A view of the French countryside in winter, gamma-corrected on the left and uncorrected on the right

Encoders and decoders

Image compression, like other types of compression, requires two pieces of software: an encoder that converts the input image into a compressed stream of bytes and a decoder that takes a compressed stream of bytes and converts it back to an image that the computer can display.

This system is sometimes referred to as a *codec*, which stands for *coder/decoder*.

When discussing image compression techniques of such a dual system, the main thing to keep in mind is that each compression technique imposes different constraints and considerations on both the encoder and decoder, and we have to make sure that those constraints are realistic.

For example, a theoretical compression technique that requires a lot of processing to be done on the decoder's end may not be feasible to implement and use in the context of the Web, since decoding on, e.g., phones, would be too slow to provide any practical value to our users.

Color Profiles

How does the encoder know which color space we referred to when we wrote down our pixels? That's where something called *International Color Consortium (ICC)* or color *profiles* come in.

These profiles can be added to our images as metadata and help the decoder accurately convert the colors of each pixel in our image to the equivalent colors in the local display's "coordinate system."

If the color profile is missing, the decoder cannot perform this conversion, and as a result, its reaction varies. Some browsers will assume that an image with no color profile is in the sRGB color space and will automatically convert it from that space to the local display's color space. At the same time, other browsers will send the image's pixels to the screen as they are, effectively assuming that the color profile the images were encoded in matches the screen's. That can result in some color distortion, so where color fidelity is important, color profiles are essential for cross-browser color correctness.

On the other hand, adding a color profile can add a non-negligable number of bytes to your image. A good tradeoff is to make sure your images are in the sRGB color space and add a fairly small sRGB (*http://bit.ly/2ax0sPH*) color profile to them.

We will discuss how you can manage and control your images' color profiles more in Chapter 14.

Alpha Channel

We discussed all the possible options we have to represent colors, but we left something out. How do we represent lack of color?

In some cases we want parts of our image to be transparent or translucent, so that our users will see a nonrectangular image, or otherwise will be able to see through the image onto its background.

The representation of the absence of color is called an *alpha channel* (see Figure 2-10). It can be considered a fourth color, where the zero value means that the other three colors are fully transparent, and a maximal value means that the other three colors are fully visible.

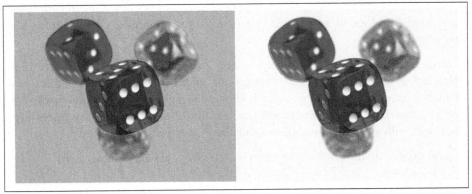

Figure 2-10. An image with an alpha channel over different backgrounds; note the different colors of the dice edges (image taken from Wikipedia (http://bit.ly/2aWYdIO))

Frequency Domain

As we now know, we can break our images into three components: one brightness component and two color ones. We can think of each component as a two-dimensional function that represents the value of each pixel in the spatial domain, where the x- and y-axis are the height and width of the image, and the function's value is the brightness/color value of each pixel (see Figure 2-11).

Figure 2-11. The Y component of an image, plotted as a 2D function

Therefore, we can apply certain mathematical transforms on these functions, in order to convert them from the spatial domain into the frequency domain. A frequency domain-based representation gives us the frequency at which each pixel value is changing rather than its value. Conversion to the frequency domain can be interesting, since it enables us to separate high-frequency brightness changes from low-frequency changes.

It turns out that another characteristic of human vision is that we notice high-frequency brightness and color changes significantly less than we notice low-frequency ones. If brightness or color is changing significantly from one pixel to the next and then back again, our eye will tend to "mush" these neighboring pixels into a single area with an overall brightness value that is somewhere in between.

We will expand on how this works when we talk about JPEGs in Chapter 4.

Image Formats

In the following chapters we will discuss the various image formats that are in common use today. But before we can dive into the details of each format, let's explore the slightly philosophical question: what is image compression and why it is needed?

Why Image-Specific Compression?

As you may have guessed, image compression is a compression technique targeted specifically at images. While many generic compression techniques exist—such as Gzip, LZW, LZMA, Bzip2, and others—when it comes to raster images, we can often do better. These generic compression algorithms work by looking for repetitions and finding better (read: shorter) ways to represent them.

While that works remarkably well for text and some other types of documents, for most images, it's not enough. That kind of compression can reduce the number of used bytes for bitmap images that have lots of pixels of *exactly* the same color right next to one another. While that's great, most images—especially those representing real-life photography—don't exhibit these characteristics.

So, pretty early on, various image compression techniques and related formats began to form and eventually a few formats were standardized. Many of these image compression techniques use generic compression techniques internally, but do so as part of a larger scheme that maximizes their benefits.

Raster Versus Vector

Raster versus vector-based images is the first fundamental divide when discussing image formats and compression techniques.

As previously mentioned, a raster image comprises a rectangular matrix called a bitmap. Each value in that matrix represents the color of a certain pixel that the computer can then copy to its graphics memory to paint to the screen.

Unlike raster images, vector images don't contain the colors of individual pixels. Instead, they contain mathematical instructions that enable the computer to calculate and draw the image on its own.

While vector images can have many advantages over raster images in various scenarios, raster images are more widely applicable. They can be used for both computer-generated graphics as well as real-life photos, whereas vector images can only be efficiently used for the former.

Therefore, throughout the book, unless otherwise specified, we will mostly be referring to raster images, with the main exception being Chapter 6.

Lossy Versus Lossless Formats

Another characteristic that separates the various formats is whether or not they incur a loss of image information as part of the compression process. Many formats perform various "calculated information loss" in order to reduce the eventual file size.

Quite often that loss in image information (and therefore image precision and fidelity to the original) aims to reduce information that is hardly noticed by the human eye, and is based on studies of human vision and its characteristics. Despite that, it's not unheard of for precision loss to be noticeable, which may be more critical for some applications than others.

Therefore, there are both lossy and lossless image formats, which can answer those two different use cases: image compression that maintains 100% fidelity to the original versus compression that can endure some information loss while gaining compression ratio.

Lossy Versus Lossless Compression

While the formats themselves can be lossy or lossless, there are various examples where images can undergo lossy as well as lossless compression, regardless of the target format. Metadata that is not relevant to the image's display (where the image was taken, camera type, etc.) can be removed from images, resulting in arguably lossless compression even if the target format is lossy. Similarly, image information can be removed from the image before it is saved as the target format, resulting in lossy compression of a lossless image format.

One exception to that case is that you cannot save an image losslessly in a format that only has a lossy variant. This is because these formats usually apply some degree of loss as part of their encoding process, and that cannot be circumvented.

We will further discuss lossless and lossy compression in Chapter 14.

Prediction

Often, the encoding and decoding processes both include some guess of what a pixel value is likely to be, based on surrounding pixel values, and then the actual pixel value is calculated as the offset from the "expected" color. That way we can often represent the pixel using smaller, more compressible values.

Entropy Encoding

Entropy encoding is a very common generic compression technique that is used to give the most frequent symbols the shortest representation, so that the entire message is as compact as possible. Entropy coding is often used in image compression to further compress the data after the main image-specific parts are performed.

Since entropy encoding requires us to know what the most frequent symbols are, it typically involves two steps. The first pass gathers statistics regarding the frequency of words in the data, and then creates a dictionary translating those words into symbols from the frequency data. The second pass translates the words into shorter symbols using the previously created dictionary.

In some domains, where word frequency is known in advance with a good enough approximation, the first step is skipped and a ready-made frequency-based dictionary is used instead. The result is a potentially slightly larger data stream, but with the advantage of a single-pass algorithm that is faster and possible to perform on the fly.

When you are compressing content using entropy encoding, the dictionary used for the encoding has to be present in the decoder as well. Sending the dictionary data adds a "cost" to entropy encoding that somewhat reduces its benefits.

Other types of entropy encoding permit adaptive encoding, where a single pass over the data is enough. Such encodings count the frequency and assign codes to symbols as they go, but change the code assigned to each symbol as its frequency changes.

Relationship with Video Formats

One important thing to keep in mind about image formats is that they share many aspects with video formats. In a way video formats are image formats with extra capabilities that enable them to represent intermediary images based upon previous full images, with relatively low cost. That means that inside every video format, there's also an image format that is used to compress those full images. Many new efforts in the image compression field come from adopting compression techniques from the video compression world, or adopting the still image encoding parts (called *I-frame encoding*) from video formats and building an image format based on that (e.g., WebP, which we will discuss later on).

Comparing Images

Comparing the quality of an image compressed using different settings, different encoders, or different formats is not a trivial task when it comes to lossy compression. Since the goal of lossy image compression is achieving quality loss that, to some extent, flies under most people's radar, any comparison has to take both the visual quality of the image and its eventual byte size into account.

If you're trying to compare the quality and size of a single image, you can probably do so by looking at the image output of different encoding processes and trying to "rank" the variants in your head, but that is hardly scalable when you have many images to compare, and it is impossible to automate.

As it turns out, there are multiple algorithms that try to do just that. They give various "scores" when comparing the compressed images to their originals, enabling you to tune your compression to the visual impact compression would have on the image, rather than to arbitrary "quality" settings.

PSNR and MSE

The Peak Singal-to-Noise Ratio (PSNR) is a metric that estimates the ratio of error introduced by the compression alogorithm. It often uses Mean-Square-Error (MSE) in order to do that. In a nutshell, MSE is the average mathematical distance of the pixels in the compressed image from the original one. PSNR calculates that and uses the ratio between the maximum possible pixel value to the MSE in order to estimate the impact of compression on the image.

That method works to estimate divergence from the original, but it's not necessarily tied to the impact of that divergence on the user's perception of the compressed image. As we'll see later on, some formats rely on further compressing parts of the image that are less noticeable by the human eye in order to achieve better compression ratios with little perceived quality loss. Unfortunately, PSNR and MSE don't take that into account, and therefore may be skewed against such formats and techniques.

SSIM

Structural Similiarity (SSIM) is a metric that tries to take the image's structure into account when calculating the errors in the image. It operates under the assumption that human visual perception is adapted to extract structural information, and therefore deterioration in the structural contents of an image would mean that it would be perceived as a lower-quality image.

The algorithm estimates structural changes by comparing the intensity and contrast changes between pixel blocks in both the original and compressed image. The larger the intensity and contrast differences are, the more "structural damage" the compressed image's pixel blocks have sustained.

The result of the algorithm is an average of those differences, providing a score in the range of 0 to 1.

When the result is 1 the compressed image is a perfect replica of the original image, and when it is close to 0 very little structural data remains.

So when using SSIM for compression tuning, you want to aim at close to 1 values for "barely noticeable" compression, and lower values if you're willing to compromise image quality for smaller files.

SSIM also has a multiscale variant (MS-SSIM), which takes multiple scales of both images into account when calculating the final score.

There's also the Structural Dissimilarity metric (DSSIM), which is very similar to SSIM, but has an inverse range, where 0 is the perfect score and 1 means that the compressed image has no resemblance to the original.

Butteraugli

Butteraugli is a recent visual comparison metric from Google that aims to be even more accurate than SSIM in predicting perceived image quality. The metric is based on various anatomic and physiological observations related to the human eye structure.

As a result, the algorithm "suppresses" the importance of some colors based on the differences in location and density of different color receptors, calculates frequency domain image errors (putting more weight on low-frequency errors, as they are more visible than high-frequency ones), and then clusters the errors, as multiple errors in the same area of the image are likely to be more visible than a single one.

It is still early days for that metric, and it is mostly tuned for high-quality images, but initial results look promising.

Summary

In this chapter, we went through the basic terms and concepts we use when discussing digital images and the various image formats. In the following chapters we will make good use of this knowledge by diving into the details of what each format does and how.

CHAPTER 3

Lossless Image Formats

Tim Kadlec

In the previous chapter, you learned about the difference between lossy and lossless image formats. Lossy image formats lose image information during their compression process—typically taking advantage of the way we perceive images to shave away unnecessary bytes. Lossless image formats, however, do not have that benefit. Lossless image formats incur no loss of image information as part of their compression process.

In this chapter, we'll dig deeper into GIF and PNG, the two primary lossless image formats on the Web. We'll talk about how they're constructed and compressed, and what to do to ensure we keep them as lightweight as possible.

GIF (It's Pronounced "GIF")

When it comes to image formats on the Web, the Graphic Interchange Format (GIF) may no longer be the king of the castle, but it certainly is its oldest resident. Originally created in 1987 by CompuServe, the GIF image format was one of the first portable, nonproprietary image formats. This gave it a distinct advantage over the many proprietary, platform-specific image formats when it came to gaining support and adoption on first Usenet, then the World Wide Web.

The GIF format was established at a time of very limited networks and computing power, and many of the decisions about how to structure the format reflect this. Unfortunately, as we'll see, this limits its ability both to portray rich imagery as well as to compress.

Block by Block

The building blocks of the GIF format are...well, they're blocks. A GIF file is composed of a sequence of data blocks, each communicating different types of information. These blocks can be either optional or required.

The first two blocks of every GIF file are required, and have a fixed length and format.

Header block

First up is the *header* block. The header takes up 6 bytes and communicates both an identifier of the format and a version number. If you were to look at the header block for any given GIF, you would almost certainly see one of the following sequences:

```
47 49 46 38 39 61
```

```
47 49 46 38 37 61
```

The first three bytes (47, 49, 46) are the GIF's signature and will always equate to "GIF." The last three bytes indicate the version of the GIF specification used—either "89a" (38, 39, 61) or "87a" (38, 37, 61). Generally speaking, image encoders will use the older 87a for compatibility reasons unless the image is specifically taking advantage of some features from the 89a specification (such as animation).

Logical screen descriptor

Immediately following the header block is the *logical screen descriptor*, which is 7 bytes long and tells the decoding application how much space the image will occupy.

The *canvas width* and *canvas height* can be found in the first two pairs of bytes. These are legacy values that stem from the belief that these image viewers may render multiple images in a single GIF, on the same canvas. Most viewers today ignore these values altogether. The only time in practice that a GIF contains multiple images is if it is animated, but in those cases each image is either a frame or in image libraries. (We'll explore this in more detail later in the chapter.)

The next byte is actually four fields of data crammed together. By converting the byte to a binary number, you get a series of boolean switches to indicate four distinct pieces of data.

The first bit is the *global color table flag*. If the bit is 0, there is no global color table being used in the image. If the bit is one, then a global color table will be included right after the logical screen descriptor.

GIF is a palette-based image format; that is, the colors that the image uses have their RGB values stored in a *palette*— or *color—table*. These tables contain the colors in the image, as well as a corresponding index value starting at zero. So, if the first pixel of an image is the color green, then in the color table, the color green will have a corresponding index value of 0. Now, whenever the image is being processed and encoded, any time that color is discovered, it can be represented by the number 0.

In the case of the GIF format, each table can hold up to 256 entries. This 256-color limit made a great deal of sense when the GIF format was established—hardware was far less capable than it is today—but it severely limits GIF's ability to display images that contain much detail.

Hacking GIF's Color Limit

While GIFs are restricted to a 256-color palette, it is technically possible for you to save a true color GIF. Because the GIF format allows for multiple image blocks, and each of those image blocks can have its own 256-color palette, you can technically layer these blocks on top of each other, creating a true color image.

However, keep in mind that sometimes things that sound like a good idea really aren't. Creating a true color GIF is one of those things. Because of the layering and all those color palettes, the resulting file will be gigantic. In addition, not all image editors even handle multiple image blocks correctly. Put it all together, and creating true color GIFs is a better answer to a really technical trivia question than it is an actual approach.

GIFs can feature both a global color table as well as a number of local color tables if multiple images are being used (typically in animation). While the global color table is not required, it is almost always included in the image, so this bit is typically the number 1.

The next three bits are the *color resolution*, which is used to help determine the size of the global color table. The formula for the number of entries in the global color table is $2^{(N+1)}$ where N is equal to the number indicated in the color resolution bits. For example, if the color resolution bit is 0, then the size of the color table is 2 ($2^{(0+1)}$). If the color resolution bit is 3, the size of the color table is 16 ($2^{(3+1)}$).

Following the color resolution is the *sort flag*: another single bit that is used to indicate if the colors in the global color able are sorted, typically by how frequently they occur in the image, or not.

The last two bytes, the *background color index* and *pixel aspect ratio*, are mostly unused. The background color index only comes into play if you're trying to composite several subimages—something that was anticipated when the GIF format was created, but never really utilized.

The pixel aspect ratio is also mostly ignored, and the GIF standard isn't exactly forthcoming on what their thinking was for including it in the first place.

But wait, there's more!

Following the header and logical screen descriptor blocks are a number of optional blocks, as well as the actual image data. These blocks range from the optional global and local color tables, to extensions that enable transparency, animation, and even comments for including human-readable metadata within the image. We'll touch on some of the extensions when we look at animation.

The very last block in any GIF is always the *trailer*, which is a single byte with the value of *3B*, providing decoders with an indicator that they've reached the end of the file.

GIF is a *palette-based* image format; that is, the colors that the image uses have their RGB values stored in a palette table.

Animation

Animated GIFs are everywhere on the Web today. Thanks to social media, they've seen a resurgence in popularity. It makes good sense, too: they're pretty easy to make and because they're GIF files, they work in every major browser without any need for additional development work.

Animation was built into the *GIF89a* file format. The way it works is that each *frame* of the animation is a separate image, stored within the file. A series of extension blocks are used to tell decoders how to transition between these images.

The application extension block is used to indicate how many times the animation should loop. Immediately following the application extension block, you'll find a graphic-control extension, which provides information about how the file should move between the different images (or frames) in the file and how long the delay should be.

While the portability and broad support of the format may seem appealing, there are much better options.

Remember: the GIF format is showing its age. It has a limited color palette that makes it poorly equipped to show detailed images, and it was formalized before incredibly useful compression techniques, such as chroma subsampling (which you'll learn about in Chapter 4) or specific compression techniques targeted at video data.

With every frame of the animation requiring another image to be stored inside the GIF file, and with the format itself lacking many of these advanced compressed techniques, animated GIFs very quickly become frighteningly heavy and bloated.

An increasingly popular (and more bandwidth friendly) alternative is to use a video instead—something like the MP4 format. Much like image formats have specific compression steps built in that are tailored for compressing image data, video formats have additional compression techniques available that are tailored for compressing video. As a result, using an MP4 can significantly reduce the size of the file.

Consider the image of Eadweard Muybridge's famous "The Horse in Motion" in Figure 3-1. Sadly, you'll have to take our word that it's an animated GIF. Just squint and use your imagination to pretend the horse is galloping.

Figure 3-1. An animated GIF of "The Horse in Motion"

The animated GIF contains 15 frames—which means there are actually 15 images bundled up in this file. Compressed, it weighs in at a whopping 568 KB.

We can use the open source tool `FFmpeg` to convert the GIF to an MP4 file (Example 3-1).

Example 3-1. Using FFmpeg to convert GIF to an MP4 file

```
fffmpeg -f gif -i horse.gif horse.mp4
```

The resulting MP4 is only 76 KB—around 14% of the size of the GIF itself. Not bad for a one-line command.

You can now use the `<video>` element to include your new, bandwidth-friendly animation (Example 3-2).

Example 3-2. Using video element to include animation

```
<video autoplay loop>
        <source src="horse.mp4" type="video/mp4" />
</video>
```

Transparency with GIF

The GIF format also allows for transparency. Just as with animation, transparency support is indicated within a graphic control extension block, this time using a transparency color flag that is either set to "0" if there is no transparency in the file, or "1" if we would like the image to have a transparent component.

In Chapter 2, you learned that transparency can be handled using an alpha channel—an additional byte of information for each color indicating the level of transparency. The GIF format, however, takes a different approach.

In GIF images, we accomplish transparency by signifying that one color in the palette should be treated as transparent. For example, we may indicate that any white pixels should be transparent. This has the advantage of not requiring nearly as much additional data as having a full-blown alpha channel, but it also brings a significant limitation. Having a single color represent a transparent pixel removes any ability for partial transparency: it's all or nothing. As a result, transparency in GIFs frequently looks very jagged and low resolution.

LZW, or the Rise and Fall of the GIF

The GIF format boasted a lossless compression algorithm known as Lempel-Ziv-Welch, or more commonly, LZW. This algorithm allowed GIF to improve compression significantly over other lossless formats of the time, while maintaining similar compression and decompression times. This file savings, paired with GIF's interlace option, which allowed a rough version of an image to be displayed before the full image had been transmitted, made GIF a perfect fit for the limited networks and hardware of the Web's early days.

Unfortunately, the same compression algorithm that made it such a great format for the Web also directly led to GIF's fall from grace. As it turns out, the algorithm had been patented by Unisys. In December 1994, Unisys and CompuServe announced that developers of GIF-based software (e.g., compression tools) would be required to pay licensing fees. As you might imagine, this didn't sit well with developers and the community at large.

There were many repercussions of this announcement, but none more notable than the creation of the PNG image format in early 1995.

The PNG File Format

Depending on who you ask, PNG either stands for Portable Network Graphics or, as a bit of recursive humor, PNG not GIF (we programmers have a very finely tuned sense of humor). The PNG format was the community's response to the licensing issues that arose around GIF.

The early goal of creating the format was pretty straightforward: create an open alternative to GIF to avoid all the licensing fees. It didn't take long for everyone involved to realize that they wouldn't be able to do this and maintain backward compatibility in any way. While everyone loves a seamless fallback, the advantage was that this meant the folks creating the PNG format could be more ambitious in their aims—if they weren't going to be able to maintain backward compatibility, why not make PNG better in every possible way? For the most part, it would seem, they succeeded.

Understanding the Mechanics of the PNG Format

PNGs are composed of a PNG signature followed by some number of chunks.

PNG Signature

The PNG signature is an 8-byte identifier that is identical for every single PNG image. This identifier also works as a clever way to verify that the PNG file has not been corrupted during transfer (whether over the network or from operating system to operating system). If the signature is altered in any way, then the file has been corrupted somewhere along the line.

For example, the first value in the PNG signature is "137"—a non-ASCII, 8-bit character. Because it is a non-ASCII character, it helps to reduce the risk of a PNG file being mistakenly identified as a text file, and vice versa. Since it is 8 bits, it also provides verification that the file was not passed over a 7-bit channel. If it was, the 8th bit would be dropped and the PNG signature would be altered.

The full list of bytes of the PNG signature is presented in Table 3-1.

Table 3-1. PNG signature bytes

Decimal value	Interpretation
137	8-bit, non-ASCII character
80	P
78	N
71	G
13	Carriage-return (CR) character
10	Line-feed (LF) character
27	Ctrl-Z
10	Line-feed (LF) character

Chunks

Other than the first 8 bytes that the PNG signature occupies, a PNG file is made entirely of chunks—the building blocks of the PNG format.

Each chunk composes the same set of four components:

Length field
    The length field takes up 4 bytes and refers to the length of the chunk's data field.

Type field

The type field takes up 4 bytes and indicates to the decoder what type of data the chunk contains.

Chunk data

The chunk data contains the bytes of data that the chunk is trying to pass along. This can range anywhere from 0 bytes to 2 GB in size.

Cyclic Redundancy Code (CRC)

The CRC is a 4-byte check value. The decoder calculates the CRC based on the chunk data and chunk type—the length field is not used in the calculation. If the calculated CRC value matches the 4-byte CRC field included in the chunk, the data has not been corrupted.

Cyclic Redundancy Code Algorithm

The actual algorithm used to calculate the CRC makes for pretty dry reading (says the guy writing about the nuances of PNG compression), but if that's your cup of tea, you can find the exact alogrithm online (*https://www.w3.org/TR/PNG/#5CRC-algorithm*).

Ancillary and critical chunks

The type field communicates a decent amount of information about the chunk within its 4 little bytes. Each byte has a designated purpose. In addition, each byte has a simple boolean value of information that is turned on and off by the capitalization of the character occupying that byte.

The first byte is the *ancillary bit*. Just as with blocks in the GIF format, not all chunks are essential to succesfully display an image. Each chunk can either be *critical* (uppercase) or *ancillary* (lowercase). A *critical* chunk is one that is necessary to successfully display the PNG file. An *ancillary* chunk is one that is not—instead, its purpose is to provide supporting information.

The second byte is the *private bit*. The private bit informs the decoder if the chunk is public (uppercase) or private (lowercase). Typically private chunks are used for application-specific information a company may wish to encode.

The third byte is a reserved bit. Currently this bit doesn't inform the coder of anything other than conformance to the current version of PNG, which requires an uppercase value here.

The fourth byte is the *safe-to-copy bit*. This bit is intended for image editors and tells the editor whether it can safely copy an unknown ancillary chunk into a new file (lowercase) or not (uppercase). For example, an ancillary chunk may depend on the image data in some way. If so, it can't be copied over to a new file in case any of the critical chunks have been modified, or reordered, or new critical chunks have been added.

The capitalization means that two chunk types that look nearly identical can be very different. Consider iDAT and IDAT. While they appear similar, the first byte makes them distinct chunk types. iDAT is an ancillary chunk type—it's not essential to properly display the image. IDAT, on the other hand, starts with the first character capitalized, indicating that it is a critical chunk type and therefore if it is missing, any decoder should throw an error since it won't be able to display the image.

The PNG specification defines four critical chunk types (see Table 3-2), three of which are required for a PNG file to be valid.

Table 3-2. Critical chunks

Chunk type	Name	Required
IHDR	Image header	Yes
PLTE	Palette	No
IDAT	Image data	Yes
IEND	Image trailer	Yes

The IHDR chunk is the first chunk in any PNG image and provides details about the type of image (more on that in a bit), the height and width of the image, the pixel depth, the compression and filtering methods, the interlacing method, whether the image has an alpha channel (transparency), and whether the image is true color, grayscale, or color-mapped.

The IDAT chunk contains the compressed pixel data for the given image. Technically, the IDAT chunk can contain up to 2 GB of compressed data. In practice, however, IDAT chunks rarely reach that size.

The final required chunk is the IEND chunk. IEND is as simple as you can possibly get when it comes to chunks—it contains no data at all. Its entire purpose is to indicate that there are no more chunks in the image.

Pairing these three required chunks—IHDR, IDAT, IEND—with a PNG signature gives you the simplest PNG file possible. In fact, these three chunks are all you need to build a true color or grayscale PNG file.

However, like its predecessor GIF, PNG can also take advantage of color palettes. If a color palette is being used, then the PNG file also needs to include the PLTE (palette) chunk. The PLTE chunk houses a series of RGB values that may be included in the image.

While these four chunks—IHDR, IDAT, IEND, and PLTE—are the primary ones, and the only critical chunks specified, that doesn't mean they're the only chunks in your files. Image editors tend to create all sorts of ancillary chunks containing everything from histogram-related data to the oh-so-very-helpful chunk Photoshop adds that tells you that the image was made in Photoshop. Removing any chunks that have no influence over the visual appearance of your image is an essential first step in reducing PNG bloat, and any PNG optimization tool worth its salt will take care of this step for you.

Filters

The not-so-secret secret of compression is that the more repetitive data an object contains, the easier it will be to compress. Image data by itself is typically not very repetitive, so the PNG format introduces a precompression step called filtering. The goal of the filtering process is to take the image data and try to make it easier to compress.

The PNG filtering process uses what is called *delta encoding*; that is, it compares each pixel to the pixels surrounding it, replacing the value with the difference to those pixels.

Clear as mud? Here's an example.

Let's say we had a set of numbers:

    1 2 3 4 5 6 7

Every value in the set is unique, so when a compression algorithm comes through, it's not going to have any luck reducing the size.

But what if we had a filter run through and replace each number with the difference between its value, and the value of the number preceding it? Then our set of numbers would look like:

    1 1 1 1 1 1 1

Now this is much more promising! A compression algorithm can whittle this down to almost nothing, giving us a huge savings. That's delta encoding (albeit a very idealistic example), and that's what the PNG filters set out to accomplish.

The PNG format has five filters that may be applied line by line:

None
> Each byte is left unchanged.

Sub
> Each byte is replaced with the difference between it and the value of the byte just to the left of it.

Up
>   Each byte is replaced with the difference between it and the value of the byte just above it (in the preceding row).

Average
>   Each byte is replaced with the difference between it and the average of the bytes just to the left and just above it.

Paeth
>   Each byte is replaced with the difference between it and the Paeth predictor (a function of the bytes above, to the left, and to the upper left).

These filters can vary from line to line of the image, based on the content of that line and what filter would have the greatest impact.

Interlacing

Both GIFs and PNGs have an *interlacing* feature that, similar to the progressive JPEG feature you'll learn about in the next chapter, enables an image to be rendered quickly as a low-resolution version, and then be progressively filled in at each successive pass. This interlacing approach allows the browser to give the user some sense of the makeup of the image earlier than the typical top-down approach to image rendering.

The GIF approach to interlacing is a one-dimensional scheme; that is, the interlacing is based on horizontal values only, focusing on a single row at a time. GIF's approach to interlacing has four passes. First, every eighth row is displayed. Then, every eighth row is displayed again—this time offset by four rows from the first pass. For example, in an image composed of eight rows of pixels, pass one would display row one and pass two would display row five.

The third pass displays every fourth row, offset by two rows from the top. So in our 8-px by 8-px example, pass three would fill in the third and seventh rows. The fourth and final pass displays every other row. You can see how each row of an image is displayed using GIF interlacing in Figure 3-2.

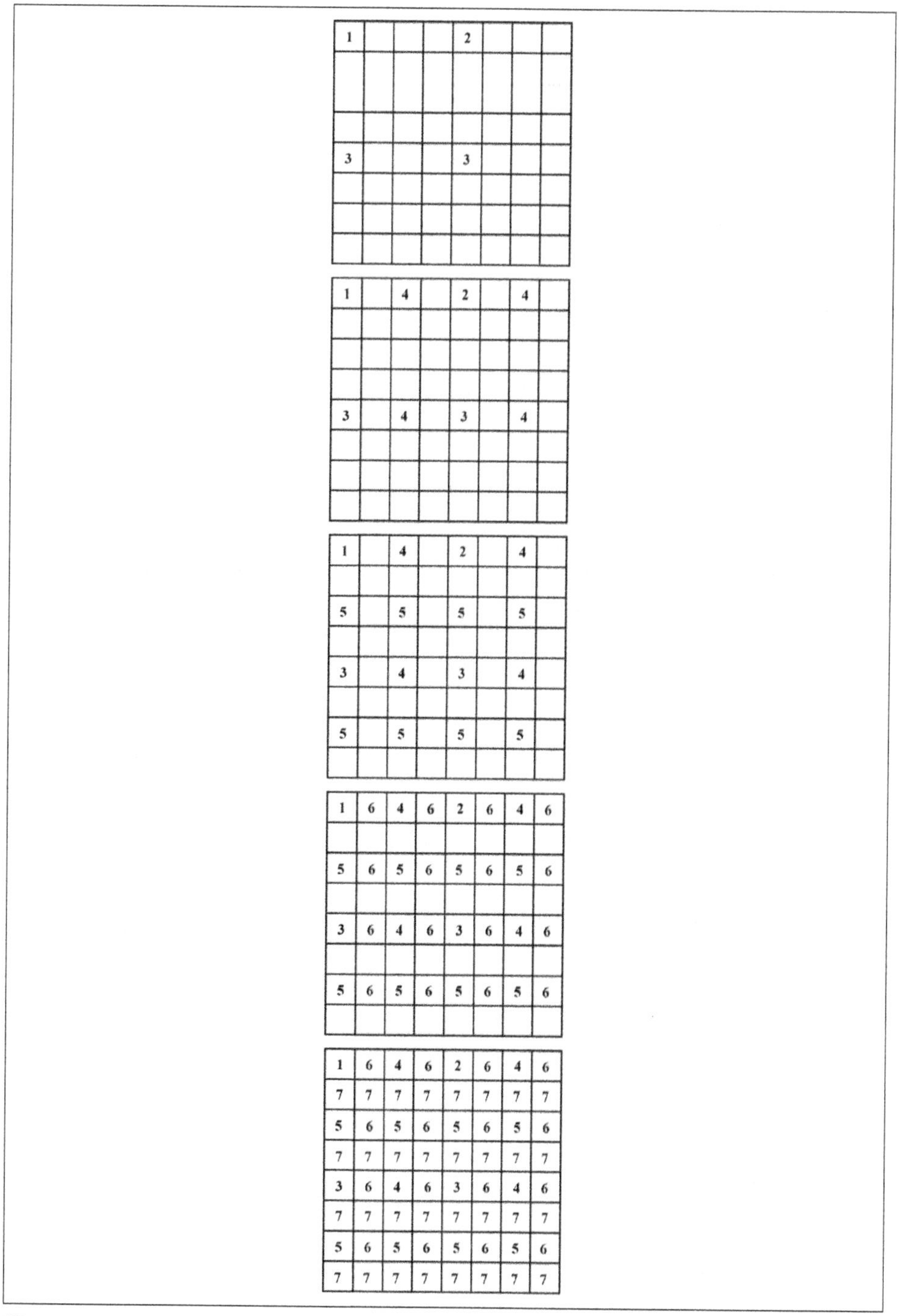

Figure 3-2. How rows of an image are displayed using GIF interlacing

In contrast, PNG's interlacing method is a two-dimensional scheme. Instead of analyzing a single row at a time, PNG's interlacing method involves looking at the individual pixels within the row.

The first pass involves filling in every eighth pixel—both horizontally and vertically. The second pass fills in every eighth pixel (again horizontally and vertically) but with an offset of four pixels to the right. So given an image eight pixels wide and eight pixels high, pass one would fill in the first pixel in the first row, and pass two would fill in the fifth pixel on the first row.

The third pass fills in the pixels that are four rows below the pixels filled in by the first two passes. Using the same 8×8-pixel image, pass three would fill in the first pixel on row five as well as the fifth pixel on row five.

The fourth pass displays the pixels that are offset by two columns to the right of the first four pixels, and the fifth pass fills in the pixels that fall two rows below each of the prior displayed pixels.

Pass six fills in all remaining pixels on the odd rows, and the seventh and final pass fills in all pixels on the even rows.

That's a lot of numbers, and is quite possibly as clear as mud at this point. For those more visually minded, Figure 3-3 shows which pixels are filled in for each pass.

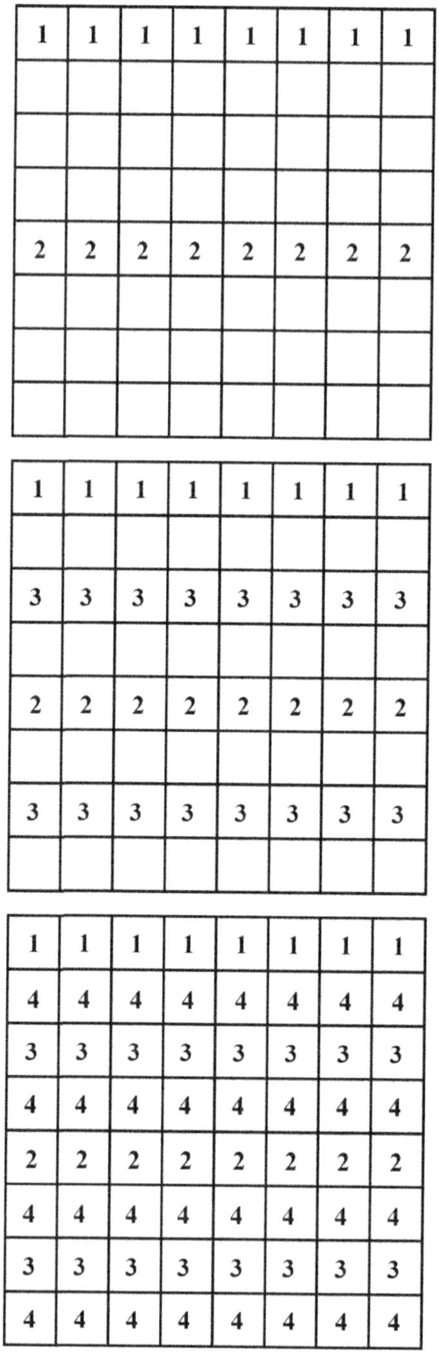

1	1	1	1	1	1	1	1
2	2	2	2	2	2	2	2

1	1	1	1	1	1	1	1
3	3	3	3	3	3	3	3
2	2	2	2	2	2	2	2
3	3	3	3	3	3	3	3

1	1	1	1	1	1	1	1
4	4	4	4	4	4	4	4
3	3	3	3	3	3	3	3
4	4	4	4	4	4	4	4
2	2	2	2	2	2	2	2
4	4	4	4	4	4	4	4
3	3	3	3	3	3	3	3
4	4	4	4	4	4	4	4

Figure 3-3. A visual of which pixels are filled in per pass

While the PNG method of interlacing involves more passes, if you were to assume the same network conditions and compression levels, an interlaced PNG image would be on pass four by the time the GIF image had completed its first pass. Why? Because the first pass of GIF interlacing involves 1/8 of the data of the GIF image itself (1 in every 8 rows), whereas the first pass of PNG interlacing involves only 1/64 of the data (1 pixel in every 64 pixels—8 pixels horizontally multiplied by 8 pixels vertically). The impact is particularly noticeable on any images with text, as the text becomes readable much more quickly using the PNG approach to interlacing.

Progressive loading, higher fidelity much earlier than the GIF counterpart—PNG interlacing sounds great, right? Unfortunately, it's not all sunshine and roses. The consequence of PNG's approach to interlacing is that it can dramatically increase the file size because of its negative impact on compression.

Remember all those filters we talked about? Because each pass in the PNG interlacing process has different widths, it's far simpler to treat each pass as a completely separate image for filtering. The consequence is that the filtering process has less data to work with, making compression less effective. On top of that, the benefits of progressively loading images have been debated with no definitive conclusion. When you combine the severe reduction in compression with the questionable value of interlacing in the first place, PNG interlacing starts to make a lot less sense. Typically, you're better off ignoring interlacing on both PNGs and GIFs altogether.

Image Formats

PNG images can be saved in five different formats: indexed, grayscale, grayscale plus alpha, truecolor, and truecolor plus alpha.

The difference is in how many bytes are needed to describe each pixel's color and, optionally, transparency.

Indexed PNGs use a palette to list all the colors included in the image. These palette-based PNGs are commonly grouped together as PNG8, which is technically short for 8-bit PNGs. Somewhat confusingly, that doesn't necessarily mean that each pixel value is actually 8 bits deep. You can actually have 1-, 2-, and 4-bit pixels as well. Each just means you have potentially smaller color tables. For example, an 8-bit PNG can support 256 colors, while a 2-bit PNG can only support up to 4 colors.

Grayscale PNGs are similar in that they use a palette, but they also add support for 16-bit pixels for highly detailed grayscale-based imagery (think things like medical imagery).

Truecolor PNGs are what are referred to when you hear about PNG-24s, and they do not use a palette at all. Instead of referring to a palette table, each pixel directly specifies a color using the RGB format. This provides the ability for PNG-24s to cover the full color spectrum (hence "truecolor"), but is also the reason why PNG-24s are much heavier than their 8-bit counterparts.

> ## Keep That Color Count Down
>
> If you've ever run the Posterize filter in Photoshop, you've likely noticed that even if you don't see any visual difference, the outputted file size is much smaller.
>
> That's because what the `Posterize` filter is doing is looking for similar colors and combining them, reducing the unique color count. The more similar colors in an image, the better it will compress.

Transparency with PNG

Like the GIF format, PNGs support transparency. The PNG format, however, is much more powerful and flexible in its support.

If you recall, we accomplish transparency in GIFs by specifying an individual color in the color table to be displayed as transparent—it's entirely binary, leaving room for partial transparency.

On the other hand, PNG support for transparency takes a few different flavors.

For palette-based images, we handle transparency by adding one or more entries of alpha information to the tRNS chunk. Truecolor and grayscale images can also use the tRNS chunk, but only to define a single value as transparent. Because we're referring to specific entries in the palette table, you don't have the ability to make, say, two different white pixels in your image display with two different alpha values.

If you want more flexibility and access to partial transparency, the truecolor and grayscale formats also allow for the addition of an alpha channel—each pixel now receiving its own alpha value. This is much more costly than the indexed approach to transparency, as we're not adding merely a table, but a full channel of information to every single pixel.

Knowing this, as well as the golden rule of image compression (the more similar colors, the better), we can take a few steps to ensure that our transparent PNGs are as light as possible.

As we just discussed, if you're using a truecolor PNG and making a large number of those pixels fully transparent, that alpha value is added to each individual pixel. But what about all the RGB data? That doesn't go away. Even if we marked those pixels as fully transparent so that they will not display, there may still be dozens and dozens of unique RGB data values associated with them.

To maximize compression, we can use an image editor to convert all of those fully transparent pixels to be the same color—red, for example. Now, when we make them fully transparent, their full RGBA values will be identical and PNG's compression algorithms will happily gobble up all that unnecessary data, leaving us with a much smaller file size.

There Can Be Only One!

So given all the preceding information, here's the ultimate question: when do you use a GIF and when do you use a PNG? The answer is to favor PNGs for all except the smallest of images. Likewise, if you want to use animation at all, GIF is the way to go (though as we've seen above, you could argue MP4s are even better).

Basically, while the GIF format helped pave the way for formats like PNG, its time has come and gone. If you are ever considering putting a GIF in a page, take a step back and consider if another alternative would work better.

Summary

In this chapter we looked at the two most popular and widely supported lossless image formats on the Web, GIFs and PNGs. We looked at how each format is encoded and compressed, as well as what tweaks we can make to maximize those savings. Now that you know all about lossless formats, not only can you impress your friends with your in-depth knowledge of filtering and compression algorithms, but you can also start to save precious bytes with every image you produce.

In the next chapter, we'll dig into JPEGs—the Web's favorite lossy image format—and learn how to optimize them as much as possible.

CHAPTER 4

JPEG

Yoav Weiss

JPEGs are the Web's most abundant image file format. According to the HTTP archive (*http://httparchive.org*), at the time of this writing, they make up 45% of all image requests, and about 65% of image traffic. They are good candidates for full-color images and digital photos, making them the go-to image format whenever people want to share important moments in their lives (e.g., what they are having for brunch) over the Internet. JPEG's capability of lossily compressing images to save bandwidth (without losing too much quality in the process) has gained the format worldwide adoption.

History

The need for photographic image compression was clear from the early days of personal computing. Multiple proprietary formats were devised in order to achieve that, but eventually, the need to share these images between users made the case for a standard format clear.

Even before the Internet was widespread, corporations shared images with their users over CD-ROMs with limited storage capacity, and wanted the users to be able to view these images without installing proprietary software. In the early days of the Internet (then mostly at 9,600 baud speeds), it was apparent that a standard format could not come soon enough.

A few years earlier, back in 1986, the Joint Photographic Experts Group was formed, and after six years of long debates, it published the ITU T.81 (*http://www.w3.org/Graphics/JPEG/itu-t81.pdf*) standard in 1992. The group's acronym was adopted as the popular name of this new format: JPEG.

The JPEG Format

The bytestream of files that we call JPEG nowadays (often with extensions such as *.jpg* and *.jpeg*) is not a direct result of a single standard. These files are composed of a container and payload. The payload corresponds to the original T.81 standard (or, to be more accurate, to a subset of that standard that is supported by browsers), while the container is defined by other standards entirely, and is used to, well, "contain" the payload and important metadata about the image that the decoder needs in order to decode it.

Containers

The T.81 standard actually defined a standard JPEG container called JIF, for JPEG Interchange Format. But JIF failed to gain traction, mostly because it was overly strict and failed to provide some information that was required for the decoding process. Luckily JIF was built with forward compatibility in mind, so it was soon succeeded by other, backward-compatible container formats.

There are two commonly used types of JPEG containers today: JFIF and EXIF.

JFIF stands for JPEG File Interchange Format, and is the older and more basic of the two containers. EXIF stands for Exchangeable Image File Format, and can contain far more metadata than JFIF, such as where the image was taken, the camera's settings, copyright, and other metadata that might be relevant for humans editing and manipulating the image, but is not required to display the image in a browser.

Later, we will see how lossless optimization often trims that data in order to reduce its size. What is common to all these container types is their internal structure, which is somewhat similar and comprised of markers.

Markers

Each JPEG file, regardless of container, is composed of markers. These markers all start with the binary character 0xff, where the following character determines the marker's type. The JFIF and EXIF parts are contained in "application markers" comprising segments that hold container-specific information. Decoders that weren't created to interpret or use JFIF- or EXIF-specific markers simply ignore them and move on to the next marker.

Here are a few markers that are fairly important in the JPEG world:

SOI

The "Start of Image" marker represents the start of the JPEG image. It is *always* the first marker in the file.

SOF

"Start of Frame" represents the start of the frame. With one nonpractical exception, a JPEG file will contain a single frame.

DHT

"Define Huffman Table" contains the Huffman tables. We'll discuss them in detail in "Entropy Coding" on page 53.

DQT

"Define Quantization Table" contains the quantization tables, which we'll discuss in "DCT" on page 56.

SOS

"Start of Scan" contains the actual image data. We'll discuss its content shortly.

EOI

"End of Image" represents the end of the JPEG image, and should always be the last marker of the file.

APP

Application markers enable extensions to the basic JIF format, such as JFIF and EXIF.

The terms *image*, *frame*, *scan*, and *component* can be confusing, so let's clarify them. Each JPEG is a single *image*, which contains (in all practical cases) a single *frame*, and a frame can contain one or many *scans*, depending on the encoding mode, which we'll discuss momentarily. On top of that, each scan can contain multiple components. Quite the Russian doll.

One thing that is often surprising is that the JPEG's pixel dimensions can be buried rather deep inside the bytestream, as part of the Start of Frame (SOF) marker's header. That means that for JPEGs with a lot of data before that marker (notably EXIF-based JPEGs with a lot of metadata), the information regarding the JPEG's dimensions may come in pretty late (see Figure 4-1). That can be a problem if you're processing the JPEG on the fly, and particularly, large chunks of EXIF data can often mean that the browser knows the image dimensions significantly later than it could have if the (irrelevant) EXIF data wasn't there.

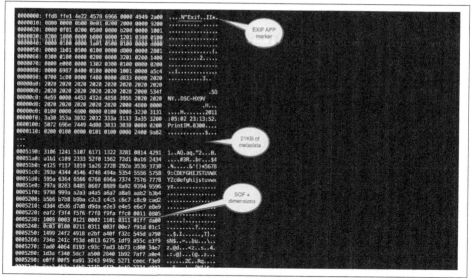

Figure 4-1. A JPEG with EXIF data

Since browsers use the presence of image dimensions for layout changes in certain cases, as well as for triggering various internal processing events, the presence of EXIF metadata in your images can have a significant negative impact on your site's performance.

Color Transformations

Another key concept about JPEGs is that they convert the input image from its origin RGB color model to the YCbCr color model, breaking the image into brightness, blue chroma, and red chroma components.

As discussed in Chapter 2, the human eye is more sensitive to luminance details than it is to details in color components. That means that we can generally get away with relatively high color component detail loss, while the same is not always true for the luma component.

JPEG takes advantage of that and applies different (and often harsher) compression on the color components of the image.

As we've seen, one disadvantage of YCbCr versus other, more modern color models (e.g., YCgCo) is that YCbCr is not binary fraction friendly. Those mathematical operations, when carried out by a computer, are bound to lose some precision, and therefore an RGB to YCbCr to RGB conversion is somewhat lossy in practice. That adds to the lossy aspect of the format.

Subsampling

One of the major ways that compression of the color components is performed is through *subsampling*. Sampling, which you learned about in Chapter 2, is about fitting an analog signal (e.g., a real-life image of continuous color) into an inherently discrete medium, such as a pixel bitmap, a process which by definition loses detail and precision.

Subsampling is about losing even more precision during the sampling (or resampling) process, resulting in less detail, entropy, and eventually bytes to send to the decoder.

When we discuss subsampling in JPEG, we are most often talking about chroma subsampling: subsampling of the color components. This process reduces the color component sampling precision, which is OK since the human eye tends to be more forgiving of lost color precision details.

How is subsampling done in JPEG? There are multiple patterns for possible subsampling in the JPEG standard. In order to understand what these subsampling patterns mean, let's start by drawing a 4×2-pixel row of the Cb (blue chroma) component (see Figure 4-2).

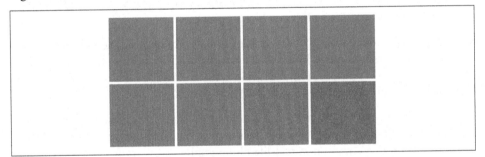

Figure 4-2. A 4×2-pixel block

As you can see, each pixel has a different value. Subsampling means that we coelesce some of those colors into a single intensity value.

The notation given to the various subsampling patterns is *J:a:b*, where:

- *J* is the number of pixels in each row. For JPEG that number is often 4. There are always 2 rows.
- *a* represents the number of colors used from the first row.
- *b* represents the number of colors used in the second row.

In case you're dozing off, let's look at a few examples. Figure 4-3 shows a few subsampling patterns with that notation.

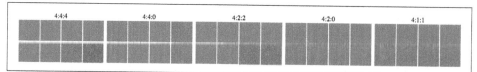

Figure 4-3. Various subsampling results of 4×2-pixel block from Figure 4-2

If you were paying attention, you may have noticed that the 4:4:4 example is exactly the same as the original. In fact, 4:4:4 means that for each row of four pixels, four colors are picked, so no subsampling is taking place.

Let's take a look at what other subsampling patterns are doing.

4:4:0 means that color intensity is averaged between every two vertical pixels in the 4×2 block. In 4:2:2 intensity is averaged between two horizontally neighboring pixels. 4:2:0 averages intensity between the pixels in each 2×2 block inside the 4×2 block. And finally, 4:1:1 means that intensity is averaged between four vertically neighboring pixels.

This example is tainted to make it clear that we're talking about *chroma* subsampling, but you should note that each pixel in the example represents the intensity of only one of the color components. That makes it significantly easier to average the pixel color intensity without losing too much color precision.

Also, as you can notice from these examples, not all subsampling methods are created equally, and some are more likely to be noticeable than others. In practice, most JPEGs "in the wild" (*http://bit.ly/2b5Gxt5*) exhibit either 4:4:4 subsampling (so no subsampling at all) or 4:2:0 (see Figure 4-4).

Note that some color combinations become impossible to represent with subsampling—for example, 1-pixel-wide red lines over a blue background. However, such patterns are not that common in real-life photography.

We have seen that we lose precision by subsampling, but what do we gain from it?

By getting rid of pixels in the chroma components we effectively reduce the size of the color component bitmap by half for 4:2:2 and 4:4:0 subsampling and by three-quarters (!) for 4:2:0 and 4:1:1. That drop in pixel count equates to significant byte size savings as well as significant memory savings when we're dealing with the decoded image in memory. We'll further discuss these advantages in Chapter 9.

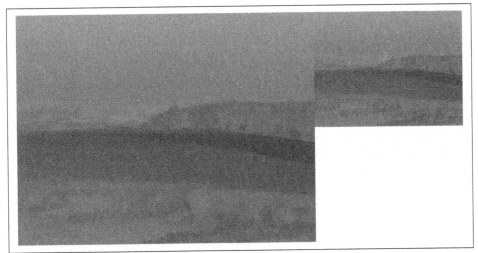

Figure 4-4. To the left, the original (untainted) Cb component; to the right, the same component after 4:2:0 subsampling

Entropy Coding

As discussed in Chapter 2, entropy coding is a technique that replaces data stream symbols with codes, such that common symbols get shorter codes.

The JPEG standard includes two different options for entropy encoders: Huffman encoding and arithmetic encoding.

Huffman encoding has been around since 1952, and is based on the idea that once the frequency of the symbols in the data stream is known, the symbols are sorted by their frequency using a binary tree. Then each symbol gets assigned a code that represents it, which is shorter the more frequent the symbol appears in the encoded data stream. One more important quality is that no code is a prefix of another, longer code. That is, no two or more codes, when concatenated, comprise another, longer code. That fact avoids the need to add length signals for each code, and makes the decoding process straightforward.

Huffman encoding is widely used and has lots of advantages, but suffers from one downside: the codes assigned to each symbol are always comprised of an integer number of bits. That means that they cannot reflect with complete accuracy the symbol frequency, and therefore, leave some compression performance on the table.

Huffman Encoding in Detail

Let's sink our teeth into a specific case in order to better understand what that means. Let's say we have an alphabet consisting of the letters A, B, and C, and the probability to appear in the stream is the same for all symbols: 1/3.

With Huffman encoding, we would use a tree structure to arrange them so that the symbols with the highest probability are closest to the tree's root, and then assign symbols accordingly. Since all symbols have the same probability, we'll end up with the tree shown in Figure 4-5.

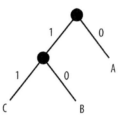

Figure 4-5. A Huffman tree used to code our alphabet

As we can see from this tree, A would be assigned the symbol 0, B would be assigned the symbol 10, and C would be assigned the symbol 11. That means we're "spending" more bits than needed on B and C, while "spending" less than required on A. B and C are subsidizing A, if you will. Huffman encoding is still a huge win, but if we compare the number of bits it takes us to encode a symbol, we're not reaching this theoretical ideal due to this difference between each symbol's probability and the number of bits we encode it with.

Arithmetic encoding to the rescue!

Arithmetic encoding is able to encode a symbol using fractions of a bit, solving that problem and achieving the theoretical encoding ideal. How does arithmetic coding do that "fractions of a bit" magic? It uses an (extremely long) binary fraction as the code representing the entire message, where the combination of the fraction's digits and the symbol's probability enable decoding of the message.

Arithmetic Encoding in Detail

To illustrate the way that works, the encoding process starts with the current interval being set to the range between 0 and 1, with the output binary fraction set to 0.

Each symbol is then assigned a range on the current interval that corresponds with the probability that it will appear in the data stream. The lower limit of the current symbol in the data stream is added to the output, and the current interval is set to the range of the current symbol. The process then repeats itself until all symbols are encoded (see Figure 4-6).

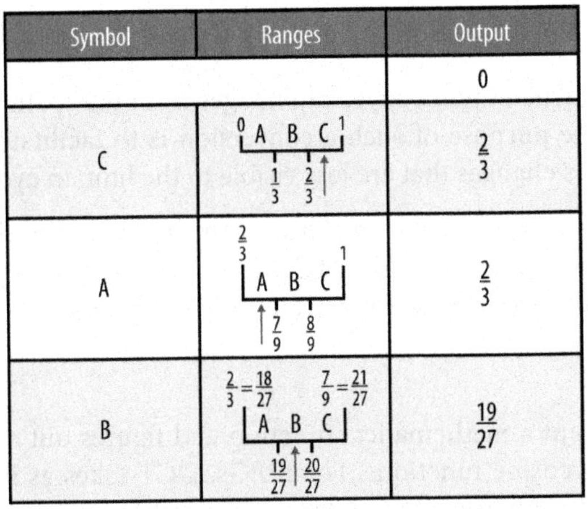

Symbol	Ranges	Output
		0
C	0 A B C 1 $\frac{1}{3}$ $\frac{2}{3}$	$\frac{2}{3}$
A	$\frac{2}{3}$ A B C 1 $\frac{7}{9}$ $\frac{8}{9}$	$\frac{2}{3}$
B	$\frac{2}{3}=\frac{18}{27}$ $\frac{7}{9}=\frac{21}{27}$ A B C $\frac{19}{27}$ $\frac{20}{27}$	$\frac{19}{27}$

Figure 4-6. The process of encoding the message "CAB" in an alphabet consisting of A, B, and C using arithmetic encoding

Unfortunately, when it comes to JPEGs, Huffman encoding is the option that is most often used, for the simple fact that arithmetic encoding is not supported by most JPEG decoders, and specifically not supported in any browser. The reason for that lack of support is that decoding of arithmetic encoding is more expensive than Huffman (and was considered prohibitively expensive in the early days of JPEGs), and it was encumbered by patents at the time that JPEG was standardized. Those patents have long expired, and computers are way better at floating-point arithmetic than they used to be in 1992; however, support in decoders is still rare, and it would also be practically impossible to introduce arithmetic encoding support to browsers without calling these JPEGs a brand new file format (with its own MIME type).

But even if arithmetic encoding is rarely used in JPEGs, it is widely used in other formats, as we'll see in Chapter 5.

While entropy codings can be adaptive, meaning that they don't need to know the probabilities of each symbol in advance and can calculate them as they pass the input data, Huffman in JPEG is not the adaptive variant. That means that often the choice is between an optimized, customized Huffman table for the JPEG, which has to be calculated in two passes over the data, and a standard Huffman table, which only requires a single pass but often produces compression results that are not as good as its custom, optimized counterpart.

Huffman tables are defined in the DHT marker, and each component of each scan can use a different Huffman table, which can potentially lead to better entropy encoding savings.

DCT

In Chapter 2, we touched upon converting images from the spatial domain to the frequency domain. The purpose of such a conversion is to facilitate filtering out high-frequency brightness changes that are less visible to the human eye.

In JPEG, the conversion from the spatial domain to frequency domain and back is done by mathematical functions called Forward Discrete-Cosine Transform (FDCT) and Inverse Discrete-Cosine Transform (IDCT). We often refer to both as DCT.

How does DCT work?

DCT takes as its input a mathematical function and figures out a way to represent it as a sum of known cosine functions. For JPEGs, DCT takes as input the brightness function of one of the image components (see Figure 4-7).

Figure 4-7. The Y component of an image, plotted as a 2D function

How does DCT do its magic?

DCT defines a set of basis functions: special cosine functions that are orthogonal to each other.

That means that:

- There's no way to represent any of the waveforms that these functions create as a sum of the other functions.
- There's only one way to represent an arbitrary 1D function (like sound waves or electrical currents) as the sum of the basis functions, multiplied by scalar coefficients.

This allows us to replace any n value vector by the list of n coefficients that can be applied to the basis functions to re-create the function's values.

The DCT basis functions are ordered from the lowest frequency one to the left up to the highest frequency one to the right, as shown in Figure 4-8.

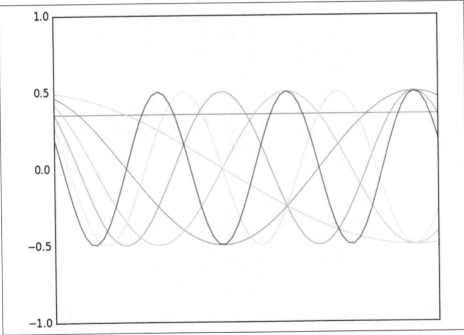

Figure 4-8. The basis functions of one-dimensional DCT

Each DCT value is a scalar multiplier of one of the basis functions. The first value, which correlates to the constant function we've seen earlier, is called the *DC component,* since when discussing electrical currents, that constant function represents the direct current part. All other values are called the *AC components*, since they represent the alternating current component.

The reason we're using electrical terms such as DC and AC is that one-dimensional DCT is often used to represent electrical signals, such as analog audio signals.

While one-dimensional DCT is not very interesting in and of itself, when discussing images, we can extend the same concept to two-dimensional functions (such as the brightness function of an image). As our basis functions we can take the eight one-dimensional DCT functions we saw earlier and multiply them to get 8×8 basis functions. These functions can then be used in a very similar way to represent any arbitrary set of 8×8 values as a matrix of 8×8 coefficients of those basis functions (see Figure 4-9).

One small difference in image data with regard to audio waves or electrical currents is that our function's possible output range is from 0 to 255, rather than having both positive and negative values. We can compensate for that difference by adding 128 to our function's values.

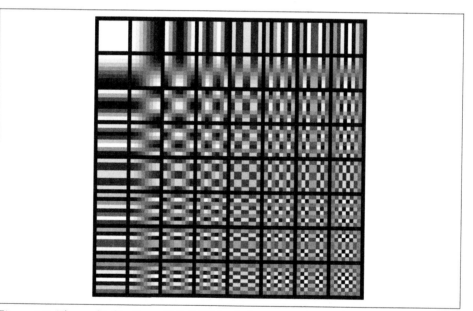

Figure 4-9. The multiplication of 1D DCT basis functions creates the following 8×8 matrix of 2D basis functions

As you can see in the upper-left corner, the first basis function is of constant value. That's the two-dimensional equivalent of the DC component we've seen in one-dimensional DCT. The other basis functions, because they result from multiplying our one-dimensional basis functions, are of higher frequency the farther they are from that upper-left corner. That is illustrated in Figure 4-9 by the fact that their brightness values change more frequently.

Let's take a look at the brightness values of a random 8×8-pixel block in Figure 4-10:

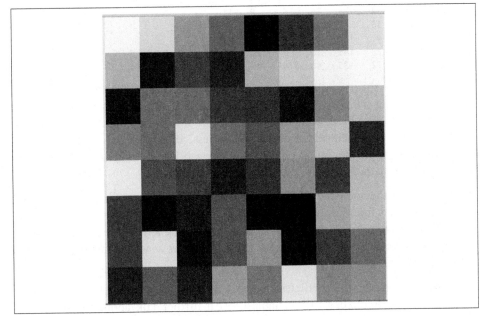

Figure 4-10. A random 8×8-pixel block

```
240   212   156   108     4    53   126   215
182    21    67    37   182   203   239   243
 21   120   116    61    56    22   144   191
136   121   225   123    95   164   196    50
232    89    70    33    58   152    67   192
 65    13    28    92     8     0   174   192
 70   221    16    92   153    10    67   121
 36    98    33   161   128   222   145   152
```

Since we want to convert it to DCT coefficients, the first step would be to center these values around 0, by substracting 128 from them. The result is:

```
 112    84    28   -20  -124   -75    -2    87
  54  -107   -61   -91    54    75   111   115
-107    -8   -12   -67   -72  -106    16    63
   8    -7    97    -5   -33    36    68   -78
 104   -39   -58   -95   -70    24   -61    64
 -63  -115  -100   -36  -120  -128    46    64
 -58    93  -112   -36    25  -118   -61    -7
 -92   -30   -95    33     0    94    17    24
```

Applying DCT on the preceding matrix results in:

-109	-114	189	-28	17	8	-20	-7
109	33	115	-22	-30	50	77	79
56	-25	0	3	38	-55	-60	-59
-43	78	154	-24	86	25	8	-11
108	110	-15	49	-58	37	100	-66
-22	176	-42	-121	-66	-25	-108	5
-95	-33	28	-145	-16	60	-22	-37
-51	84	72	-35	46	-124	-12	-39

Now every cell in the preceding matrix is the scalar coefficient of the basis function of the corresponding cell. That means that the coefficient in the upper-left corner is the scalar of the constant basis function, and therefore it is our DC component. We can regard the DC component as the overall brightness/color of all the pixels in the 8×8 block. In fact, one of the fastest ways to produce a JPEG thumbnail that's 1/8 of the original JPEG is to gather all DC components of that JPEG.

We've seen that the coefficient order corresponds with the basis function order, and also that the basis function frequency gets higher the farther we are in the right and downward directions of the matrix. That means that if we look at the frequency of the coefficients in that matrix, we would see that it increases as we get farther away from the upper-left corner.

Now, when serializing the coefficient matrix it's a good idea to write the coefficients from the lowest frequency to the highest. We'll further talk about the reasons in "Quantization" on page 62, but suffice it to say that it would be helpful for compression. We achieve that kind of serialization by following a zig-zag pattern, which makes sure that coefficients are added from the lowest frequency to the highest one (see Figure 4-11).

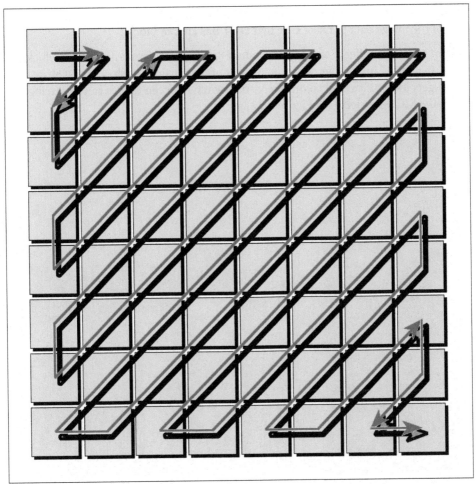

Figure 4-11. The zig-zag pattern used by JPEG to properly order lower-frequency components ahead of higher-frequency ones

Minimal coding units

So, we can apply DCT to any 8×8 block of pixel values. How does that apply to JPEG images that can be of arbitrary dimensions?

As part of the DCT process each image is broken up into 8×8-pixel blocks called *MCUs*, or *minimal coding units*. Each MCU undergoes DCT in an independent manner.

What happens when an image width or height doesn't perfectly divide by eight? In such cases (which are quite common), the encoder adds a few extra pixels for padding. These pixels are not really visible when the image is decoded, but are present as part of the image data to make sure that DCT has an 8×8 block.

One of the visible effects of the independent 8×8 block compression is the "blocking" effect that JPEG images get when being compressed using harsh settings. Since each MCU gets its own "overall color," the visual switch between MCUs can be jarring and mark the MCU barriers (see Figure 4-12).

Figure 4-12. Earlier image of French countryside with rough compression settings; note the visible MCU blockiness

Quantization

Up until now, we've performed DCT, but we didn't save much info. We replaced representing sixty-four 1-byte integer values with sixty-four 1-byte coefficients—nothing to write home about when it comes to data savings.

So, where do the savings come from? They come from a stage called *quantization*. This stage takes the aforementioned coefficients and divides them by a *quantization matrix* in order to reduce their value. That is the lossy part of the JPEG compression, the part where we discard some image data in order to reduce the overall size.

Figure 4-13. French countryside in winter

Let's take a look at the quantization matrix of Figure 4-13:

```
 3   2   8   8   8   8   8   8
 2  10   8   8   8   8   8   8
10   8   8   8   8   8   8   8
 8   8   8   8   8   8   8   8
 8   8   8   8   8  10   9   8
 8   8   8   8   8   9  12   7
 8   8   8   8   9  12  12   8
 8   8   8   8  10   8   9   8
```

But that image is the original that was produced by the digital camera, and is quite large from a byte size perspective (roughly 380 KB). What would happen if we compress that JPEG with quality settings of 70 to be 256 KB, or roughly 32% smaller? See Figure 4-14.

Figure 4-14. Same image with a quality setting of 70

And its quantization matrix?

```
10    7    6   10   14   24   31   37
 7    7    8   11   16   35   36   33
 8    8   10   14   24   34   41   34
 8   10   13   17   31   52   48   37
11   13   22   34   41   65   62   46
14   21   33   38   49   62   68   55
29   38   47   52   62   73   72   61
43   55   57   59   67   60   62   59
```

As you can see from the preceding quantization matrices, they have slightly larger values in the bottom-right corner than in the upper-left one. As we've seen, the bottom-right coefficients represent the higher-frequency coefficients. Dividing those by larger values means that more high-frequency coefficients will finish the quantization phase as a zero value coefficient. Also, in the $q=70$ version, since the dividers are almost eight times larger, a large chunk of the higher-frequency coefficients will end up discarded.

But, if we look the two images, the difference between them is not obvious. That's part of the magic of quantization. It gets rid of data that we're not likely to notice anyway. Well, up to a point at least.

Compression levels

Earlier we saw the same image, but compressed to a pulp. Wonder what the quantization matrix on that image looks like?

```
160  110  100  160  240  255  255  255
120  120  140  190  255  255  255  255
140  130  160  240  255  255  255  255
140  170  220  255  255  255  255  255
180  220  255  255  255  255  255  255
240  255  255  255  255  255  255  255
255  255  255  255  255  255  255  255
255  255  255  255  255  255  255  255
```

We can see that almost all frequencies beyond the first 20 are guaranteed to be quantified to 0 (as their corresponding quantization value is 255). And it's even harsher in the quantization matrix used for the chroma components:

```
170  180  240  255  255  255  255  255
180  210  255  255  255  255  255  255
240  255  255  255  255  255  255  255
255  255  255  255  255  255  255  255
255  255  255  255  255  255  255  255
255  255  255  255  255  255  255  255
255  255  255  255  255  255  255  255
255  255  255  255  255  255  255  255
```

It is not surprising, then, that the image showed such blockiness. But what we got in return for that quality loss is an image that is 27 KB or 93% (!!!) smaller than the original. And you could well argue that the result is still recognizable.

Note that the compression level and quality settings of the different JPEG encoders mean that they pick different quantization matrices to compress the images. It's also worth noting that there's no standard for what quantization matrices should be picked and what quality levels actually mean in practice. So, a certain quality setting in one encoder can mean something completely different (and of higher/lower visible quality) when you're using a different encoder.

One more thing of note is that encoders can (and often do) define a different quantization matrix for different components, so they can apply harsher quantization on the chroma components (which are less noticeable) than they would apply on the luma component.

Dropping zeros

How does zeroing out the coefficients help us better compress the image data? Since we are using a zig-zag pattern in order to sort the coefficients from lower frequency to high frequency, having multiple zero values at the end of our coefficient list is very easy to discard, resulting in great compression. JPEG further takes advantage of the fact that in many cases zero values tend to gather together, and adds a limited form of *run-length encoding*, which discards zeros and simply writes down the number of preceding zeros before nonzero values. The remaining values after quantization are also smaller numbers that are more amenable to entropy encoding, since there's higher probability that these values are seen multiple times than a random 0–255 brightness value.

Dequantization

At the decoder, the reverse process happens. The quantified coefficients are multiplied by the values of the quantization matrix (which is sent to the decoder as part of the DQT marker) in a process called *dequantization*, which recontructs an array of coefficients. The accuracy of these coefficients versus the coefficients encoded varies based on the values of the quantization matrix. As we've seen, the larger these values are, the further are the dequantized coefficients from the original ones, which results in harsher compression.

Lossy by nature

It is important to note that quantization is a lossy process, and YCbCr color transformations may also be lossy depending on the implementation. That means that if we take a JPEG and compress it to the same quality (so, using the same quantization tables) over and over, we will see a significant quality loss after a while. Each time we encode a JPEG, we lose some quality compared to the original images. That's something worth bearing in mind when constructing your image compression workflow.

Progressive JPEGs

Sequential JPEGs are JPEGs in which each MCU is sent in its entirety in a single scan. Such JPEGs can be decoded as they come, creating a partial image (Figure 4-15).

Figure 4-15. Image truncated after 60 KB of data

Progressive JPEGs, on the other hand, are JPEGs in which MCU data is sent over in multiple scans, enabling the decoder to start decoding an approximate image of the entire JPEG after receiving just one of the scans. Future scans further refine the image details. That enables supporting browsers to optimize the first impression of the user, without compromising the eventual image quality (see Figure 4-16).

Figure 4-16. Image truncated after 60 KB of data using progressive mode

We can see that the image is not perfect, but it is fairly complete.

There are two forms of sending JPEG data progressively: *spectral selection* and *successive approximation*. Spectral selection means that the parts of the MCU data that are sent first are the low-frequency coefficients in their entirety, with the higher-frequency coefficients sent as part of a later scan. Successive approximation means that for each coefficient, its first few bits are sent as part of an early scan, while the rest of its bits are sent at a later scan.

These two methods are not mutually exclusive, and can be combined for ideal progressive results. Some coefficients are sent in their entirety, while others are sent over multiple scans.

One significant advantage of progressive JPEGs is that each scan can have its own dedicated Huffman table, which means that progressive JPEGs can have a higher compression ratio, as each part of the JPEG can have a highly optimal Huffman table.

It is worth noting that, as the popular saying goes, there's more than one way to scan a JPEG. There's a very large number of combinations for possible scans, differing from one another in the coefficients that get sent in their entirety and the coefficients that get sent progressively using successive approximation, as well as which components get sent first.

This allows us to squeeze some extra compression from JPEGs. Finding the ideal combination of progressive scans and their relative Huffman compression performance is a nontrivial problem. Fortunately, the search space is not huge, so smart encoders just brute-force their way to find it. That is the secret of the lossless optimizations performed by tools like jpegrescan, which are now integrated as part of MozJPEG (which we'll soon discuss).

Unsupported Modes

The JPEG standard includes two more modes, but those are rarely supported by encoders and decoders, meaning they are rarely of practical use.

Hierarchical mode

Hierarchical operation mode is similar to progressive encoding, but with a significant difference. Instead of progressively increasing the quality of each MCU with each scan being decoded, the hierarchical mode enables progressively increasing the spatial resolution of the image with each scan.

That means that we can provide a low-resolution image and then add data to it to create a high-resolution image! Here's how it works: the first scan is a low-resolution baseline image, while each following scan upsamples the previous scan to create a prediction basis upon which it builds. This way, each scan other than the first sends only the difference required to complete the full-resolution image.

Unfortunately, it is not very efficient compared to other JPEG modes. It is also limited in its utility, since upsampling can only be done by a factor of two.

Lossless mode

The lossless operation mode in JPEG is another rarely supported operation mode. It is quite different from the other operation modes in the fact that it doesn't use DCT to perform its compression, but instead uses neighboring pixels–based prediction (called *differential pulse code modulation*, or *DPCM*) in order to anticipate the value of each pixel, and encodes only the difference between prediction and reality. Since the difference tends to be a smaller number, it is more susceptible to entropy coding, resulting in smaller images compared to the original bitmap (but still significantly larger than lossy, DCT-based JPEGs).

JPEG Optimizations

As we've seen in Chapter 2, lossy image formats such as JPEG (ignoring its irrelevant lossless mode of operation) can undergo both lossy and lossless types of compression. In this section we'll explore various optimization techniques that are often used to reduce the size of JPEG images.

Lossy

As far as lossy optimization, JPEG images can be optimized by undergoing the regular DCT-based high-frequency reduction, only with more aggressive quantization tables. Quantization tables with higher numeric values lead to higher loss of high-frequency brightness changes, resulting in smaller files with more visible quality loss.

Therefore, a common way to optimize JPEGs is to decompress them and then recompress them with lower "quality" values (which translate into higher numeric value quantization tables).

Lossless

There are multiple ways to losslessly optimize a JPEG:

- Optimize its Huffman tables for current scans.
- Rescan it, in order to achieve the ideal combination of progressive JPEG scans and Huffman tables.
- Remove nonphotographic data such as EXIF metadata.

We already discussed the first two when we talked about Huffman tables and progressive JPEGs, so we'll expand on the third here.

EXIF metadata is added to JPEGs by most, if not all, modern digital cameras and by some photo editing software. It contains information regarding when and where the image was taken, what the camera settings were, copyright, and more. It may also contain a thumbnail of the image, so that a preview image can be easily displayed.

However, when you're delivering images on the Web, all that info (perhaps besides copyright information) is not really relevant. The browser doesn't need that information and can display the image just fine without it. Furthermore, users cannot access that information unless they explicitly download the image to look for it (and disregarding very specific and niche use cases, they would not care about it).

Also, as we saw earlier, that metadata may appear in the JPEG before the information regarding the JPEG dimensions, which can lead to delays in the time it takes the browser to learn what the image dimensions are, and can result in a "bouncy" (or "bouncier") layout process.

So, it makes good sense to remove this metadata from web-served images. There are many software utilities that enable you to do that, and we'll further discuss them in Chapter 14.

You should note that EXIF data may also contain orientation information that in some cases can alter the orientation of the image when it's displayed in the browser. At least today, most browsers (with the notable exception of mobile Safari) ignore orientation information for images that are embedded in the document (either content images or background images), but they respect it when the user navigates directly to the image. Firefox also respects orientation information when an (experimental) CSS property called `image-orientation` indicates that it should.

Therefore, dropping orientation info can cause user confusion or content breakage in various scenarios. It is advisable to maintain it intact when processing JPEGs.

MozJPEG

We already mentioned that JPEG has been around for a long while, and JPEG encoders have existed for just as long. As a result, many of them have not been updated with new features and improvements in recent years. At the same time, various browser-specific image formats (which we'll discuss in the next chapter) were sparking interest in image compression and since their encoders were being written from scratch, they included more recent algorithms, which presented a non-negligable part of the reason these formats performed better than JPEG.

Mozilla, reluctant to introduce support for these newer formats, decided to start improving JPEG's encoding and bring it up to the current state of the art, so that we can at least compare the different formats on a level playing field.

Hence they started the MozJPEG project, with the goal of increasing JPEG's compression performance and creating smaller, similar quality files compared to other encoders, without hurting JPEG's compatibility with all existing browsers. In order to reduce unnecesary development, and increase compatibility with existing image compression workflow, the project is a fork of the libjpeg-turbo project and a drop-in replacement of it in terms of binary interface.

The project uses various encoding optimizations to achieve improved compression rates:

- Lossless compression based on ideal progressive scan patterns that produce smaller files
- Trellis quantization, an algorithm that enables the encoder to pick better adapted quantization coefficients, in order to minimize image distortion for the current image
- Quality tuning based on visual metrics, such as SSIM
- Deringing of black text over white background
- And more

Summary

In this chapter we looked into how JPEGs are constructed, which methods they use in order to achieve their impressive compression ratios, and how they can be optimized further.

Practical takeaways of this chapter include:

- Progressive JPEGs can show the full image in lower quality sooner, providing a better user experience than sequential JPEGs.
- Progressive JPEGs can have a smaller byte size than sequential ones.
- JPEG encoders' quality metric is often only an indication of the quantization table used, and its impact on various images may vary greatly.
- Lossless optimization, such as EXIF removal, can have significant implications on byte size as well as the browser's ability to calculate the image's layout as early as possible.
- Chroma subsampling can significantly reduce the size of JPEG's color components.
- JPEG compression is a lossy process, and each consecutive reencoding results in some quality loss.
- If you have an image compression workflow that's producing JPEGs, MozJPEG should probably be a part of it.

In the next chapter we will see how other, newer image formats are taking similiar methods further (by incorporating algorithmic knowledge that the compression industry has accumulated since 1992) to accomplish even better compression ratios.

CHAPTER 5

Browser-Specific Formats

Nick Doyle

While the traditional image formats used on the Web—GIF, JPEG, and PNG—have served us well and will continue to be useful long into the future, there are a number of new formats that can be particularly useful on the Web today. The most notable and useful of these formats are Google's WebP, Microsoft's JPEG XR, and JPEG 2000. All three of these formats improve on the features of GIF, JPEG, and PNG while often also improving compression and fidelity.

The biggest improvement these formats all provide to the Web is that they all support lossy compression with alpha transparency. Traditionally, to have an image on the Web with alpha transparency, the only option was to use PNG. While this enabled alpha transparency, it came at the cost of dramatically heavier images because PNG's compression is lossless. Now, with these new formats, it's possible to get the best of both worlds: alpha transparency at a fraction of the byte size.

The second improvement WebP, JPEG XR, and JPEG 2000 provide is smarter and more robust image compression. We've learned a lot about image compression since JPEG was first introduced in 1992, and these three formats have capitalized on that. While these formats each use a different approach to compression, they often outperform JPEG at comparable fidelity levels for byte savings.

There's one drawback to these formats, though, at least on today's Web: not all browsers support them. Actually, for the most part, any of today's major browsers will support only one, if any, of these formats. This means that, if you want to use any of these formats and get their benefits, you'll need to be smart about how the images get delivered. If you serve the wrong format to the wrong browser, you'll end up with a broken image at the added expense of transferring all of those image bytes to the end user for nothing. Bummer!

When these formats are used properly, however, there are substantial byte savings to be had. Let's discuss these three new formats in more detail.

WebP

WebP, developed and promoted by Google, was the first browser-specific image format to gain any substantial adoption and mindshare from web developers. It's based on Google's VP8 video codec; specifically, it wraps VP8's intraframe image coding in a RIFF image container.

Today, there are effectively three different variations of WebP: basic, extended, and animated. The basic variation is very simple: it supports encoding a single lossy opaque image, much like JPEG. The extended variation adds support for lossless compression and, more importantly, full transparency. Finally, animated WebP images are built on top of the extended variation and add animation support; this makes animated WebP images a good replacement for animated GIFs if the browser has support.

These three variations show that WebP is happy to evolve to improve and add features, but it also shows a tricky compatibility landscape. Different versions of different browsers have varying support for the different variations of WebP.

WebP Browser Support

Browser support for WebP extends primarily to Google- and Blink-based browsers: Chrome, Android Browser, and Opera. The current support matrix is shown in Table 5-1.

Table 5-1. WebP browser version support

	Basic	Extended	Animated
Chrome (desktop)	>= 17	>= 23	>= 32
Chrome (Android)	>= 25	>= 25	>= 32
Chrome (iOS)	>= 29 and < 48	>= 29 and < 48	No
Android	>= 4.0	>= 4.2	No
Opera (desktop)	>= 11.10	>= 12.10	>= 19
Safari	(< =10): No	No	No
Firefox	(< =10): No	No	No
Internet Explorer	(< =10): No	No	No
Edge	(< =10): No	No	No

WebP Support on Chrome for iOS

Chrome for iOS dropped WebP support in the transition from UIWebView to iOS 8's WKWebView. WKWebView brought performance and stability, but unfortunately, it uses the native Safari rendering engine and does not allow much in the way of customization. The result is that WebP support in iOS was dropped in version 48. All versions of Chrome for iOS, however, do support JPEG 2000.

Google suggests using the Accept HTTP request header and checking if it contains image/webp to determine if a server should serve a WebP image to a client. While this works for many cases, it has problems relating to the evolving nature of WebP. If a client sends an Accept: image/webp header, you can assume it supports up to the extended variation of WebP, but it is impossible to know (with the Accept header alone) if the client supports WebP animation. If new features are added to WebP (like improved VP9 coding), then this problem compounds and it will be impossible to determine support by Accept header alone.

Because of this deficiency with the Accept header and because most other browser-specific formats don't use the Accept header, the most robust solution generally is to, unfortunately, parse User-Agent strings to determine image support in addition to the Accept header. The Accept header is discussed in more detail in Chapter 13.

WebP Details

The most interesting variation of WebP when talking about optimizing for the Web is the extended variation. This variation is important because it supports both lossy encoding and full transparency. With these two features, WebP becomes a great format to replace both JPEG and PNG. You get the byte savings of JPEG (and then some) and the transparency support previously only available in the byte-heavy PNG format. The lossless compression modes are useful in many contexts, but web performance isn't particularly one of them. WebP offers good byte savings for its lossless encoding when compared to other lossless encodings, but the image weight is usually impractical for normal web use. The lossless encoding features of WebP are more interesting and relevant for image archiving purposes.

At its core, lossy WebP is encoded very similarly to how JPEG is encoded with some important differences. As in JPEG encoding, the Discrete Cosine Transform (DCT) is also used in WebP encoding. Instead of JPEG's 8×8-pixel blocks, WebP uses 4×4-pixel blocks for performing the DCT. WebP also allows for a variety of zig-zag patterns to traverse the pixels in a block compared to JPEG's single zig-zag pattern. The biggest improvement over JPEG is that WebP will try to predict the pixels in a block using pixels above and to the left of the block and a number of predetermined prediction algorithms. After WebP makes a prediction of a particular block, that block can be precisely described as a difference from this prediction. While JPEG applies the DCT to the raw pixels, WebP applies the DCT to this prediction difference. WebP's approach means that the coefficients produced by the DCT are generally much smaller and contain more zeros than JPEG's approach. This is one of the primary compression improvements of WebP over JPEG.

The second major difference between WebP and JPEG is the compression algorithm used to encode all of these DCT coefficients. JPEG uses Huffman encoding, whereas WebP uses the superior arithmetic encoding. The JPEG specification allows for JPEGs to be encoded using arithmetic encoding, but this capability was never implemented by anything other than very specialized encoders and decoders. The reason arithmetic encoding never caught on with JPEG is because, at the time, there were a number of patents protecting the algorithm and licensing the technology would have been costly. Because of this, virtually all JPEGs are encoded using Huffman encoding, and changing that would involve an almost impossible shift in JPEG compatibility and legacy JPEG code. By the time WebP hit the scene, patents surrounding arithmetic encoding had expired, allowing for a fresh start.

WebP isn't perfect, though: there are two important features of JPEG that are missing with (lossy) WebP. The first missing feature is configurable chroma subsampling. VP8 encoding specifies that a chroma subsampling of 4:2:0 will always be used; this means that all WebP images are also encoded using 4:2:0 chroma subsampling. For the vast majority of images this is a great choice and, among other benefits, provides very sizeable byte savings with minimal visual degradation. There are a number of image types, though, that don't lend themselves well to this aggressive chroma subsampling. Images with hard edges between black or white and solid color often have noticeable artifacts along these edges. With this chroma subsampling, there's often a dark ring in the colored edge that is unacceptable to many people. This is most commonly seen with solid colored text in images.

The inability to configure chroma subsampling in WebP means that either you have to live with this degradation or you have to use another image format for them. Thankfully, there's been recent work toward improving WebP's chroma subsampling. The latest version of the cwebp tool offers a -pre 4 option that uses a new chroma subsampling algorithm that dramatically reduces this degradation at the expense of longer image encoding time.

The second important feature that JPEG has that is missing from WebP is progressive loading. Instead of loading the image in full fidelity in a single pass, JPEG can load progressively, starting with an entire low-quality image that gradually improves in quality as data is received. This ability to show an early, full, low-quality image is great for the perception of fast loading; it makes people think the image has loaded much sooner than it really does. This feature is entirely absent from WebP. It can be argued that WebP images load faster than a comparable JPEG simply because WebP images are much lighter weight, bytewise. This argument doesn't necessarily hold up for large images, though, where it is more important to get a quicker sense of *completeness* at the expense of lower fidelity (which will later be improved) than it is to display the full-fidelity final image line-by-line as the data comes in.

The absence of progressive loading also makes some more interesting optimizations impossible. For example, with HTTP/2 it is possible to be clever about how image resources are prioritized and multiplexed. A smart HTTP/2 server might give a higher priority to the beginning of an image that can be progressively loaded and a lower priority to the remaining bytes. This allows the low-quality portion of the image to load quickly while also reducing bandwidth contention for other resources. This is, unfortunately, impossible with WebP.

WebP Tools

The tooling for working with WebP images is pretty good—better than all of the other tools for working with browser-specific image formats. The two main tools are *libwebp* and *ImageMagick*. libwebp is a C library for encoding and decoding WebP images but has useful standalone tools bundled with it. These tools are cwebp and dwebp for encoding and decoding WebP images, respectively. If you're familiar with cjpeg for creating JPEG images, then cwebp will feel very familiar. ImageMagick actually uses libwebp internally to provide WebP support. If you are already using ImageMagick for some of your image processing, then using it to take advantage of WebP is very convenient.

JPEG XR

JPEG XR is Microsoft's take on a new image format. The *XR* stands for *eXtended Range*, which was one of the primary goals of the format. JPEG XR allows for higher bit depths per color channel than JPEG, which leads to an extended range of possible colors that can be represented. While this extended range is the feature prominent in the format's name, it isn't the feature that's most interesting from a web performance perspective. As with WebP, the important features of JPEG XR above and beyond JPEG are improved lossy encoding and transparency support, making it a good replacement for both JPEG and PNG images.

JPEG XR Browser Support

The only browsers that support JPEG XR today are Microsoft's browsers, specifically Internet Explorer 10 and higher and the new Edge browser. While Internet Explorer 9 does support JPEG XR partially, there were rendering bugs that made the format unusable for most purposes. Internet Explorer 9 would display an unsightly grey border around all JPEG XR images; this was fixed in Internet Explorer 10. The current support matrix is shown in Table 5-2.

Table 5-2. JPEG XR browser version support

Internet Explorer	>= 10
Edge	Yes
Chrome	No
Android	No
Opera	No
Safari	No
Firefox	No

Internet Explorer and the Edge browser will send an `Accept: image/jxr` header with HTTP requests for images. This header could be used by a server to decide if a JPEG XR image should be served to a client. Unfortunately, Internet Explorer 10 and earlier don't send this header, so, in general, it's more practical to parse `User-Agent` strings if you want to cover the widest supported user base.

JPEG XR Details

JPEG XR supports all of the important features of JPEG while improving lossy encoding byte savings and adding support for full transparency. Unlike WebP, JPEG XR does support a full range of chroma subsampling options as well as progressive loading.

A number of new approaches are taken to compress images using JPEG XR, many of which are designed to enable—but not force—lossless encoding. Firstly, while JPEG uses YCbCr to describe pixel data, JPEG XR uses a similar but slightly different color space: YCgCo. Just as Cb is *blueness* and Cr is *redness*, Cg is *greenness* and Co is *orangeness*. YCgCo accomplishes a lot of the same goals as YCbCr but is able to do so in a completely lossless way.

Secondly, instead of using the Discrete Cosine Transform like JPEG, JPEG XR uses a modified version called Photo Core Transform (PCT). PCT is similar to DCT except that the process is entirely lossless as well. All lossiness in JPEG XR is entirely due to PCT coefficient quantization. A lossless JPEG XR image is the special case where all quantizations are set to 1—no quantization. JPEG XR improves on JPEG by allowing a certain amount of overlap when working with blocks of pixels. This overlap helps reduce the infamous blocking effect in low-quality JPEG images.

To improve compression, JPEG XR allows for different PCT coefficient ordering patterns instead of JPEG's single zig-zag pattern. JPEG XR also has a certain amount of block prediction to help reduce the magnitude of the PCT coefficients. Both of these techniques, if even at just a conceptual level, are mirrored in WebP. JPEG XR does not mirror WebP with the final entropy encoding, though. JPEG XR, like JPEG, still uses Huffman coding to compress the final PCT coefficient data instead of using the superior arithmetic encoding.

JPEG XR Tools

JPEG XR's tools are its biggest downfall. They are definitely the most difficult tools to use among all the browser-specific formats. Microsoft provides software called *jxrlib* with bundled tools called JxrEncApp and JxrDecApp to encode and decode JPEG XR images, respectively. The software is very rarely updated and is provided as source code only. Anyone who wants to use these tools will have to go through the process of building the software themselves for their own system.

ImageMagick advertises JPEG XR support, but it isn't particularly useful. ImageMagick supports only lossless encoding, so it isn't useful for web performance. ImageMagick actually just delegates all encoding and decoding work to the JxrEncApp and JxrDecApp tools if it's able to find them. This delegation seems to work inconsistently, however. It's often worth the effort to use the JxrEncApp and JxrDecApp tools directly even though they are rather difficult to use.

JPEG 2000

JPEG 2000 was developed by the Joint Photographic Experts Group as their follow-up to JPEG. In addition to a completely new way of encoding images, a number of new features were added to JPEG 2000 that weren't available in JPEG, like lossless encoding, higher-channel bit depths, and full transparency support.

JPEG 2000 Browser Support

Support for JPEG 2000 is available in all of Apple's recent browsers. Support has been available in desktop and mobile Safari since version 5. An interesting side effect of this Safari support is that Chrome for iOS also supports JPEG 2000. This is because Chrome for iOS is built on top of Safari instead of Blink, which means it's the only browser that supports more than one browser-specific format: JPEG 2000 and WebP. The current support matrix is shown in Table 5-3.

Table 5-3. JPEG 2000 browser version support

Safari	>= 5
Chrome (iOS)	Yes
Chrome (non-iOS)	No
Internet Explorer	No
Edge	No
Android	No
Opera	No
Firefox	No

Safari doesn't send any hints in HTTP headers about what image formats it will accept. Unlike recent versions of Chrome and Edge, Safari doesn't send any Accept header with image requests. This means that the most practical way for a server to determine whether or not it should send a JPEG 2000 image is by parsing the User-Agent string.

JPEG 2000 Details

JPEG 2000 maintains all of the important features of JPEG, including configuration options for chroma subsampling and progressive loading, which are absent from WebP. Support for full transparency has been added, which, as with WebP and JPEG XR, makes JPEG 2000 another great alternative to JPEG and PNG.

While the feature set of JPEG 2000 is similar to the other browser-specific formats, under the hood it is the most different format as far as encoding of the actual image is concerned. JPEG 2000 doesn't use DCT or any variation of DCT; instead, JPEG 2000 uses a Discrete Wavelet Transform (DWT) at the core of its encoding. It's best to think of DWT as a transform that takes an image (like the one shown in Figure 5-1) and divides it into four parts (Figure 5-2). The first part is the original image at one-half the width and one-half the height. The other three parts are all also individually one-half the height and one-half the width of the original image, but, combined, contain the *details* necessary to exactly construct the full-size image from the first part. One part has horizontal details, one part has vertical details, and the last part has diagonal details.

Figure 5-1. Original image before Discrete Wavelet Transform

Figure 5-2. Image after Discrete Wavelet Transform (details enhanced for demonstration purposes)

You can see in Figure 5-2 that the three detail parts are mostly empty and black. This emptiness allows for a lot of opportunities for compression. To extract even more sparse details, we can repeat this DWT process recursively on the first newly scaled image part. After we've recursively applied DWT a number of times, the detail parts are quantized much like DCT coefficients are quantized in JPEG. After quantization, arithmetic encoding is used for final compression.

JPEG 2000 Tools

The tools for encoding JPEG 2000 are in the middle of the road as far as ease of use and features go. The *OpenJPEG* project provides a C library and the `opj_compress` and `opj_decompress` tools for encoding and decoding images, respectively. These tools don't abstract the concept of "quality" to a simple 1–100 scale like most image encoders; instead, quality is described using compression ratios or PSNR values. The current release is also missing important features like transparency and chroma sub-sampling support, although transparency support is available if you build the latest unreleased version from the project's source control repository.

ImageMagick has decent JPEG 2000 support and, in fact, uses the *OpenJPEG* C library behind the scenes. This means that ImageMagick has the same limitations as OpenJPEG when working with JPEG 2000 images but provides a simpler interface if you're already familiar with ImageMagick.

Finally, *Kakadu Software* makes a popular full-featured JPEG 2000 encoder that people and businesses can license for a fee. While features like chroma subsampling are available, learning how to use them is difficult. This encoder is also much faster for encoding than OpenJPEG.

Summary

The web continues to evolve and move forward, so it makes sense that our image formats will as well. While the GIF, JPEG, and PNG have served us well so far, there's always room for improvement. The WebP, JEPG XR, and JPEG 2000 formats each bring new and improved approaches to compression that can provide signficant savings in terms of file size.

While they face an uphill battle in terms of both browser support and tooling, you can still take advantage of these formats to provide improved performance to the browsers that do support them and in Chapter 11, we'll look at exactly how to do that.

In the next chapter, however, let's turn our attention away from raster images and explore what vector formats bring to the table.

CHAPTER 6

SVG and Vector Images

Tim Kadlec

So far our focus has been on raster image formats—and for good reason. Raster formats are the dominant image format on the Web. They're capable of representing highly detailed and photographic images, whereas vector formats are not. Combine that with the large ecosystem of tooling and editors supporting them, and it's little wonder that they've reigned supreme.

However, raster images are not without limitations. They don't scale well, and there is an almost linear relationship between display size and file size. Both of these issues have become glaringly obvious thanks to the rapid increase in the diversity of devices accessing the Web. Confronted with the variety of screen sizes being used, web designers and developers have become painfully aware of these issues. There have been two major outcomes of this:

- New responsive image standards have evolved.
- There has been an increased interest in vector formats, most notably the *Scalable Vector Graphics (SVG)* format.

We will be discussing the responsive image standards in Chapter 11, *Responsive Images*. In this chapter, let's take a look at how vector formats overcome the limits of raster formats, and how and when to use them.

The Trouble with Raster Formats

As we saw in Chapter 2, raster images are composed of a matrix of pixels. This matrix matches the dimensions of the actual image, and each cell represents a single pixel of the image. While this matrix enables raster formats to represent detailed photographic images, it also causes issues when trying to scale raster images.

If a browser or other application needs to scale a raster image beyond the size of that matrix, it needs to create new pixels. For example, scaling a 100x100-pixel image to 120x120 means the browser needs color data for an additional 4,400 pixels (120x120–100x100) that are not represented in the original matrix.

Lacking the proper information for these additional pixels, the browser does the next best thing: it guesses. The browser looks at the surrounding pixels to get an idea of what color values are present, and then uses that information to figure out approximately what color values these additional pixels should contain. The result of all these extra pixels, with their approximated values, is that a scaled raster image will appear blurry and full of digital artifacts.

If a developer wants to serve a raster image intended to be displayed at a variety of sizes without scaling artifacts, he or she will need to produce the image at a number of different dimensions and serve them using the appropriate responsive standards (discussed in Chapter 11). This helps to minimize the scalability issues, but it highlights another limitation of raster formats: the almost linear relation between image dimensions and file size.

Imagine you were going to include a simple square image on your site. The square would need to be displayed at 100x100 pixels on the smallest screen, 700x700 pixels on the largest, and 400x400 pixels somewhere in between. Even though the image is not complex at all, the way raster formats work means that all pixels will need to be processed, compressed, and outputted to the final file. This means our 700x700 version of the square is likely to be significantly heavier than our 100×100 pixel version of the square—it has to store 490,000 pixels (700×700) of data compared to 10,000 pixels of data (100×100) for the smaller image.

What Is a Vector Image?

Vector formats help to address these limitations by describing how an image should be constructed, rather than storing all the pixel data. Vector images comprise a series of points, lines, curves, shapes, and colors that are described by mathematical expressions. This allows the client to calculate how the image should be displayed, maintaining these basic expressions no matter the size of the image ultimately being displayed.

Let's go back to our square. Using a vector format like SVG, the instruction for building the square would look like this:

```
<svg xmlns="http://www.w3.org/2000/svg"
  width="100" height="100" viewBox="0 0 100 100">
  <rect height="100" width="100" fill="#f00" />
</svg>
```

If the specific markup there doesn't make sense to you yet, don't worry—we'll get to the basics of the SVG format in a minute. For now, it's enough to know that these three lines of code describe a perfect square, filled in with the color red. This same markup accurately describes the square no matter the resolution; whether displayed at 100x100 or 700x700, these commands are all the client needs to determine just how to draw the image—no difference in file size necessary.

There's no such thing as a free lunch, though—there is a tradeoff being made here. While using markup to describe the content of an image can greatly reduce the file size, it does require the client to do more work processing that information and drawing it out to the screen. Typically, this process involves the data in the SVG being software rendered to a bitmap (rasterized), and then uploaded to the GPU. The more complex the image, the more instructions the software needs in order to perform rasterization. The more instructions, the longer it will take to process and follow them all. This is why you will frequently see poor performance on older browsers, particularly on low-powered mobile devices, for SVG. It's a complex task that can tax the device.

Thankfully, this situation is improving. Browsers are continuing to evolve and improve the efficiency of how they display and process SVG images, eliminating the bulk of the on-device overhead. Still, it's a good idea to remember that the more complex your SVG image, the more work you'll be requiring the client to do in order to display it. That complexity also means a heavier file size. As a result, vector formats should be used primarily on simple images: those with a limited number of colors and shapes.

SVG Fundamentals

On the Web if you want to use a vector format, it's going to be SVG. There aren't any other contenders with any semblance of cross-browser support. Before we get into the specifics of how to optimize SVG files for performance, let's spend a few pages getting to understand a few core concepts of the format.

Hungry for More SVG Information?

It's beyond the scope of this chapter to try to provide a comprehensive, detailed resource for the SVG format—we're primarily focused on the basics and the performance impacts. If you'd like to dig deeper, Sara Souedian has done a tremendous job writing detailed posts on her blog (*https://sarasoueidan.com/tags/svg/index.html*).

If you're just starting to get familar with the SVG format, it can be useful to remember that it's markup, like HTML. In HTML, a root element (<html>) and any number of other elements enable you to define particular sections of your page. A distinct paragraph goes in the <p> element. A table is marked up with the <table> element.

SVG works similarly. There is a root element (<svg>) and a number of different core elements. The difference is that in the case of SVG, those core elements are describing shapes and lines. Just as with elements in an HTML page, we can style the individual elements within an SVG document using CSS and interact with them using JavaScript. This not only enables far more granular control over how the individual pieces constituting an SVG element are displayed, but also allows you to animate or otherwise alter these elements.

Whither Thee DOCTYPE?

You may be wondering if I've overlooked another key component of XML-based languages like SVG and HTML: the document type.

While it's true that SVG technically has a DOCTYPE element that can be included, in practice it's rarely a good idea due to misuse. In fact, in the latest specs for SVG, the document type has been removed entirely.

The Grid

SVG elements are positioned based on a coordinate system. The top-left corner, for example, has the coordinates (0,0). Any element positioned within the document is measured from that top-left corner. If you're thinking that sounds similar to what you learned in school about graphs, you're right—with one wrinkle. In SVG, the x attribute pushes you to the right and the y attribute pushes you toward the bottom—the opposite of what you may be used to.

Consider, again, a simple red square:

```
<rect x="10" y="10" height="100" width="100" fill="#f00" />
```

This element would result in a square that starts 10 px from the left and 10 px from the top, then spans 100 px to the right and 100 px down. Where things get interesting is when you consider the canvas that the coordinate system relates to.

Understanding the Canvas

In the context of a web page, there are two variables in terms of size: the dimensions of the page itself, and the dimensions that can be viewed at a single moment in time. For example, you may have a web page that, with all content and images loaded, is 3,000 px high. Yet the browser window itself may only show 800 px vertically at a single time. Similarly, your page may be wider than the width of the browser. In either case, some content will not be visible—it'll be cut off from view.

The same is true of SVG. You have a canvas that can be thought of as infinite in height and width, and you have a viewport that defines what part of that SVG canvas is actually visible—anything that lies outside of that viewport area is cut off.

To define the viewport, you apply the width and height attributes to the root <svg> element:

```
<svg xmlns="http://www.w3.org/2000/svg"
  width="100" height="100">
  <!-- super exciting SVG content to be drawn -->
</svg>
```

This example establishes a viewport of 100x100 pixels. In addition, by establishing the viewport, we've also initialized two different coordinate systems: the initial viewport coordinate system and the initial user coordinate system.

Height and Width Matters

The height and width attributes are incredibly important. It can be tempting to remove these attributes, and in fact many software applications, such as Adobe Illustrator, offer the option to do so when you export an SVG image from the application. Removing them is almost never a good idea, however.

If an SVG image is served in a browser, and there are no height and width attributes applied, the browser will scale the SVG to fill the width of the browser viewport. You can override this behavior using CSS, but if the SVG image is displayed before the CSS is applied, you'll get a very unseemly flash of this obnoxiously large, unstyled SVG.

If, however, the height and width attributes are present, the browser will display the SVG at the dimensions specified by those attributes. If and when CSS is applied, the CSS still overrides the dimensions set by those attributes. The only difference is that you no longer have a situation where the browser is trying to scale the SVG to massive proportions.

The initial viewport coordinate system is based on the viewport. Its origin is the top-left corner of the viewport—point (0,0). The initial user coordinate system is based on the SVG canvas. Initially, it's identical to the viewport coordinate system and has the same origin point of (0,0). The primary difference between the two is that the user coordinate system can be altered via the viewBox attribute.

viewBox

The viewBox attribute accepts a value made up of four parameters: min-x, min-y, width, and height. The first two parameters, min-x and min-y, set the upper-left corner of the viewbox, while the final parameters, width and height, determine the dimensions. *The viewBox attribute is crucial—without it browsers will not scale SVG elements.*

If we revisit our example from before, we could set the viewBox to be identical to the SVG viewport by applying the viewBox attribute as follows:

```
<svg xmlns="http://www.w3.org/2000/svg"
  width="100" height="100" viewBox="0 0 100 100">
  <!-- super exciting SVG content to be drawn -->
</svg>
```

That in itself is not particularly interesting. Where it gets fun is when we start to alter the viewBox so that it has different dimensions from the viewport or shift it from the top-left corner a bit.

For example, let's alter the viewBox to be a quarter of the size of the viewport itself:

```
<svg xmlns="http://www.w3.org/2000/svg"
  width="100" height="100" viewBox="0 0 25 25">
  <!-- super exciting SVG content to be drawn -->
</svg>
```

In this example, because we've kept min-x and min-y set to "0" (the first two values of the viewBox attribute), the top-left corner of the viewBox is still the same point as the viewport: (0,0). However, the dimensions of the viewBox itself are only a quarter of the size of the full viewport.

You can imagine the viewBox in this case to be an instruction to the client to zoom in on a certain portion of the viewport area. In this case, the selected area will be the first 25x25 area, starting at the top-left corner. Anything that is part of the SVG element that does not lie within the viewBox will be ignored.

With that 25x25 area selected, the next thing that happens is that the client will zoom in on it—scaling it up until the area within the viewBox is stretched to fill the full 100x100-pixel viewport of the SVG itself (see Figure 6-1). What we've essentially done here is select a subset of the SVG image and zoom in by a factor of four.

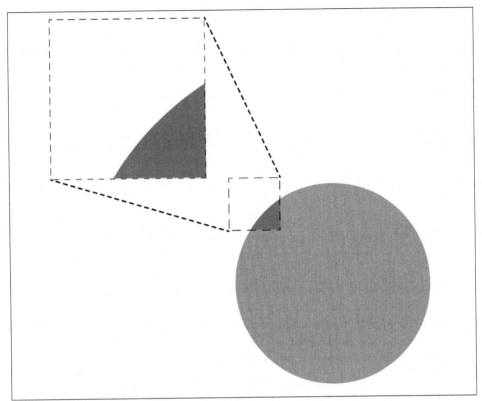

Figure 6-1. Zoomed in area of an SVG image subset

We've also changed the user coordinate system. It no longer matches the viewport coordinate system. Instead, one user coordinate unit is equivalent to four units in the viewport coordinate system (because we zoomed in by a factor of four).

Sara Soueidan has compared this to Google Maps. You can choose a specific region within a given map, and Google Maps will zoom in on it. The rest of the map is still there, it's just not visible as it extends beyond the viewport. This is exactly what happens here: the rest of the content within the SVG file still exists, it's just not visible. It's cropped out.

It's a Matter of Scale

Just as you'll often want to keep the height and width attributes around, you'll almost certainly want to make sure the viewBox attribute is present and accounted for. If a browser sees an SVG image without a defined viewBox, it will not scale that image—effectively defeating one of the primary reasons why the SVG format exists.

Getting into Shape

Most drawing within an SVG image is done by including a number of different elements that correspond to various shapes. The basic shapes included within SVG are listed in Table 6-1.

Table 6-1. Basic SVG shapes

Basic shape	Corresponding element	Example
Rectangle	rect	`<rect x="0" y="0" width="50" height="50"/>`
Circle	circle	`<circle cx="50" cy="75" r="20"/>`
Ellipse	ellipse	`<ellipse cx="75" cy="75" rx="20" ry="5"/>`
Straight line	line	`<line x1="0" y1="110" x2="20" y2="150"/>`
Group of connected lines	polyline	`<polyline points="0,0  30,0  15,30"/>`
Polygon	polygon	`<polygon points="10,0  60,0  35,50"/>`

In addition to the basic shapes, there is also the `<path>` element. If using basic shapes is roughly the equivalent of tracing predefined stencils on a paper, then the `<path>` element is the equivalent of handing you a pencil and letting you draw whatever you wanted. Because of this, the `<path>` element is incredibly powerful and expressive. That power comes at the cost of complexity, though.

For example, if you wanted to draw a 100x100-pixel red square using the `<rect>` element, the code would look something like this:

```
<svg xmlns="http://www.w3.org/2000/svg"
  width="100" height="100" viewBox="0 0 100 100">
  <rect height="100" width="100" fill="#f00" />
</svg>
```

In contrast, accomplishing the same thing with the `<path>` element would involve quite a bit more information:

```
<svg xmlns="http://www.w3.org/2000/svg"
  width="100" height="100" viewBox="0 0 100 100">
  <path d="M 0 0 H 100 V 100 H 0" fill="#f00" ></path>
</svg>
```

Let's break down that `<path>` description attribute (d) to see exactly what's happening here:

M 0 0

> The M represents the "MoveTo" command and moves to a specific point within the coordinate system. It's necessary at the start of a path description to establish the starting point. Here, we've specified that the starting point should be the top-left corner of the user coordinate system—point (0,0).

```
H 100
```

H is a shortcut for drawing a horizontal line. In this case, we're telling the client to draw a horizontal line 100 px wide, starting at the current position (which we defined using the initial "MoveTo" command).

```
V 100
```

At this point, we've drawn a 100 px horizontal line from point (0,0), bringing us to point (100,0). Now we need to tell the client to draw a vertical line, which we do using the V command. In this example, we've just told the client to draw a 100 px vertical line, bringing us to point (100,100).

```
H 0
```

We're almost there! All we need to do now is tell the client to draw one more horizontal line, back to point (0,100). We don't need to tell it to close the shape—it will connect the final point to the origin by default.

With the `<rect>` element, we didn't have to go through the process of explaining each individual command. That's because the `<rect>` element is essentially a shortcut—it understands the basic process of drawing out a rectangular shape, so all it needs are the starting point and the dimensions.

This is true of each basic shape: they're essentially recipes. They know the steps needed to construct a very specific type of shape and, as a result, don't need as many detailed instructions as required with the `<path>` element.

Our square example wasn't too unwieldy, but that's not always the case: the more complex the path you are describing, the more instructions you'll need to provide. This can lead to significant bloat within the file. It also makes the client work harder to rasterize those paths. Basic shapes aren't just shortcuts for you, the person coding the SVG files—they're shortcuts that the browser can take as well.

For this reason, whenever possible, you'll want to favor using basic shapes for drawing purposes—lightening the load over the network as well as the load on the client to display the image once it has been downloaded. Save the `<path>` element for more complex shapes and use them sparingly.

This isn't necessarily a hard and fast rule—it would be boring if it were that easy. There are exceptions. The most typical are the polygon and polyline shapes, both of which can get rather complicated for more complex shapes. At times in those situations, the `<path>` element may actually be less complicated and bloated. As with anything in terms of performance, be sure to measure the impact to ensure you're getting the results you're after.

Grouping Shapes Together

One of the really nice features of SVG is that you can group and reuse elements within the SVG image, helping you avoid unnecessarily repetitive markup. There are four basic elements that enable this behavior: <g>, <use>, <defs>, and <symbol>. These elements will become particularly important in Chapter 10 when we discuss SVG sprite sheets.

The <g> element

Let's say that we've re-created the basic shape of the Olympic rings in SVG using the following markup:

```
<svg xmlns="http://www.w3.org/2000/svg"
    viewBox="0 0 120 65">
    <circle stroke-width="3" fill="none" cx="25"
      stroke="rgb(11,112,191)" cy="25" r="15"></circle>
    <circle stroke-width="3" fill="none" cx="40"
      stroke="rgb(240,183,0)" cy="40" r="15"></circle>
    <circle stroke-width="3" fill="none" cx="60"
      stroke="rgb(0,0,0)" cy="25" r="15"></circle>
    <circle stroke-width="3" fill="none" cx="75"
      stroke="rgb(13,146,38)" cy="40" r="15"></circle>
    <circle stroke-width="3" fill="none" cx="95"
      stroke="rgb(214,0,23)" cy="25" r="15"></circle>
</svg>
```

Each circle is its own separate element. We define the position of each circle and apply a colored stroke to create our rings. When viewed together they appear as the Olympic rings (see Figure 6-2). Since we really want them as a unified object in this case, we can group them together using the group element (<g>), which is intended for logically grouping related elements together.

Figure 6-2. Five individual circle elements are used, but the resulting image is one uni-fied group

Here's what our markup looks like if we group the circles together:

```
<svg xmlns="http://www.w3.org/2000/svg"
  viewBox="0 0 115 65">
  <g id="rings">
    <circle stroke-width="3" fill="none" cx="25"
      stroke="rgb(11,112,191)" cy="25" r="15"/>
    <circle stroke-width="3" fill="none" cx="40"
      stroke="rgb(240,183,0)" cy="40" r="15"/>
    <circle stroke-width="3" fill="none" cx="60"
      stroke="rgb(0,0,0)" cy="25" r="15"/>
    <circle stroke-width="3" fill="none" cx="75"
      stroke="rgb(13,146,38)" cy="40" r="15"/>
    <circle stroke-width="3" fill="none" cx="95"
      stroke="rgb(214,0,23)" cy="25" r="15"/>
  </g>
</svg>
```

Nothing has changed visually; we've just added a little more structure to our image by grouping those circles together and providing an id to refer to the group.

Structure is nice from a maintenance perspective, but by grouping these elements, we can also simplify our markup a little. If you notice, while the position and color of each circle differ, the fill and stroke-width remain the same. Attributes that are applied to a group element also apply to descendants of the group element. We can take advantage of this and pull out the stroke-width and fill, applying them to the group instead:

```
<svg xmlns="http://www.w3.org/2000/svg"
   viewBox="0 0 115 65">
  <g id="rings" stroke-width="3" fill="none">
    <circle cx="25" stroke="rgb(11,112,191)" cy="25" r="15"/>
    <circle cx="40" stroke="rgb(240,183,0)" cy="40" r="15"/>
    <circle cx="60" stroke="rgb(0,0,0)" cy="25" r="15"/>
    <circle cx="75" stroke="rgb(13,146,38)" cy="40" r="15"/>
    <circle cx="95" stroke="rgb(214,0,23)" cy="25" r="15"/>
  </g>
</svg>
```

Our markup is now both easier to read and less repetitive. Grouping also provides the benefit of making it much easier to transform these elements in CSS, or make them interactive using JavaScript. Instead of having to wrangle each individual element, we can apply our CSS or attach our JavaScript directly to the group element, and the descendants will all follow along.

The use element

Grouping these elements together also allows us to easily repeat the group by taking advantage of the <use> element.

In order to use the xlink:href attribute without any errors, you'll need to include the xlink namespace on the root svg element like so:

```
<svg xmlns="http://www.w3.org/2000/svg"
   xmlns:xlink="http://www.w3.org/1999/xlink">
```

The <use> element allows you to refer to other content (like a group element) using the xlink:href attribute. You can then use the x and y attributes to move the new group's origin to a new location. It's important to note that the x and y coordinates are relative to the position of the original element.

For example, if we wanted to add another set of rings below our first set, we could expand our viewBox slightly and then reuse the group like so:

```
<svg xmlns="http://www.w3.org/2000/svg"
   xmlns:xlink="http://www.w3.org/1999/xlink"
   viewBox="0 0 115 130">
  <g id="rings" stroke-width="3" fill="none">
    <circle cx="25" stroke="rgb(11,112,191)" cy="25" r="15"/>
    <circle cx="40" stroke="rgb(240,183,0)" cy="40" r="15"/>
    <circle cx="60" stroke="rgb(0,0,0)" cy="25" r="15"/>
    <circle cx="75" stroke="rgb(13,146,38)" cy="40" r="15"/>
    <circle cx="95" stroke="rgb(214,0,23)" cy="25" r="15"/>
  </g>
  <use x="0" y="65" xlink:href="#rings" />
</svg>
```

In this example, we reference the `rings` group using the `xlink:href` attribute. We then specify that we want the starting *x* coordinate to be identical to the starting *x* coordinate of the original element (x="0") and that we'd like to shift the image down from the starting *y* coordinate of the original element (y="65"). The result is two sets of identical rings, stacked vertically (Figure 6-3).

Figure 6-3. By using the use element, we're able to duplicate the original group of rings without having to repeat ourselves in the markup

We could also have referenced an external SVG file inside our `use` element. The following snippet shows how you would do that:

```
<use x="0" y="65" xlink:href="/other/svg/file.svg#rings" />
```

Depending on what you're trying to accomplish, referencing these files externally may be the ideal option, as it enables each SVG file you are using to be cached individually. There are browser support issues (in Internet Explorer prior to version 11) to be aware of, but we'll discuss how to navigate those when we explore SVG spriting.

The defs element

Hopefully by now it's becoming clear how useful the group element can be. However, you may have also noticed a catch: the group element is rendered onto the canvas. In the examples we've been showing, that's OK. There are times, though, where you may want to have a pattern grouped together that you don't want to render until you've included it elsewhere using the `<use>` element. To accomplish this, we can wrap the group element within a `<defs>` element—allowing us to define the rings as a set of grouped elements without having them rendered:

```
<svg xmlns="http://www.w3.org/2000/svg"
  xmlns:xlink="http://www.w3.org/1999/xlink"
  viewBox="0 0 115 65">
  <defs>
    <g id="rings" stroke-width="3" fill="none">
      <circle cx="25" stroke="rgb(11,112,191)" cy="25" r="15"/>
      <circle cx="40" stroke="rgb(240,183,0)" cy="40" r="15"/>
      <circle cx="60" stroke="rgb(0,0,0)" cy="25" r="15"/>
      <circle cx="75" stroke="rgb(13,146,38)" cy="40" r="15"/>
      <circle cx="95" stroke="rgb(214,0,23)" cy="25" r="15"/>
    </g>
  </defs>
  <use x="0" y="65" xlink:href="#rings" />
</svg>
```

In this example, we've wrapped our group within a `defs` element, which stops it from being rendered. It's defined but not displayed. This alters the way the x and y coordinates on the `use` element behave. With group elements, since they are displayed, the x and y coordinates on the `use` element are relative to the original group. Now that the `defs` element has stopped the group from being displayed, however, there is no original element to position relative to. Instead, we're back to the familiar process of positioning our `use` element relative to the user coordinate system.

The symbol element

The final element related to grouping and reuse is the `symbol` element. The `symbol` element has some similarities both to the `<g>` element and the `defs` element. Like the `<g>` element, it is intended as a way to logically group related elements together. Like the `defs` element, however, any `symbols` that are defined are not rendered until they're referenced later by a `use` element.

The symbol element also differs from the group element in that it can have its own viewBox and preserveAspectRatio attributes, letting you alter the way it fits within the viewport.

Other than that, it's used in the same way as the <g> element, so the markup is nearly identical:

```
<svg xmlns="http://www.w3.org/2000/svg"
  xmlns:xlink="http://www.w3.org/1999/xlink"
  viewBox="0 0 115 65">
  <symbol id="rings">
    <circle stroke-width="3" fill="none" cx="25"
      stroke="rgb(11,112,191)" cy="25" r="15"/>
    <circle stroke-width="3" fill="none" cx="40"
      stroke="rgb(240,183,0)" cy="40" r="15"/>
    <circle stroke-width="3" fill="none" cx="60"
      stroke="rgb(0,0,0)" cy="25" r="15"/>
    <circle stroke-width="3" fill="none" cx="75"
      stroke="rgb(13,146,38)" cy="40" r="15"/>
    <circle stroke-width="3" fill="none" cx="95"
      stroke="rgb(214,0,23)" cy="25" r="15"/>
  </symbol>
  <use x="0" y="0" xlink:href="#rings" />
</svg>
```

We'll go into more detail about some of the other differences and gotchas around each of these grouping elements in Chapter 10.

Filters

If you've ever opened Photoshop (or something similar), you're probably familiar with the idea of *filters*—graphic operations such as drop shadows and blurs that you can apply to your image. The advantage of a vector format in this regard is that the filtering can be done through markup or applied with CSS.

Filters are essentially post-processing steps for your images. For an HTML page to be loaded within a browser, the browser needs to go through a series of steps to construct the page: grab all the elements, apply the styles, lay out the elements on the screen, and finally render the page. Filtering introduces one more step in the process. Just before the page is displayed on the screen, the filter is overlaid on any images it is being applied to.

Applying filters

You can apply filters to your SVG images in one of two ways. The first is to use the filter element to define a filter that can then be referred to later in the SVG file.

Here's an example of what a drop shadow might look like when applied to our Olympic rings:

```
<svg xmlns="http://www.w3.org/2000/svg"
  viewBox="0 0 115 65">
  <defs>
    <filter id="dropShadow">
      <feGaussianBlur in="SourceAlpha" stdDeviation="1"></feGaussianBlur>
      <feOffset dx="1" dy="1" result="offsetblur"></feOffset>
      <feFlood flood-color="#000000"></feFlood>
      <feComposite in2="offsetblur" operator="in"></feComposite>
      <feMerge>
        <feMergeNode></feMergeNode>
        <feMergeNode in="SourceGraphic"></feMergeNode>
      </feMerge>
    </filter>
  </defs>
  <g id="rings" stroke-width="3" fill="none" filter="url(#dropShadow)">
    <circle cx="25" stroke="rgb(11,112,191)" cy="25" r="15"/>
    <circle cx="40" stroke="rgb(240,183,0)" cy="40" r="15"/>
    <circle cx="60" stroke="rgb(0,0,0)" cy="25" r="15"/>
    <circle cx="75" stroke="rgb(13,146,38)" cy="40" r="15"/>
    <circle cx="95" stroke="rgb(214,0,23)" cy="25" r="15"/>
  </g>
</svg>
```

The only thing we changed regarding our original group of rings is that we've added the `filter` attribute, referring to the `id` of the new filter we just defined. The rest of the magic is happening inside that `filter` element. Let's walk through it.

The fourth line defines the filter and gives it an `id` of `"dropShadow"` so that we can refer to it later.

Lines 5 through 10 are *filter primitive elements*. The filter primitives are what actually describe the work to be done. The browser will walk through each primitive, applying it step by step, to create the overall filter. Digging deep into all of the native filters is a little beyond the scope of this chapter: we're introducing this concept only to highlight a few performance gotchas. The result of each of those primitives in this case is a small drop shadow. When we apply it to our rings group, each individual circle will have a drop shadow applied.

You can achieve a similar effect by taking advantage of CSS filter effects. In fact, the whole thing becomes much simpler. Here's a drop shadow applied to our rings using CSS (see Figure 6-4):

```
<svg xmlns="http://www.w3.org/2000/svg"
  viewBox="0 0 115 65" style="-webkit-filter: drop-shadow(2px 5px 7px black);">
    <g id="rings" stroke-width="3" fill="none">
      <circle cx="25" stroke="rgb(11,112,191)" cy="25" r="15"></circle>
      <circle cx="40" stroke="rgb(240,183,0)" cy="40" r="15"></circle>
      <circle cx="60" stroke="rgb(0,0,0)" cy="25" r="15"></circle>
      <circle cx="75" stroke="rgb(13,146,38)" cy="40" r="15"></circle>
      <circle cx="95" stroke="rgb(214,0,23)" cy="25" r="15"></circle>
```

```
    </g>
  </svg>
```

Unfortunately, support for CSS filters is still limited at the time of writing, with most browsers that do support them having hidden them behind a prefix or configuration flag.

Figure 6-4. We can apply filters with CSS or the SVG filter element to add effects such as blurring and drop shadows

Performance concerns

Because this does introduce a new step in the process of displaying a page, you want to be careful with how many filters you apply: they're not free. Usually, if you're careful about how many filters you apply, it's not too much of an issue. Where it becomes a bit more serious is when you try applying any filter that involves some sort of blurring—effects such as applying a drop shadow or, well, a blur. This is because the process of creating the blur is rather involved.

Let's say you apply a 10-pixel blur to your SVG image. In order for the browser to display it properly, it needs to walk through the original image, pixel by pixel. For each pixel of the original image, it must also look at the surrounding 10 pixels in every direction in order to properly calculate the colors to be displayed. This process becomes more unwieldy the larger the radius. The browser will try to optimize this process as much as possible, but you can still run into some rather serious performance issues—particularly on an underpowered device.

The wrong way to do filters

Filters are incredibly powerful and useful. Mostly, if they're kept in check, the performance isn't too bad, other than those filters involving some level of blurring. If you're using a graphics editing program to apply these filters, you'll want to pay very close attention to the outputted code: it may not be doing exactly what you think.

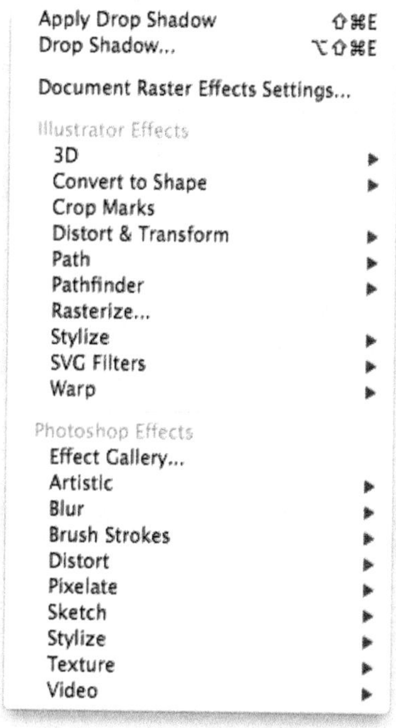

Figure 6-5. Adobe Illustrator has many image effects you can choose from, but you'll want to be very careful to double-check the resulting code

For example, Adobe Illustrator has a number of filters and image effects listed in the Effect menu option (see Figure 6-5). If you apply a drop shadow from here and then view the resulting code, you'll see something like this:

```
<svg xmlns="http://www.w3.org/2000/svg"
  viewBox="0 0 115 65" style="-webkit-filter: drop-shadow(2px 5px 7px black);">
    <g id="rings" stroke-width="3" fill="none">
      <image overflow="visible" width="451" height="212"
      xlink:href="78ABE.png"  transform="matrix(1 0 0 1 37 146)">
      </image>
      <circle cx="25" stroke="rgb(11,112,191)" cy="25" r="15"></circle>
      <circle cx="40" stroke="rgb(240,183,0)" cy="40" r="15"></circle>
      <circle cx="60" stroke="rgb(0,0,0)" cy="25" r="15"></circle>
      <circle cx="75" stroke="rgb(13,146,38)" cy="40" r="15"></circle>
      <circle cx="95" stroke="rgb(214,0,23)" cy="25" r="15"></circle>
    </g>
</svg>
```

Instead of using the native SVG filters, the effect creates a rasterized image of the drop shadow (78ABE.png) that is then linked to and layered into the final image. In this example, that external image was 22 KB. For reference, the original example where we used the `filter` element weighs in at a mere 853 bytes uncompressed. On top of the file size differences, we've seen that rasterized images don't scale as efficiently. Needless to say, this output is less than ideal.

If you're applying filters inside of Illustrator, make sure you explicity instruct Illustrator to use an SVG filter by using the Effects → SVG Filters option. From there you can handcode your filter and have that applied, avoiding the inefficiency of Illustrator's default process (see Figure 6-6).

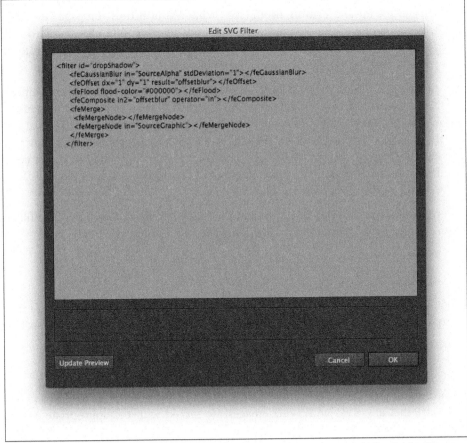

Figure 6-6. Using Illustrator's SVG Filters option will allow you to handcode the filter to be applied to the image

SVG Optimizations

We've covered most of the basics of the SVG format. Along the way we touched on a few things for you to keep in mind in terms of performance, but it's time now to take a deeper look at specific optimizations that you can apply to reduce the footprint and performance impact of your SVG images.

Enabling GZip or Brotli

One of the advantages of the SVG format being text-based is that it compresses very well. As we've seen, the SVG format is an XML-based format and XML formats tend to be fairly repetitive. This plays right into the hands of compression algorithms such as GZip and the up-and-coming Brotli (see "What About Brotli?" on page 103). As a result, applying one of these compression methods to your SVG files should be the very first optimization that you consider by default. Even if you were to do nothing else, you would still see a significant savings in file size.

You can apply GZip to your SVG files ahead of time, or have your server compress the files when served. If you compress them ahead of time (which is ideal, because it means you can use the high-efficiency Zopfli compressor), it's recommended that you use the .svgz extension to helpfully distinguish between the compressed and uncompressed SVG files you're providing. You'll also need to make sure that the server communicates to the browser that the image has GZip applied to it. Otherwise, the browser will not be able to display it.

If you're using Apache, you'll want to add the following lines to your .htaccess file to ensure the browser knows that any SVGZ images have GZip applied to them:

```
<IfModule mod_mime.c>
  AddEncoding gzip svgz
</IfModule>
```

If you want the server to apply compression on the fly, you'll need to configure it to do so. In Apache, that means making sure the following lines are in your .htaccess file:

```
<IfModule mod_filter.c>
  AddOutputFilterByType DEFLATE "image/svg+xml"
</IfModule>
```

Regardless of whether you're compressing ahead of time or on the fly, you'll also want to ensure that any SVG and SVGZ images are served with the appropriate MIME type:

```
AddType image/svg+xml svg svgz
```

You can verify that SVG files are being served appropriately, with GZip correctly applied, by checking to make sure that any SVG images are sent with the following headers:

```
Content-Type: image/svg+xml
Vary: Accept-Encoding
```

Any SVGZ files passed from the server should also carry the `Content-Encoding` header:

```
Content-Type: image/svg+xml
Content-Encoding: gzip
Vary: Accept-Encoding
```

If you're seeing these headers correctly returned and your images are displaying, you're successfully reaping the rewards of GZip compression on your SVG images.

What About Brotli?

Brotli is a new compression algorithm with a higher rate of compression than GZip is capable of providing. At the time of writing, support for Brotli is limited and the modules necessary for on-the-fly compression on servers could use a little time to stabilize.

Setting your server up to provide SVG files that have been precompressed with Brotli is a similar process to enabling GZip, with the exception being that you would want the `Content-Encoding` header to advertise that it uses Brotli, not GZip:

```
Content-Type: image/svg+xml
Content-Encoding: br
Vary: Accept-Encoding
```

While enabling compression and minifying your SVG files will greatly reduce the file size, they don't help in terms of reducing the complexity of the image to begin with. There are, however, a few simple optimizations you can apply that will help on that front.

Reducing Complexity

Many of the optimizations you can apply to the SVG format all revolve around the same basic principle: reduce complexity. We touched on this briefly when we discussed the basic shapes defined in SVG and compared them to the `path` element. Using the basic shapes wherever possible not only makes it easier for browsers during the rasterization process, but it also reduces the complexity and amount of markup necessary to produce the image in the first place.

There are several other optimizations that accomplish the same basic goal:

Simplify paths
> If you use paths within your image (and you'll need to in order to draw anything a bit more complex), you'll want to try to keep those paths as simple as possible.

The fewer points and commands you include in a path, the less markup you'll use and the fewer instructions the client will have to parse through and decipher. The end result will be a lighter image that displays more quickly.

Another Downside to Complex Paths

Complex paths are so difficult to rasterize efficiently that browsers like Chrome will actually change the rasterization process entirely to minimize the imapct.

In Chapter 10 we'll see that the browser will often try to offload some of the work involved in displaying images to the GPU for better efficiency. However, if an SVG image contains too many paths, or those paths have certain characteristics related to their complexity, trying to shift some of the work to the GPU can actually be incredibly expensive. For this reason, Chrome and other browsers that use the Blink rendering engine may decide to forgo the potential benefits of shifting work to the GPU if the paths of the SVG image in question look too complex. The risk outweighs the potential reward.

Reduce the number of decimal points

> If you're using a graphics editing program (like the popular Adobe Illustrator) to produce your SVG images, you'll likely see that many of the points defined within the various shapes and paths are incredibly precise. Rarely is that level of precision needed. In most cases, you can safely round off to one or two decimal points without any noticeable visual degradation in the image. It sounds fairly trivial, but removing those unnecessary decimal points can really add up in terms of file size.

Combining similar paths

> If an SVG image has several paths of a similar shape and style, it may make sense to merge them together—reducing the number of paths necessary for the SVG image to be drawn. You'll want to be careful with this one, though: if paths overlap, then trying to merge them can result in some serious visual degredation. This is one optimization you'll want to do by hand.

Converting Text to Outlines

SVG makes including actual text pretty trivial. In fact, it can be as simple as using the `<text>` element, like so:

```
<svg xmlns="http://www.w3.org/2000/svg"
  viewBox="0 0 100 100">
  <text font-family="Times New Roman" font-size="10" x="0" y="20">
    Hi. I'm text.
  </text>
</svg>
```

That's it. That's all there is to it. We set our font styling, and type out our text, and it's now included within our SVG image. Beyond making it easy to add text to an SVG image, the <text> element adds a few other benefits as well:

- Because the <text> element allows you to embed your text plainly, it's searchable and accessible.
- The <text> element relies on the font itself. Many well-designed fonts have features, like hinting, that enable them to adjust the display for different sizes, maximizing visual appeal and readability.

Unfortunately, this second feature also causes some problems. If the font is not one that is available on the system, the text will revert to the system default. Considering that this text lives in an image, and is therefore most likely specifically chosen to appear in a certain way, this is not exactly ideal.

Now it is entirely possible to use a web font to render that text, but that requires the additional request and weight associated with making that request—and when it comes to web fonts, that weight is usually not trivial.

In order to ensure that your text appears as styled, no matter the font available on the viewer's operating system, you can elect to convert that text into outlines. This process involves the graphic editor creating an outline of the text, then creating a path that matches the shape of that outline.

This eliminates the need for the additional request and weight needed to include the web font, but it does mean that the SVG file itself becomes substantially more complex. This tradeoff is quite frequently acceptable when viewed purely from a performance standpoint: as we've discussed, SVG compresses incredibly well and the extra bloat within the SVG file itself is not likely to come anywhere near the size of the actual font.

You also lose a bit of the accessibility that the <text> element provides. Because the text is no longer text, but instead a path comprising a series of points, the text becomes inaccessible and unsearchable. You can bring that back to an extent by using the <title> element and including an appropriate textual representation of the image there.

Automating Optimization Through Tooling

There are a few options for SVG optimization tools, but SVG Optimizer (SVGO) stands above the rest for its large number of optimizations and the wide range of tools that take advantage of it. At its core, SVGO is a Node.js-based tool, but there is also a web app, a Grunt task, a Gulp task, and plug-ins for Sketch, Illustrator, and Inkscape. For the purpose of this section, we'll zero in on the command-line interface provided by the core tool and the web app: SVGOMG.

Installing the SVGO Node Tool

If you have Node.js already installed on your machine, then you can install SVGO using the npm install command (optionally using sudo):

```
[sudo] npm install -g svgo
```

You can verify that it's properly installed by entering svgo into your command line and pressing Enter. If SVGO is ready to go, you'll see a list of options that can be used with SVGO.

To run SVGO on an SVG image, you type the svgo command followed by the file name:

```
svgo myimage.svg
```

Even if you run SVGO using the default configuation, you're almost certainly going to see some performance gains in terms of file size. Just about every optimization we've discussed—reducing decimal points, merging and simplifying paths—can be done automatically by SVGO.

You will want to pay close attention to the defaults, however, because it's unlikely that everything is going to be set up the way you want. While many of the default optimizations are harmless, a few are riskier to automate. I've seen many cases where combining shapes ended up distorting the image in some way. Other "optimizations," such as removing the viewBox, can actually be detrimental for reasons we've already discussed.

You can override the default configuration by creating your own configuration and passing that file to the SVGO command. The configuration file can be as simple as a list of the SVGO plug-ins you'd like to execute, stored in a Yet Another Markup Language (YAML) file. For example:

```
plugins:
  - removeDoctype
  - removeComments
  - cleanupAttrs
  - minifyStyles
  ....
```

If we stored this in a file called *myconfig.yml*, we could then pass that configuration to SVGO using the --config flag as follows:

```
svgo --config myconfig.yml myimage.svg
```

SVGOMG: The Better to See You With, My Dear

The command-line interface, as well as the Grunt and Gulp tasks built on top of it, is an excellent option for automation. If you need to dig deeper into a specific file, though, then the web app SVGOMG, built by Jake Archibald and shown in Figure 6-7, may be a better option.

Figure 6-7. SVGOMG provides a nice GUI on top of the powerful SVGO Node.js tool

SVGOMG provides all the functionality of the underlying SVGO Node.js tool, but with one notable improvement: it lets you visualize the difference both in the code and the image itself.

Using SVGOMG, you upload your SVG file and are immediately presented with it in all its visual glory. You can then select and deselect SVGO options to see what, if any, difference they make visually as well as in terms of file size.

SVGOMG also allows you to view the code of the optimized SVG image. The code is updated as each SVGO optimization is toggled on or off, allowing you to see exactly what is being changed.

When you're done tweaking the image, you can download it back to your machine.

Pick Your Flavor

Whichever of the many SVGO-based tools you decide to use, including SVGO in your workflow will greatly simplify the process of optimizing every last little byte of the images you produce. It's an essential tool for anyone producing SVG images.

Summary

In this chapter we dug deeper into the differences between raster formats and vector formats. We walked through the basics of the SVG format, and talked about how you can minimize the performance impact through a series of optimizations.

You now have a really solid understanding of the various image formats and how to effectively compress them. In Part II of this book, we'll shift our focus to how those images are actually loaded by the browser.

Image Loading

Colin Bendell

There are many different image formats you can use, each with different features and functionality. Using the best format and the right quality is not just the responsibility of the creative team, since these decisions can also impact the performance of a web page.

In this second half of the book, we'll discuss everything that happens *after* you've created and optimized your images. We'll explain how images are downloaded and rendered in a browser, show how this affects performance, and discuss techniques to accelerate this process. We'll specifically focus on loading images on mobile devices and cellular networks, as mobile images are especially challenging.

Note that while these techniques are primarily oriented toward web pages, many of the same concepts and technologies can apply to native apps or other types of clients.

Browser Image Loading

Guy Podjarny and Yoav Weiss

Before we discuss image delivery, we should discuss how browsers load images. We'll cover several performance best practices as we do so, but this chapter will serve primarily as a foundation for advice in later chapters.

Referencing Images

The primary two ways a web page can load an image are:

- An HTML `<img>` tag
- A CSS `background-image`

Both techniques will trigger the download and display of an image, but each has some important unique characteristics, which we'll explain next.

It's worth noting there are several newer ways to load images, focusing on the "responsive images" practice of downloading images sized appropriately to the current display. These include the `image-set` CSS property, `<picture>` element, and `srcset` attribute, all of which will be discussed in Chapter 11.

JavaScript Image Object

Another often-used technique to load an image is using the Java-Script `new Image()` constructor. While this constructor is standardized and widely supported, it's actually just another way to create an `HTMLImageElement`, and is functionally equivalent to `document.createElement("img")`.

<img> tag

The simplest way to load an image is to use the HTML `<img>` tag. This tag requires only a single `src` attribute (which points to the image location), and doesn't even need to be closed (see Example 7-1 and Figure 7-1).

Example 7-1. Simple <img> tag

```
<img src="book.jpg">
```

Figure 7-1. Result of Example 7-1

The full `<img>` tag supports various other attributes, most notably `alt`, `height`, and `width` (see Example 7-2 and Figure 7-2). The `alt` attribute holds a textual description of the image, to be displayed as a placeholder and used by screen readers and other accessibility tools. The `height` and `width` attributes explicitly indicate the dimensions of the image.

Example 7-2. Full <img> tag

```
<img src="book.jpg" alt="A Book" height="200" width="100">
```

Figure 7-2. Result of Example 7-2

The `alt` attribute has no real performance impact, though it does affect our ability to implement alternate image loading techniques, as we'll see further on.

The `height` and `width` attributes, however, do impact performance. If these attributes were omitted, the browser would have no way of knowing how much area it should allocate for the image, until it actually downloads the image file and sees its dimensions. This browser would reserve some arbitrary (and usually small) space, and once enough of the image data arrives (i.e., enough for the browser to conclude the image's dimensions) it would update the layout—also known as *reflow*. Reflows have computational cost and take time, but more importantly, they make for a very poor user experience, as page parts move around while the user is trying to read them, possibly being pushed below the visible area. Therefore, an important best practice is to *always specify dimensions in your `<img>` tag*.

Note the `width` and `height` of an image can also be specified in the CSS rules of the page. If you believe that the dimensions of an image have more to do with how it's laid out on the page than the image itself, than CSS is a more logical place to state them. That is especially true in responsive layouts, where the image's display dimensions may depend on the current breakpoint and are often relative to its container or the viewport. On the other hand, if the image is of fixed dimensions and those dimensions are tied to the actual visual—the contents of the image—then element attributes may be the way to go.

From a performance perspective, the source of the `height` and `width` matters very little. Specifying the dimensions in CSS means the browser won't see them until it has downloaded and processed all the relevant CSS files, making the attribute path theoretically faster. However, the browser doesn't perform the initial layout until all CSS is fully processed anyway, and so in practice, it doesn't help to know the dimensions earlier.

We won't be discussing layout much in this book, but if you'd like to learn more about how rendering is handled in the browser, check out the "Critical Rendering Path" (*http://bit.ly/2awvQj0*) article on Web Fundamentals (*http://bit.ly/2bitF5V*).

CSS background-image

Another prevalent path to load images is the CSS `background-image` property (see Example 7-3 and Figure 7-3). This styling instruction was originally used as a richer alternative to a background color, but is now used for many different purposes, ranging from rounded corners to logos to rich photography positioned behind the page's content.

Example 7-3. Simple background-image

```
<style>
#title {
        background-image: url("stars.jpg");
        background-size: contain;
        color: white
}
</style>
<h1 id="title" color="white">Reach for the stars!</h1>
```

Figure 7-3. Result of Example 7-3

Background images are designed—surprise surprise—to be in the background, and much of their handling assumes they do not hold important content. In reality, however, background images often do hold critical content. Examples include tab or section titles, primary navigation icons, visual context for foreground content (e.g., a map, with foreground landmarks), and more.

In addition, background images are sometimes used for actual foreground imagery. This is usually done for performance reasons, such as image sprites or responsive images, both of which will be explained in detail in later chapters.

The use of background images for core content has various implications, with the primary impact being on file structure and accessibility.

File structure

HTML holds an mix of software and content. The software components are usually made up of portions of the HTML itself, as well as the majority of JavaScript and CSS —including the style-related images. The content includes the remaining HTML portions, as well as most of the text within the HTML, and almost all foreground images.

On most sites, the content pieces change much more frequently than the software ones. In fact, on many sites the content is queried and constructed in real time, and often personalized for the current user. It's also likely that the content authors—the people who create and edit the content—are entirely separate from those creating the software. You probably don't want your engineers to write your marketing headlines, nor would you want to allow your journalists to alter your JavaScript.

It's important, therefore, to maintain a good separation between the content and software. Such separation makes it easier to control who can edit which portions, handle different update frequencies, and so on. This separation can also improve performance, letting you set different caching instructions for each part (e.g., cache software longer than content), control loading priority (e.g., prioritize fetching content over software), and prefetch or defer software components.

Using background images as foreground images (and to a lesser extent as important background content) gets in the way of this separation. It often leads to mixing content-related and styling-related CSS rules in the same file, inlining styling instructions into the HTML, and creating content-specific CSS rules that are often hard to delete later on.

Accessibility

When you develop a web page, it's easy to forget that many users cannot see the page the way you do. Users who are visually impaired, whether they're color blind, far-sighted, or completely blind, have to rely on helper tools when interacting with the Web. The two most common tool families are screen readers, which read a page's content out loud and allow voice-based actions, and high-contrast settings, which help color blind or far-sighted individuals see the page.

For screen readers to work well, they need to understand the *intent* behind each page component. Understanding this intent is much easier when the elements are used for the declared purpose—for instance, using tables only for tabular content (but not for layout), using headlines for section headings (and not styling), and so on.

The use of a background image as content can confuse a screen reader, hindering the user's ability to interact with the page. More specifically, unlike content images, background images don't support the alt attribute, which screen readers use to articulate what this image holds. There *are* ways to communicate a background image's intent, but they are not standardized, and thus much more error prone.

High-contrast settings also rely on a meta-understanding of the page. Specifically, high-contrast settings may remove background images altogether, going on the assumption that those images are only aesthetic and do not include important content. Alternatively, such settings may eliminate transparency of images, crippling cases where the background is an important context for a foreground image (e.g., a map with landmarks).

While not related to performance, accessibility concerns are a strong reason to try to avoid using background images as actual page content, let alone as foreground image replacements.

When Are Images Downloaded?

Now that we know how to instruct a browser to download (and display) an image, let's discuss when these downloads happen. To do so, we first need to take a slight detour and understand some core concepts around how browsers process pages and their resources.

Building the Document Object Model

As soon as a browser starts receiving HTML data, it will start parsing it and constructing the Document Object Model (DOM). The DOM is the programmatic representation of the page—practically everything we see or do on a page results in reading data from it or making a change to it.

As it builds the DOM, the browser encounters references to external resources, such as external JavaScript files, links to CSS, and—of course—images. Once discovered, the browser queues the resource to be downloaded, working within the network constraints we'll discuss later in this chapter.

While both the DOM and HTML are tree structures, converting the HTML into a DOM isn't simple. HTML is a very loose language to begin with, and browsers have always been very permissive when it comes to malformed HTML. Instead of erring, browsers automatically apply fixes to the page, making changes such as closing open tags, moving elements between body and head, and even correcting common typing mistakes. For instance, most browsers today support loading an image using the non-standard <image> tag (*http://jakearchibald.com/2013/having-fun-with-image/*), most often by silently converting to an <img> tag. In general, browsers are willing to jump through hoops to make pages work, even if their content is not standard and only resembles well-formed HTML when the lights are dim and the music is loud.

One especially painful complexity with building the DOM comes from JavaScript. By design, JS code is able to read and manipulate the DOM, which is the primary means to make a web page interactive. For synchronous scripts (so <script> tags without async or defer attributes), that may mean that the script is relying on the current DOM to be in a particular state.

If the script is appending new nodes to the tree (e.g., using document.body.append Child()), they are expected to be added in a particular place in the tree. The same goes for document.write() calls, which add HTML to the HTML parser in the exact position that the script is in. Since the browser doesn't want the page to break when these things happen, it must halt the parser whenever a synchronous script is encountered, until the script has finished downloading, parsing, and executing. On top of that, synchronous script execution can be halted on in-flight CSS files, as they may impact the result of JS execution—for example, if the script is reading styling information from the DOM.

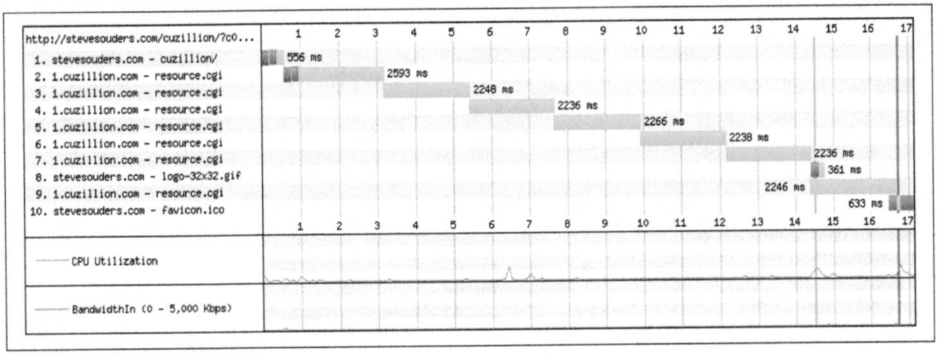

Figure 7-4. Sequential JS downloading in IE7

The waterfall in Figure 7-4 clearly shows the delay this sequential behavior causes. A very simple test page (*http://bit.ly/hpi-preloader-6js-example*) holding only six scripts (a third of today's average (*http://bit.ly/2aWr8N9*)) and an image, will be painfully slow on Internet Explorer 7. Why use IE7? Because starting with IE8 (*http://bit.ly/2bsSB7T*) (and other browsers released shortly after), browsers stopped being silly, and started using a preloader.

The Preloader

Nothing can be done to prevent synchronous scripts from blocking the building of the DOM without breaking pages. Browsers (rightfully) favor functionality over performance, and will not consider breaking pages just to speed them up. However, what can be done is to separate parsing from downloading resources—and that's precisely what the preloader does.

The preloader, also known as the "look-ahead parser," the "speculative parser," or the "preparser," is a second parser inside the browser. Just like the DOM building parser, it starts digesting the HTML as soon as it arrives, but instead of building a structure, it just tokenizes the HTML and adds subresource URLs that it encounters to the download queue. Since the preloader doesn't provide any of the page's functionality, it doesn't need to stop when it sees a script, and can simply plow along and discover all the subresources referenced in the HTML.

With this added functionality, the browser can go ahead and download resources even before it's ready to process them in full, decoupling download from execution. In addition, browsers can conceiveably do *some* processing on these resources—for instance, parsing a JS/CSS file or decoding an image.

As mentioned before, the first preloader was introduced in IE 8, and is possibly the single biggest web performance improvement we've seen in browsers. It's been further improved over the years, and now triggers additional actions such as DNS resolutions, Transmission Control Protocol (TCP) connections, Transport Layer Security (TLS) handshakes, and more. Figures 7-5 through 7-7 show the evolution of preloader-triggered downloads on the simple six-script page from the previous section, going from no preloader in IE 7, through the first generation in IE 8, to the latest iteration in IE 11.

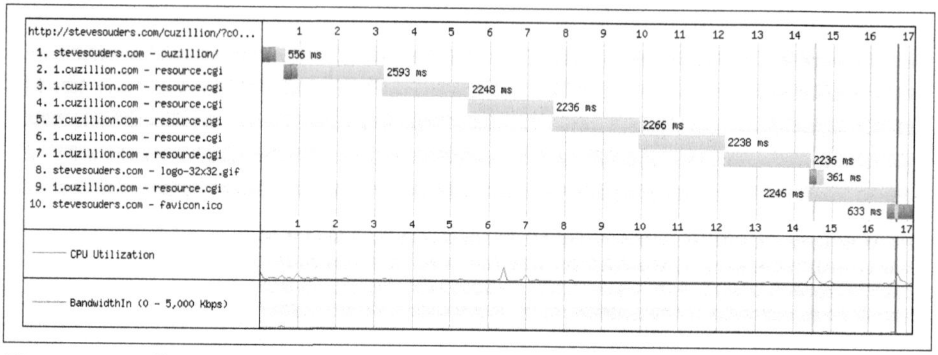

Figure 7-5. Fully sequential JS downloads in IE 7

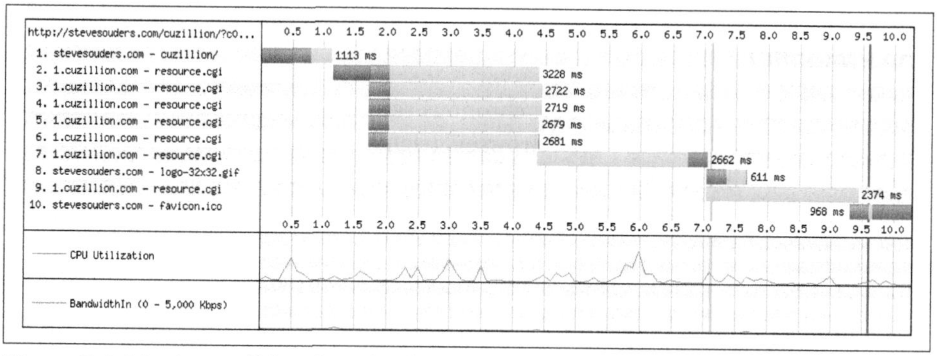

Figure 7-6. Mostly parallel JS downloads in IE 8

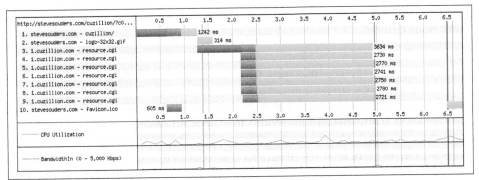

Figure 7-7. Fully parallel JS and image downloads in IE 11

While awesome, the preloader can sometimes make mistakes. As it runs ahead of the main parser, it's forced to make some simplifying assumptions. For instance, when the preloader sees two consecutive external scripts, it queues both for download right away. If it turns out the first script, when executed, navigated away from the page, it will render the second script's download unnecessary.

Cases like this happen quite often—for instance, with scripts that manipulate or change pages for A/B testing purposes, or scripts that employ client-side device detection and redirect to a mobile website. Despite this limitation, browser data indicates that the preloader is undoubtably a good way to speed up the Web. As long as its predictive downloads are accurate the vast majority of the time (which they currently seem to be), we all come out ahead.

For example, consider the following code:

```
<script>
    document.write("<-"+"-");
</script>
<img src="a_funky_sloth.jpg">
```

The preloader in this example will skip over the script and start downloading the image resource, since it assumes that it will be required later on. But, since the docu ment.write() directive starts an HTML comment, making everything that comes after it irrelevant, that download would be spurious.

Despite the preceding example, that's not a bug, but a conscious design decision. The preloader is a heuristic optimization, and is there to make the 99% cases faster, even if some edge cases will be slower as a result.

Networking Constraints and Prioritization

Between the DOM parser and the preloader, browsers can quickly build up a long list of resources to download. You may think the next step is to simply charge ahead and download all of those resources in parallel. After all, doing more in parallel leads to faster results, right?

As usual, it's not that simple. Downloading all resources at once can easily overwhelm home routers and servers and create network congestion along the way, as it effectively disables TCP's congestion avoidance mechanisms. This in turn can lead to packet loss—and so to a slower web experience. To reduce that risk, browsers limit the number of simultaneous connections they open up against a single host and (to a lesser extent) in total. Most browsers allow no more than 6–8 concurrent connections per host, and no more than 10–16 parallel connections in total (across all hosts). This browser limit led to the creation of an optimization technique called *domain sharding*, which we'll discuss more in Chapter 13.

There are also cases where a parallel download of all resources provides an inferior user experience. For instance, assume your page has 100 nonprogressive images, each 10 KB in size, and that your bandwidth is 100 KB/s. If all files are downloaded in parallel, it will take 10 seconds until all images are downloaded. Until then, no image will be fully displayed. In contrast, if only 10 images were downloaded in parallel, you would get 10 new complete images every second. It is often considered a better user experience to provide the user with some complete content as soon as possible, especially considering that there is a good chance that many of the 100 images in our preceding example might be outside of the initial viewport.

One last (but definitely not least) reason for not downloading all files in parallel is that some resources matter more than others. For example, browsers don't render anything on a page until all CSS files have been fully downloaded and processed, to avoid showing unstyled content. Images, on the other hand, don't block the rendering of anything but themselves. Therefore, it makes sense to favor the download of CSS files over those of images when you're required to make such a decision.

Browsers are constantly faced with such decisions. Given the (self-imposed) connection limit and the bandwidth concerns, prioritization often means delaying the download of certain resources until others are fully fetched. In fact, browsers assign each resource a priority, taking into account parameters, such as the resource type, whether it's async, and whether it's visible.

While resource prioritization is becoming increasingly dynamic, initial priorities are based on resource type in most cases. For images, that means that their initial priority is rather low (as other resource types, such as scripts and stylesheets, often have a larger impact on the page). Because of the preloader, when the browser starts downloading images, it is often unaware of their visibility in the initial viewport, their display dimensions, and so on. Later on, once these extra parameters become known (after the page's layout takes place), visible and high-prominence resources may get their priorities upgraded.

It's worth noting that HTTP/1.1 (and older) don't have a built-in prioritization mechanism, and so browsers can only prioritize by delaying or blocking entire resource downloads, which may underutilize the network. For example, downloading a single JS file will usually block the download of all images, even if there are available idle connections, as the browser doesn't want *any* low-priority resource to contend over bandwidth with the higher-priority script. The newer SPDY and HTTP/2 protocols provide better prioritization mechanisms.

Incosistent Image Download Handling

As we discussed, when it comes to resource prioritization, images are usually at the bottom of the pile, since they don't impact the rest of the page, and yet do take up a lot of bandwidth. In practical terms, the lower priority means image downloads are often delayed.

This manifests differently in different browsers. For instance, as of this writing, while render-blocking CSS or JS is being downloaded:

- Firefox will block all image downloads.
- Chrome will allow only one image download at a time (allow no more than one connection to download images or other noncritical resources).
- IE 11 allows any number of image downloads (until it hits the connection limit).

This inconsistency makes it hard to predict how images will be downloaded, and it'll likely increase as browsers switch to more dynamic prioritization. Therefore, this is a good case for the "Tools, Not Rules" (*https://aerotwist.com/blog/dont-guess-it-test-it/*) principle. Instead of trying to predict when your images will be downloaded, use tools such as WebPageTest (*http://www.webpagetest.org/*) to test your page load across browsers, and see when they were loaded.

HTTP/2 Prioritization

As we've seen, with HTTP/1.1, the browser has very rough control when it comes to resource prioritization, where its decision is binary: "Should this resource be requested right now or not?"

With a newer version of the HTTP protocol, that is no longer the case. HTTP/2 solves a lot of networking-related deficiencies that HTTP/1.1 suffered from:

- It can multiplex multiple requests and responses on a single connection.
- It can compress HTTP headers.
- The browser can attach fine-grained priority to each request it sends the server.

The last point emphasizes the difference in prioritization from earlier versions of the protocol. In HTTP/1.1, the browser maintains a queue of resources to be fetched, and the priorities of fetched resources are maintained internally, as part of that queue. Once a low-priority resource made it to the top of the queue (for lack of higher-priority resources that the browser is aware of), that resource was requested. And once that happened, prioritization is out the window. Even if a higher-priority resource arrived at the queue a few milliseconds later, there was no practical way to give it higher network priority than the resources already requested.

As a result some browsers preferred to hold back on requesting low-priority resources until they were sure all high-priority ones had already arrived, which led to behavior such as Chrome limiting image requests until all CSS and JavaScript components were downloaded.

With HTTP/2, the browser doesn't need a request queue at all. It can just send all the pending requests to the server, each with its priority, and let the server do the hard work of deciding which resource should be sent down first. The multiplexing capabilities also allow the server to interrupt low-priority responses whenever a higher-priority response data becomes available. The protocol also enables re-prioritization of requests—for example, when an image becomes visible in the viewport.

So for HTTP/2-enabled sites, when it comes to image priorities, the browser can actually permit itself to offload the prioritization smarts to the server, and just make sure that it sends the right priorities.

CSSOM and Background Image Download

In previous sections we talked about the preloader and the fact that it is used by the browser for early discovery of the resources that will be required later in the page. Unfortunately, since the main way it does this is by looking at HTML tokens, that doesn't work well for CSS-based resources, and in particular the preloader doesn't preload background images in any browser today.

While in theory in some cases a browser could download background images using a mix of CSS tokenization preloading and smart heuristics based on HTML tokenization, no browser actually does that. Even if it did, such heuristics run a high risk of triggering spurious downloads due to the cascading nature of CSS.

In practice that means that background images are discovered pretty late in the page's loading process, only after all CSS resources have finished downloading and the style has been calculated. So, if you have a prominent background image, how can you make sure that it's discovered in a relatively early stage and loaded as soon as possible?

Up until recently you could only do so using hacks such as including an equivalent invisible `<img>` tag in your HTML, or a `new Image().src='prominent_bg_img.jpg'` inline script. But nowadays, you can use the shiny new `preload` directive and include something like `<link rel=preload href='prominent_bg_img.jpg' as=image>` in your markup to tell the browser that it needs to load that resource while treating it as an image in terms of priority, requests headers, or the like.

Full coverage of `preload` is outside the scope of this book, but if you're curious, a recent article (*http://bit.ly/29hZUN9*) explains it in detail.

Service Workers and Image Decoding

Another recent development in the browser world is the advent of service workers (SW) (*http://www.html5rocks.com/en/tutorials/service-worker/introduction/*). In short, service workers are browser-based network proxies that you can set up to intercept and control your site's entire network traffic. While the use cases for them are wide and cover many aspects of the page loading process, we will examine a particular use case for them: using service workers to roll your own image format!

We have discussed the hardships of image format compatibility, the various browser-specific formats, and the need to serve specific formats to specific browsers. But service workers bring another possiblity to that mix: you can now ship SW-based image decoders and serve new and improved image formats only when native support is in place or when a SW-based polyfill is installed. In the latter case, you can "decorate" the outgoing requests by, for example, extending the `Accept` header, and then convert the responses to an image format that the browser recognizes.

For example, in Chapter 11 we will discuss newly developed formats that may be useful for delivering images on the Web. But, no browser actually supports these formats, which means they are of little practical use on the Web. Or are they?

With service workers, you can convert these formats to either JPEG or BMP *in the browser*, saving bytes over the network but still providing the browser with a format it can properly process and display. And even more, you can do that without any changes to your HTML or your application logic. SWs run at a lower layer, and perform all the required conversions without requiring your application's awareness.

One caveat to that approach is that JavaScript decoding implementations run a risk of being more costly than the native, highly optimized image decoders. One future browser enhancement that can help on that front is better access to low-level image decoding APIs that can speed things up: browsers could expose an API that enables decoding of video iframes or arithmetic decoding and significantly speed up decoding of new image formats that rely on these primitives.

Summary

By now, hopefully it is clear that image loading is not that simple. There are multiple ways to natively fetch and retrieve an image, and it's important that web developers use the right one for each case. Over the years, browsers have developed sophisticated logic for deciding when to download different images and how to process them, aiming to provide the fastest user experience.

This chapter looked at native and standardized ways to load images. Despite the tried-and-true and fast nature of browsers, there are quite a few image loading decisions they cannot make unilaterally. In the coming chapters we'll discuss non-native ways to load images, newer standards emerging from the mobile web, and web image performance considerations that are outside the browser's control.

Lazy Loading

Guy Podjarny

At the beginning of the book, we discussed the large percentage of requests and bytes that images account for. Much of that is due to the sheer amount of data needed to communicate a high-resolution visual. However, another significant portion is usually *wasteful*. A huge number of images are in fact never seen by the user, and do nothing but waste bandwidth and resources.

The one to blame for this waste is the scroll bar. We're all very familiar with scrolling down on pages, and today very few pages fully fit on a screen. Only 38% of an average web page is immediately visible on a typical desktop screen (see Figure 8-1). Over 80% of image requests deliver images that are not visible when the page is loaded.

This pattern is even more noticeable on mobile devices, which have smaller screens. The smaller visible area can hold less content (and fewer images), and yet website owners often try to serve the same content regardless of viewport. They often do that while avoiding horizontal scrolling, as it provides subpar user experience. Such mobile pages compensate for the lack of horizontal space with vertical space. In other words, if they can't make the page wider, they'll make it longer... which increases the portion of images not immediately visible during load.

While long pages are often the right design and UX decision, images that aren't immediately visible do have a performance cost. They compete with visible content for bandwidth and CPU, occupy TCP connections visible resources may need, and delay the documentComplete (aka onload) event and any interaction-related event handlers that await it. Note that the firing of the onload event also stops the browser's progress indicators, such as a progress bar or spinning icon. As a result, a slow loading *invisible* image can substantially delay the user being told the page is ready for use.

Figure 8-1. Sample pages, area below screen marked as sepia

The Digital Fold

The immediately visible area of a page is often referred to as being "above the fold," adopting a term from the physical newspaper world. Physical newspapers are usually large, and thus folded in two for easy stacking and carrying. The upper half of the page, the part "above the fold," is immediately visible when someone glances at a stack of newspapers, while the rest of the page requires an action—unfolding.

Web pages clearly don't have an actual fold, and browser window sizes differ greatly. Still, both web and newspaper pages have an area that is immediately visible, and a part that requires action—be it unfolding or scrolling. As a result, the parts of a web page that do and do not fit on the screen right away are often referred to as above or below the fold, respectively.

This analogy doesn't end with user action, but rather continues into the content itself. In physical newspapers, the most important stories are featured above the fold, hoping to grab consumers' attention and incite them to buy the paper. On websites, similarly, the immediately visible area often holds the content most likely to trigger an action. Be it the hottest news story, a featured product, or a corporation's key message, the "above the fold" area attempts to make the user take action.

The term *digital fold* is a hot conversation topic among web designers, with strong arguments in favor of (*http://www.nngroup.com/articles/page-fold-manifesto/*) and against (*http://www.lukew.com/ff/entry.asp?1946*) using it. For convenience, if nothing else, we will use the term *fold* in this book.

Wasteful Image Downloads

In most cases, user action includes navigating away from the current page. Since we're putting the most important content at the top, it becomes quite likely that users will click away without *ever* scrolling down. In fact, we may consider that a success, and strive to do it more! In addition, since this content prioritization/sorting is common, users have grown to expect it, and are conditioned to not bother scrolling down all the way. These two traits create a virtuous/vicious cycle, effectively encouraging people not to scroll.

Users who don't scroll turn these "below the fold" images from a performance hindrance to complete waste. Roughly 50% of users either don't scroll or barely scroll (*http://blog.chartbeat.com/2013/08/12/scroll-behavior-across-the-web/*), especially on a home page. Combining these numbers with the previous stats about visible images, we see that over 40% of image downloads on web pages are wasteful!

Why Aren't Browsers Dealing with This?

This excessive downloading of images is directly due to the way HTML, and specifically the `<img>` tag, is defined. Once a browser sees an `<img>` tag, it *must* download the image file it references. In addition, a part of the `onload` event definition is that all resources on the page, including all images, have been loaded. Therefore, browsers *cannot* avoid downloading an image the user may not see.

That said, browsers can control the *priority and order* of the downloaded resource. Browsers often use this prerogative, for instance, to prioritize downloading JS and CSS files over images. Among image downloads, browsers have historically not done much prioritization, treating them all equally. However, as we mentioned in the preloader conversation, browser prioritization is becoming increasingly dynamic, and some browsers are starting to give visible images a higher priority where possible. This is especially impactful when used in combination with HTTP2 or SPDY.

Even with such improved prioritization, browsers are still mandated to download all images on the page and delay the `onload` event until that process is complete. Several attempts were made to provide a standard way to indicate an image should only be loaded, most notably the `<img defer>` (*https://www.w3.org/Bugs/Public/show_bug.cgi?id=17842*) attribute and the `lazyload` attribute in the abandoned Resource Priorities (*http://bit.ly/2aAAwpN*). However, neither has actually made it through so far. If we want to avoid this waste, the only option we have is to take the loading of images into our own hands—and that means using JavaScript.

Loading Images with JavaScript

There are several ways to load images with JavaScript, all fairly straightforward. Let's start with a very simple example (see Example 8-1).

Example 8-1. Loading an image with JavaScript—simple case

```
<img id="the-book" alt="A Book" height="200" width="50">
<script>
document.getElementById("the-book").src = "book.jpg";
</script>
```

Note that the `<img>` tag in this example has no `src` attribute. The `<img>` will still be parsed and placed in the DOM, and the layout will still reserve the specified space for it, but without a `src` attribute the browser will have no URL to download. Later on, a script looks up this specific tag and sets its `src` attribute. Only then does the browser download the image and render it in the alloted space.

This example shows the only true requirements for loading images with JS: omitting the `src` attribute, and setting it with a script. However, it will be hard to maintain this technique for many images, as it splits the image into two separate parts: the `<img>` element and the script. To avoid this problem, we can keep the URL on the `<img>` tag itself, but use a `data-src` attribute instead (see Example 8-2).

Example 8-2. Loading multiple images with JavaScript

```
<img data-src="book.jpg" alt="A Book" height="200" width="50">
<img data-src="pen.jpg" alt="A Pen" height="200" width="50">
<img data-src="cat.jpg" alt="A Cat" height="200" width="50">
<script>
var images = document.querySelectorAll("img");
for (var i = 0; i < images.length; ++i) {
    var img = images[i];
    // Copy the data-src attribute to the src attribute
    if (!img.src && img.getAttribute("data-src"))
        img.src = img.getAttribute("data-src");
}
</script>
```

The *data-* prefix is a standard way in HTML5 (*http://bit.ly/2b5L2Ul*) to provide metadata in an element, most often to be consumed by JavaScript. By using it, we again have all the image information in the `<img>` tag, and can use a generic script to load all the images.

Deferred Loading

Of course, this function is not very useful. We moved from native loading of images to JS-based loading, but we're still loading all the images! To improve on that, let's improve the logic to only load images that are "above the fold" (see Example 8-3).

Example 8-3. Load images with JS, visible images first

```
// Test if an image is positioned inside the initial viewport
function isAboveTheFold(img) {
    var elemOffset = function(elem) {
        var offset = elem.offsetTop;
        while (elem = elem.offsetParent) {
            offset += elem.offsetTop;
        }
        return offset;
    };
    var viewportHeight = window.innerHeight || document.documentElement.clientHeight;
    var imgOffset = elemOffset(img);
    return ((imgOffset >= 0) && (imgOffset <= viewportHeight));
}

// Load either all or only "above the fold" images
function loadImages(policy) {
        // Iterate all image elements on the page
```

```
    var images = document.querySelectorAll("img");
    for (var i = 0; i < images.length; ++i) {
        var img = images[i];
                // Skip below the fold images unless we're loading all
                if (!policy.loadAll && !isAboveTheFold(img))
                        continue;
                // Copy the data-src attribute to the src attribute
                if (!img.src && img.getAttribute("data-src"))
                        img.src = img.getAttribute("data-src");
    }
}

// Load above the fold images
loadImages({loadAll: false});

// At the load event, load all images
window.addEventListener("load",function() {
    loadImages({loadAll: true});
});
```

Let's review the additional code changes we've made:

1. We added the isAboveTheFold function to test if an image is above the fold.

2. We wrapped the image loading in the loadImages function, and added an option to load images only if they're above the fold.

3. We use loadImages to load images above the fold immediately.

4. At onload, we load all images.

The first three steps create the prioritization we're looking for, only loading above the fold images, and keeping lower images from interfering. Once the page is loaded, the last step triggers and loads the remaining images for those users who do scroll down. Such loading is called *deferred loading*, and is a good way to accelerate the more important content.

Lazy Loading/Images On Demand

While deferred loading accelerates pages, it doesn't prevent waste. As we mentioned before, many users don't scroll all the way (or at all), and thus many of the images are never seen. Loading those images later would still not avoid the wasted bandwidth and battery drainage they incur.

To avoid this waste, we need to change our image loading to be "on demand," only loading an image when it comes into view. This technique is often called *lazy loading*, as we only do "the work" (downloading the image) when we absolutely must. Other common names are *images on demand* or *just-in-time images*.

Pure lazy loading will start the image download only when the image comes into view. However, doing so is likely to impact the user experience, as the user will be looking at a blank space while the image is actually downloaded and rendered. To mitigate that, we can try to anticipate user actions and download the image ahead of time. For instance, we can load images that are fewer than 200 pixels below the current visible area, trying to stay ahead of slow user scrolling. A more aggressive prefetch can improve the user experience, but will also increase the amount of wasted downloads.

In code, lazy loading requires listening to a variety of events that may change the content in view, such as scrolling, resizing, changing orientation, and more. It may also need to track application actions that impact what's in view—for instance, collapsing a page section. Each time an event fires, we need to re-examine all undisplayed images and choose which ones to load.

Lazy loading is a fairly simple concept, but it's hard to do it well. It's easy to miss a change in the visual area, as there are many events to listen on, and browsers implement them in subtly different ways. Even when you capture a change event, traversing all images to determine which is now visible is hard to do efficiently, especially when it may be called many times in sequence.

When considering lazy loading, first confirm whether deferred loading would satisfy your needs. It's much easier to implement, and is less error prone. If you still want to do lazy loading, it's recommended that you use an existing JavaScript library. A prominent example is the lazySizes (*https://github.com/aFarkas/lazysizes*) library, which lazy-loads images while playing well with the various responsive images solutions (more on that in Chapter 11). There are also automated services that can help you get lazy loading working in an optimal way with minimal effort.

If you still insist on implementing it yourself, remember to err in favor of loading the image—for instance, loading any image whose location you can't easily determine— and consider a background "cleanup" loop that will confirm you haven't missed any images every second or so.

IntersectionObserver

Traditionally, lazy loading libraries relied on the browser's scroll events to know when the user scrolled the page, and concluded from that when certain images would enter the viewport and therefore should be loaded.

However, scroll events handling is very easy to get wrong, resulting in janky scrolling, which frustrates users. The fact that many different libraries on the page were registering scroll events in order to figure out element visibility (resulting in abysmal scroll performance) prompted browsers to think about creating dedicated, highly performant primitives for that purpose.

The result of that effort is the IntersectionObserver API, which permits you to "observe" the intersection of a certain element with another element or with the viewport, and get dedicated callbacks when an element is about to enter the viewport.

You can also define custom distances for "intersections," which permits you to tell the browser things like "let me know when this element is 75% viewport height away from the current viewport."

As of this writing, the API is only shipped in Chrome, but as more browsers adopt it, lazy loading libraries are bound to move to this dedicated, jank-free API.

When Are Images Loaded?

Looking at the `loadImages` function from before, you'll notice it queries for all the images in the DOM. We would therefore want to call it only after the DOM is fully constructed, so after all HTML and synchronous JavaScript was delivered and processed. Since no image will be downloaded until this function is called, this approach can lead to a substantial delay in when the images are loaded. To mitigate this effect, we can call the function multiple times at various points in the page, though that in turn would have a computational cost. Achieving an optimal balance is doable, but hard.

Another approach would be to replace the function call with an event-driven load. Consider Example 8-4.

Example 8-4. Load visible images using image onload event

```
<script>
// Load either all or only "above the fold" images
function loadImage(img) {
        // Check if the image has a data-src attribute
        var dataSrc = img.getAttribute("data-src");

        // If the image is above the fold - load it
        if (dataSrc && isAboveTheFold(img)) {
                // Remove the onload handler, so it won't be called again
                img.onload = null;
                // Load the real image
                img.src = dataSrc;
        }
}
</script>
<div class="book-image-container">
    <img src="1px.gif" data-src="book.jpg" alt="A Book"
        onload="loadImage(this)">
</div>
```

At the bottom, you can see a modified <img> tag. Instead of omitting the src attribute, we replaced it with a tiny image file. Once it's loaded, the loadImage function in the onload attribute will be called, check if the image is above the fold, and load it if so. Since loading the new image will unnecessarily trigger the onload event again, we remove this event before updating the src attribute.

Small Image Overhead

If you are concerned about the delay caused by using the small placeholder image (*1px.gif*), don't be. The first time we download it will indeed add some latency, but if we serve that image with proper caching headers, the image can then be cached indefinitely across the entire site, avoiding future delays. If you'd still rather avoid the extra request, you can replace it with an embedded image using a data URI that looks like this: `data:image/gif;base64,R0lGODlhAQABAID/AMDAwAAAACH5BAEAAAALAAAAAA BAAEAQAICRAEAOw==`

This event-based loading is a bit more verbose, requiring us to set the onload attribute on every <img> tag, but it solves the previously mentioned delay. The browser will load the placeholder image as soon as it can, and fire the load event immediately after.

While it helps accelerate the initial load, event-driven image loading doesn't completely eliminate the need to iterate over the images. You'll still need to listen to the many events that change what's in view, such as scrolling and resizing, and then iterate images to determine if they're now in view. In addition, any type of JS-based image loading, including this one, will interfere with the preloader—which we will talk about next.

The Preloader and Images

As we mentioned in the previous chapter, browsers use the preloader to accelerate pages. The preloader parses the page ahead of the DOM builder, primarily to identify and start downloading external resources.

Not surprisingly, many of the resources the preloader finds are images. While it depends on their prioritization logic, browsers will often start downloading these images while still busy downloading and processing JS and CSS files. Even images that are not immediately fetched may be accelerated through early DNS resolution of their hostnames, pre-establishing TCP connections to those hosts, and more.

When we use JavaScript to load our images, we effectively disable the preloader. Our JS code, regardless if it's written as an onload event or a loop, will not run until the

DOM builder has actually reached the element we're handling. As a result, JS-created image tags are likely to start downloading later than native ones.

While this delay is important to consider, it's not easy to define just how impactful it will be. Different browsers implement different prioritization schemes, and many will delay image downloads until JS and CSS files have been processed anyway. As a result, an image may be delayed due to prioritization just as much as due to being hidden from the preloader, making this whole conversation moot.

To help visualize this, let's look at the waterfall chart of two simple pages, created using Steve Souders's Cuzillion (*https://stevesouders.com/cuzillion/*). Both pages hold one JavaScript file and two images, but in Page 1 the images are loaded natively (an <img> tag), while in Page 2 they are loaded using JavaScript. To better visualize the effect in the waterfall charts, subresources take 2 seconds to respond. Let's first look at the loading of the two pages in IE 11, shown in Figures 8-2 and 8-3.

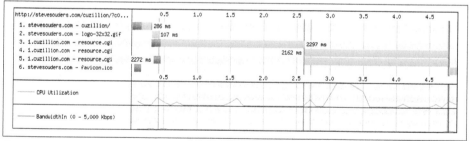

Figure 8-2. Page 1 (native images) in IE

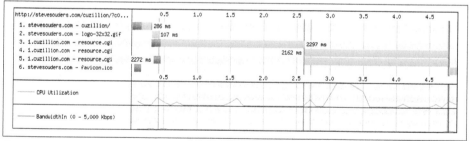

Figure 8-3. Page 2 (JS images) in IE

As is plain to see, the images created using JavaScript start their download only after the external script completed its download, dramatically delaying its rendering and also delaying the entire page load. In this case, the delay in loading images using Java-Script is very clear.

Now let's look at the two pages on Firefox (Figures 8-4 and 8-5).

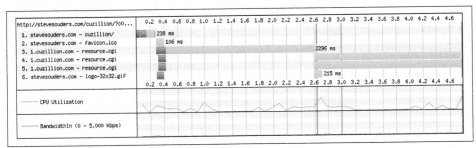

Figure 8-4. Page 1 (Native images) on Firefox

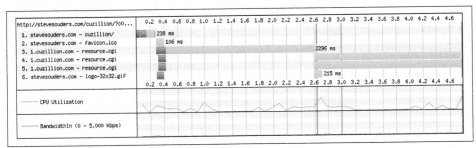

Figure 8-5. Page 2 (JS images) on Firefox

While the pages are the same as before, in this case there is practically no difference in the load time or order between the JS and native image loading. This is due to Firefox's prioritization logic, which defers all image downloads until all JS and CSS files are fully processed.

Lastly, let's take a look at how Chrome handles this page (Figures 8-6 and 8-7).

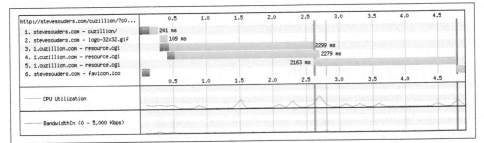

Figure 8-6. Page 1 (native images) on Chrome

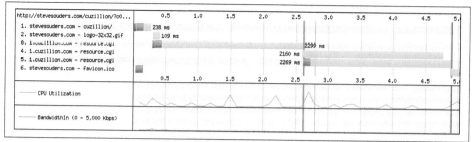

Figure 8-7. Page 2 (JS images) on Chrome

Chrome uses a more nuanced logic, wherein only one connection is allowed to download images as long as there are still JS and CSS files to fetch. As a result, the first image on this page is downloaded alongside the JS file, but the second image has to wait, resulting in slightly improved visuals but a similar total page load time.

While this is a simple page, the same behaviors take place when loading a real-world website. The key lessons we can learn are:

- The preloader makes page loads faster, and hiding images from it (by loading them with JavaScript) can delay image downloads and slow pages down. This is most clearly shown in the IE 11 example.

- Image downloads are often delayed due to prioritization anyway, reducing the impact of hiding images from the preloader. This was most clearly shown in the Firefox example.

- Browsers handle image download prioritization very differently, at least in HTTP/1.1. The only way to really know how browsers would do is to test your page with performance tools. As Paul Lewis often says, "Tools, Not Rules" (*https://aerotwist.com/blog/dont-guess-it-test-it/*).

Lazy Loading Variations

The decision between the savings lazy loading offers and the preloader crippling it causes is a tradeoff. Each website is different, and it's up to you to decide whether it's right for your site. In the next sections we'll discuss several other implications and variations of lazy loading that can help you make this decision.

Browsers Without JS

Loading images with JavaScript requires, obviously, a browser that supports Java-Script. Browsers without JS support, or ones where JS has been disabled, will clearly not run and thus not load these images.

It's hard to know exactly what portion of users fall into this group. A 2010 study by Yahoo (*http://yhoo.it/2b5Ll1C*) indicates 1.3% of users used browsers without JS support or with JS turned off. The study was repeated in 2013 by the GOV.UK team (*http://bit.ly/2aXMn0k*), which found that only 0.2% of visitors actively disabled JS, while 0.9% of visitors had enabled JS, but the script did not run nevertheless. A 2014 study by WebAIM (*http://webaim.org/projects/screenreadersurvey5/#javascript*) showed only 2.4% of screen reader users had JS turned off (mostly on Firefox, presumably using the noscript extension, or another script blocking extension).

The exact stats vary greatly by the specific audience your site caters to. To find your own number, you can repeat the Yahoo study on your own site or find that number in a different way—for instance, using Simo Ahava's guide (*http://bit.ly/2aVN517*) for using Google Analytics for this purpose. If you deem the audience big enough to care, you can still partially support them using the `<noscript>` element.

As you may know, the `<noscript>` tag holds content that will only be processed by the browser if JavaScript is disabled. We can therefore reference the image a second time inside a `<noscript>` tag, this time using a simple `<img>` tag. Example 8-5 does just that.

Example 8-5. Lazy loading with support for no-JS browsers

```
<img src="1px.gif" data-src="book.jpg" alt="A Book"
    onload="loadImage(this)">
<noscript><img src="book.jpg" alt="A Book"></noscript>
```

Using `<noscript>` is simple and has no real downsides, except for the repetition in your HTML (and maintanance costs that may come with it). Since the increase in payload size is likely minor (after compression), and since most web pages are generated using templates or code anyway (making it easy to add the `<noscript>` portion), I would recommend doing so.

Unfortunately, the `<noscript>` mitigation does not work for users that have their JavaScript support enabled, but for some reason (corporate/government firewalls, antivirus software, poor network, etc.) the scripts never fully download and run. This scenario cannot currently be fully addressed. Hopefully in the future there will be a standard way (*http://bit.ly/2al8W1a*) to define a fallback that can address this use case.

Low-Quality Image Placeholders

As you learned in Part I of the book, certain image files, most notably JPEG and WebP, can be made substantially smaller if we reduce their quality rating. Since such compression drops the least significant visuals first, the savings in file size is not linear to the loss in quality (*http://bit.ly/2aycYlb*), and you can often cut file sizes by half while slightly degrading visual quality.

If we get even more aggressive, we can often cut our image payload by a factor of 4 or more, while suffering only a 20% visual degradation. Such degradation will be noticed by most users, but it should still be clear what the image shows (see Figures 8-8 through 8-11).

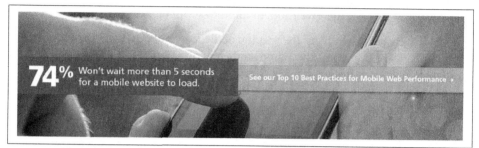

Figure 8-8. JPEG quality 90, file size 66 KB

Figure 8-9. JPEG quality 75, file size 37 KB

Figure 8-10. JPEG quality 40, file size 21 KB

Figure 8-11. JPEG quality 25, file size 16 KB

If we make our images that small, the performance impact of downloading "below the fold" images without seeing them won't be as big. In fact, it may be small enough that we'd prefer to use native image loading and the preloader benefits it carries. Once those low-quality images are loaded, we can use JavaScript to swap some of them with the original high-quality images.

This approach is called *low-quality image placeholders* (LQIP), as the low-quality images are only seen as placeholders. It consistently makes the page usable faster, and minimizes the need for lazy loading for all but the longest pages (where the number of images below the fold is especially high).

Implementing LQIP is very similar to the implementation of lazy loading, except the 1-pixel placeholders are replaced with the low-quality image variant. In addition, since we don't want the high-resolution images to interfere with the download of other page assets, we delay their download until after the page is loaded (we can also choose to lazy-load them instead). Example 8-6 shows an LQIP implementation.

Example 8-6. Low-quality image placeholders

```
<script>
// Load a placeholder image
function loadImage(img) {
// Copy the data-src attribute to the src attribute
        var dataSrc = img.getAttribute("data-src");
        if (dataSrc)
                img.src = dataSrc;
}

// Keep a registry of all image elements that need loading
var placeholderImages = [];
function registerPlaceholder(img) {
// Remove the onload handler, so it won't be called again
        img.onload = null;

        if (isAboveTheFold(img)) {
// If the image is above the fold, load it right away
```

```
                loadImage(img);
        } else {
// Register below-the-fold placeholders for deferred loading
                placeholderImages.push(img);
        }
}


// Replace all placeholder images
function replacePlaceholders() {
// Load all placeholder images (can be replaced with lazy loading)
        for (var ph in placeholderImages) {
                loadImage(ph);
        }
        placeholderImages.length = 0;
}


// At the load event, replace placeholders with real images
window.addEventListener("load",replacePlaceholders);
</script>
<img src="book-low-res.jpg" data-src="book-high-res.jpg" alt="A Book"
        onload="registerPlaceholder(this)">
```

Note that LQIP is a tradeoff, as it does include showing users a low-quality image at first. On a fast connection, the high-resolution image will quickly take its place. On a slow connection, the low-quality visual may linger, but at least the page will be usable quickly. In my opinion, it's a good way to get both speed, gained by the low-quality images, and eventual visual perfection.

Critical Images

As you've probably noticed, lazy loading is mostly a means to give visible images priority over ones outside the current viewport. The techniques we've described so far were all client-side techniques, which helps make them work well across different pages and viewport sizes. However, we can also try to guess what will be visible on the server side, and tune the page accordingly.

Guessing which images will be visible can be done in two ways: logical and technical. The logical path leverages your knowledge of the application. Does your application have a big "hero image" at the top of the page? Does a product image always show up on the top-left side? Is your logo always in the top-right corner? In many cases, we can (relatively easily) use the design guidelines to guess rather accurately which images will initially be in view.

The technical path implies loading the page in a browser, and seeing which images are within view. The most direct way to do so is using a headless browser, such as PhantomJS, in which we can load the page and see which images are loaded. The generic nature of this path allows it to run on any type of page, but doing it well requires a fair bit of R&D investment. It also assumes the page's layout is pretty straightforward, and content images are displayed in their HTML order (which is usually the case).

My advice would be not to try to implement the technical path yourself, but instead rely on existing commercial or (future) open-source solutions that would do that for you.

When we estimate an image will be immediately visible, we can change the HTML to load it using a simple (and fast) native tag, while loading the others with JS. The native images will load quickly, thanks to the preloader and the lower-bandwidth contention, while the remaining images will be loaded only if/when they're needed.

Note that while we're affecting image download priority, we're not impacting functionality. If we thought an image was visible and it wasn't, we simply downloaded it prematurely. If we incorrectly thought it was hidden, it'll still be loaded with JS shortly after. As a result, don't try to get it perfectly right from day one. Start by prioritizing (natively loading) the obviously important images (e.g., hero images, product images), and gradually tune over time.

Summary

There's little doubt that many web images today are needlessly downloaded, introducing unnecessary delay to web pages and wasteful load on servers. Lazy loading can help tune those downloads. However, due to the lack of native browser support, it requires loading images with JavaScript, which in turn carries other performance implications. Consider whether lazy loading is worth the tradeoff for you. The longer and more visually rich your web pages, the more likely it will be worthwhile.

If you've decided to implement lazy loading, find the images most likely to always be visible, and load them natively. For JS image loading, choose between lazy loading, which will conserve the most bandwidth, and deferred loading, which will provide a smoother scrolling experience. Lastly, consider using low-quality image placeholders across the board, making the page usable faster without compromising the eventual look.

Image Processing

Tim Kadlec

So far in this book, we've spent a lot of time discussing the performance impact of images in terms of requests and file size—characteristics that primarily impact the network side of things. However, there's much more work being done under the hood by the browser to get an image to be displayed on a screen. These additional steps in the image loading process can have a significant impact on the processing time and memory footprint of your site.

Decoding

As we saw in Chapters 2 and 3, when your graphic editor of choice creates the image file, it goes through a series of steps collectively called the encoding process. Consider the general steps included in the JPEG encoding process that we learned about in Chapter 4:

1. The graphic editor must covert RGB data to the YCbCr format.

2. The graphic editor applies some level of chroma subsampling to reduce file size.

3. The input is transformed from the color space to the frequency space by a Discrete Cosine Transformation (DCT) and further optimized using a quantization matrix.

4. Finally, the data goes through one last lossless compression step called Huffman encoding.

By the end of this process, the original color data has been transformed into a highly compressed bitmap. While this outputted format is exactly what we need to save the file efficiently, it's not what the browser needs. The browser needs that color data—it needs to know what to actually paint for each pixel on the screen. Specifically, the browser needs an RGBA (red, green, blue, alpha) value for each pixel of the image. To get to that data, the browser needs to walk backward through these steps and decode the image.

If we look at the JPEG format again, the decoding process looks something like this:

1. The data goes through a Huffman decoding process.

2. The result then goes through a Inverse Discrete Cosine Transformation (IDCT) and dequantization process to bring the image back from the frequency space to the color space.

3. Chroma upsampling is applied.

4. Finally, the image is converted from the YCbCr format to RGB.

Figure 9-1 illustrates the JPEG encoding and decoding process

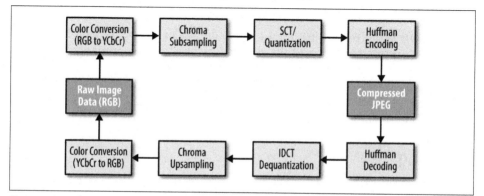

Figure 9-1. The JPEG encoding and decoding process

Whenever the browser must display an image, it has to grab this decoded data before it can draw it to the screen.

Measuring

This decode process is not cheap and can take quite a bit of time on the CPU. The amount of time the browser spends decoding images is revealed in several sets of developer tools.

Chrome

In Chrome, the image decode time is displayed inside of the Chrome Dev Tools, in the Timeline tab. If you record the loading of a new page, you can then filter using the search bar and display just the timings related to image decoding (Figure 9-2).

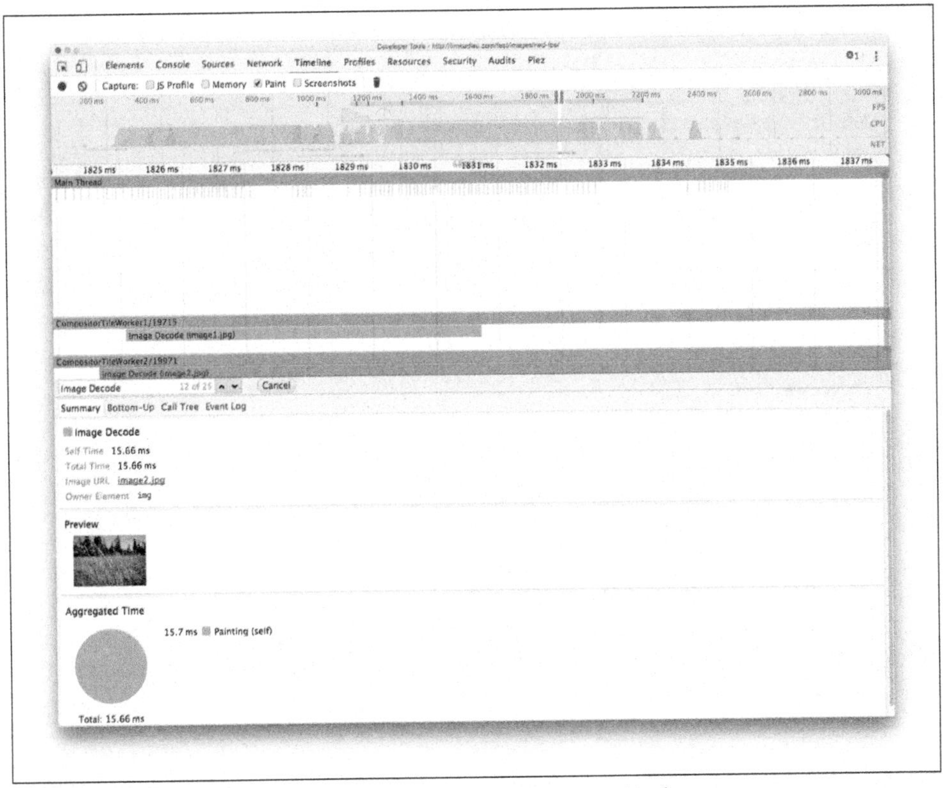

Figure 9-2. Image decode timings exposed in Chrome Dev Tools

For more detail, you can use Chrome's tracing functionality. Opening *chrome://tracing* in your browser will allow you to record a trace of all the work the browser is doing. Traces can be intimidating even to those who have spent some time digging into them, but there is an incredible amount of information in there. For our purposes, the task that holds the decode times is the *ImageFrameGenerator:decodeAndScale* task. Thankfully, we can filter down to find those timings in the massive list of information.

To do that, you'll want to select the area of the trace that you want to analyze, as shown in Figure 9-3.

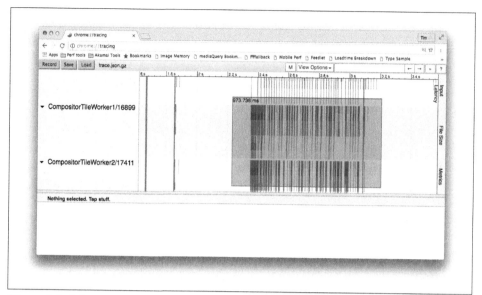

Figure 9-3. Selecting a section of a trace in Chrome for deeper analysis

With that area selected, you'll see a long list of all the "slices" (essentially, any action the browser took) revealed at the bottom (Figure 9-4).

Name ▼	Wall Duration ▽	CPU Duration ▽	Self time ▽	CPU Self Time ▽	Occurrences ▽
TileTaskManagerImpl::ScheduleTasks	0.740 ms	0.606 ms	0.740 ms	0.606 ms	45
TileTaskManagerImpl::CheckForCompletedTasks	0.406 ms	0.249 ms	0.406 ms	0.249 ms	44
TileManager::ScheduleTasks	3.447 ms	3.286 ms	2.485 ms	2.571 ms	41
TileManager::PrepareTiles	8.306 ms	8.005 ms	1.746 ms	1.669 ms	41
TileManager::AssignGpuMemoryToTiles	3.087 ms	3.035 ms	0.856 ms	1.450 ms	41
TaskSetFinishedTaskImpl::RunOnWorkerThread	2.229 ms	0.942 ms	2.229 ms	0.942 ms	135
TaskGraphRunner::RunTask	579.278 ms	479.909 ms	6.004 ms	4.138 ms	381
SoftwareImageDecodeController::ReduceCacheUsage	0.316 ms	0.177 ms	0.316 ms	0.177 ms	45
SoftwareImageDecodeController::DecodeImage	519.125 ms	443.626 ms	146.681 ms	114.812 ms	62
SchedulerStateMachine::SetNeedsPrepareTiles	0.023 ms	0.011 ms	0.023 ms	0.011 ms	4
RasterTask	46.987 ms	27.178 ms	5.681 ms	4.536 ms	184
RasterSource::PerformSolidColorAnalysis	2.195 ms	1.565 ms	2.195 ms	1.565 ms	190
RasterizerTaskImpl::RunOnWorkerThread	50.142 ms	29.566 ms	3.155 ms	2.388 ms	184
RasterBufferProvider::PlaybackToMemory	25.228 ms	21.178 ms	25.228 ms	21.178 ms	184

Figure 9-4. The list of all the actions the browser took during the selected portion of the trace.

From here, sorting by CPU Self Time will let you see which tasks took the longest on the CPU. In Figure 9-5, the top three tasks are all related to decoding images.

Name ▽	Wall Duration ▽	CPU Duration ▽	Self time ▽	CPU Self Time ▼	Occurrences ▽
ImageFrameGenerator::decodeAndScale	335.822 ms	324.289 ms	168.334 ms	163.015 ms	62
SoftwareImageDecodeController::DecodeImage	519.125 ms	443.626 ms	146.681 ms	114.812 ms	62
ImageFrameGenerator::decode	95.463 ms	90.434 ms	95.463 ms	90.434 ms	33
RasterBufferProvider::PlaybackToMemory	25.228 ms	21.178 ms	25.228 ms	21.178 ms	184
RasterTask	46.987 ms	27.178 ms	5.681 ms	4.536 ms	184
TaskGraphRunner::RunTask	579.278 ms	479.909 ms	6.004 ms	4.138 ms	381
ChildDiscardableSharedMemoryManager::AllocateLockedDiscardableSharedMemory	35.861 ms	3.683 ms	35.861 ms	3.683 ms	62
TileManager::ScheduleTasks	3.447 ms	3.286 ms	2.485 ms	2.571 ms	41
RasterizerTaskImpl::RunOnWorkerThread	50.142 ms	29.566 ms	3.155 ms	2.388 ms	184
TileManager::PrepareTiles	8.306 ms	8.005 ms	1.746 ms	1.669 ms	41
ImageDecodeTaskImpl::RunOnWorkerThread	520.903 ms	445.263 ms	1.778 ms	1.637 ms	62
RasterSource::PerformSolidColorAnalysis	2.195 ms	1.565 ms	2.195 ms	1.565 ms	190
LayerTreeImpl::UpdateDrawProperties::CalculateDrawProperties	1.974 ms	1.505 ms	1.974 ms	1.505 ms	41
ChildGpuMemoryBufferManager::AllocateGpuMemoryBuffer	16.078 ms	1.464 ms	16.078 ms	1.464 ms	18

2520 items selected | Slices (2519) | Instant Event (1)

Figure 9-5. Sorting by CPU Self Time lets you see which tasks have the highest amount of CPU overhead

You can also zoom in on an individual event within the trace to see all the related tasks that have to be run, and the timing of each. Figure 9-6 shows all the tasks being run in order to decode a pair of images.

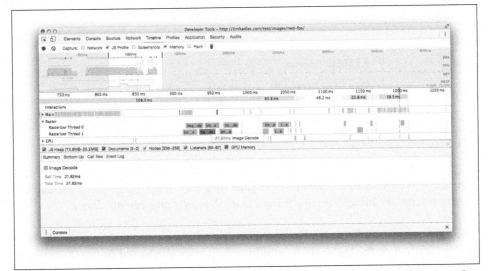

Figure 9-6. Zooming in on an individual event within the trace gives you a lot of insight into all the related tasks the browser must run

Chrome on mobile devices

Both Chrome's tracing and developer tooling allow you to easily record image decode times for mobile devices running Chrome as well.

Enabling Remote Debugging for Chrome

In order to profile a mobile device on your desktop, you'll need to make sure USB debugging is enabled. The steps vary depending on the version of Android running, but you can find the latest information on the Chrome Developer site (*https://devel oper.chrome.com/devtools/docs/remote-debugging*).

With your device connected to your machine using a USB cable, and USB debugging enabled (see "Enabling Remote Debugging for Chrome"), you can navigate to *chrome://inspect/?tracing#devices*. This will show you a list of all open tabs on the device you want to remotely debug (Figure 9-7).

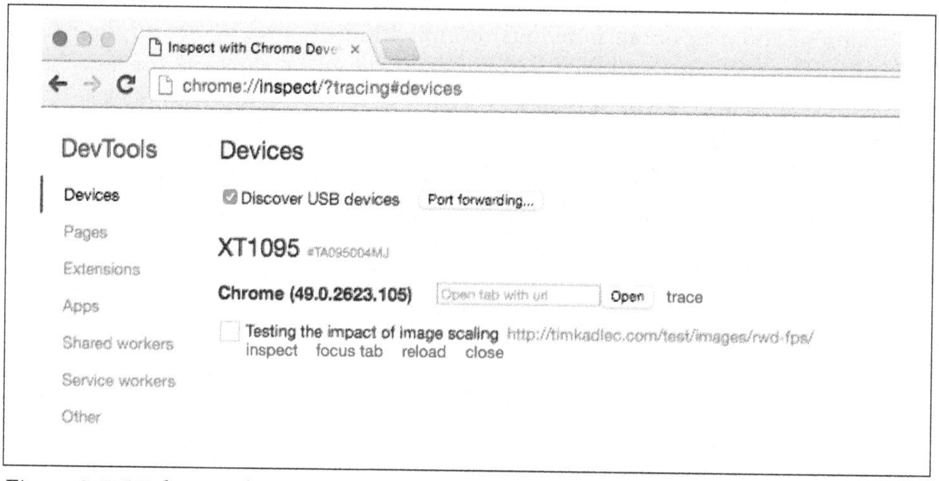

![Screenshot of Chrome inspect devices page showing DevTools sidebar with Devices, Pages, Extensions, Apps, Shared workers, Service workers, Other; and Devices panel showing XT1095 device with Chrome (49.0.2623.105) and a tab "Testing the impact of image scaling"]

Figure 9-7. With your device connected to your computer using a USB cable, you can use developer tools or Chrome's tracing feature to analyze sites on a remote device

Selecting "trace" will bring up the same tracing window you would see for desktop analysis, only now the trace will be conducted on your connected device. From here, you have all the same filtering and zooming capabilities we discussed previously.

What's This decodeToYUV Thing?

Depending on your site and the device you are remotely debugging, you may notice that instead of the familar ImageFrameGenerator:decodeAndScale task, you see a ImageFrameGenerator::decodeToYUV task instead (see Figure 9-8). That's not a bug: the browser may choose to take a slightly different route for image decoding. We'll come back to that a little later in the chapter when we discuss GPU decoding.

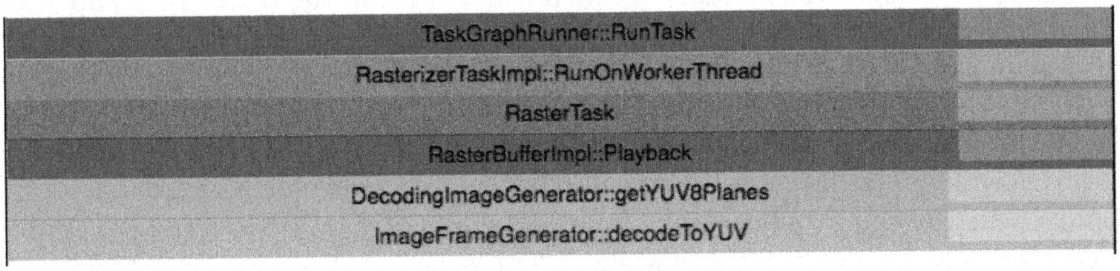

| TaskGraphRunner::RunTask |
| RasterizerTaskImpl::RunOnWorkerThread |
| RasterTask |
| RasterBufferImpl::Playback |
| DecodingImageGenerator::getYUV8Planes |
| ImageFrameGenerator::decodeToYUV |

Figure 9-8. Tracing your device may result in a slightly different decoding task called decodeToYUV

Edge

The developer tools for Microsoft Edge also display the image decode timings inside their Performance tab. Whereas the Google Dev Tools show each individual call to the decoding process, the Edge tools take the approach of showing you the total time per image—arguably a more understandable and valuable view of the data.

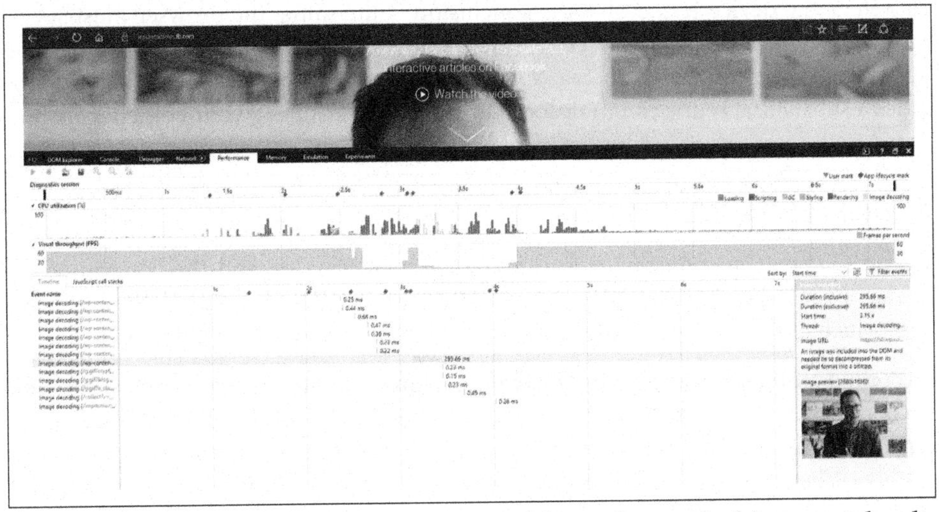

Figure 9-9. Microsoft Edge's developer tools reveal the total amount of time spent decoding each image in a given page

Firefox and Safari

At the time of writing, neither Firefox nor Safari offers the ability to analyze image decode timings.

How Slow Can You Go?

This decoding process is not cheap. It can occupy the CPU for quite a bit of time, particularly for lower-powered devices or high-resolution images. Just how slow can the decode process be? The answer ultimately depends on the complexity and size of your images, but you can get a decent idea by creating a test page of 10 images or so at different sizes and see what happens.

The simple test I ran involved using three pages, each of which displayed images at 200-pixel wide. One page served images that were resized to the exact width they would be displayed at—200 px. A second page used 400-pixel wide images, and the third page used 1,200-pixel wide images. The test was run on a Nexus 5 device, and the differences were substantial, as you can see in Table 9-1.

Table 9-1. Time spent decoding different sized images

Image size	Decode time	Percentage increase
200 px	30.38 ms	-
400 px	102.77 ms	+238.3%
1,200 px	15,534.99 ms	+4,952.6%

While the results will undoubtedly vary depending on the different images you use—as well as the device tested on—the conclusion is the same: the browser must spend *much* more time decoding images as those images get larger in size. Just as serving appropriately sized images decreases overall page weight, resizing your images provides a substantial reduction in decode time as well—ensuring your content gets rendered to the screen as quickly as possible.

Memory Footprint

Resizing images in the browser can also impact battery life and the lifespan of the device. Ever notice your phone getting warm while you're browsing an image heavy site? Much of that is from all the image decoding the browser is trying to do.

Decoding an image is a fairly involved process that the browser must go through for each and every image on the site, every time it needs to display it. Let's say you have a large hero image at the top of your page. As you scroll down, the image is no longer visible. When you scroll back up, the browser needs that decoded data again to get the image back onto your screen.

To avoid the added overhead of having to possibly decode the same image multiple times, the browser maintains an image memory pool—a preallocated space in memory where decoded image data can be stored. Now, when the browser needs to put that image back on your screen, it doesn't (necessarily) have to go through the decoding process again. Instead, it can look in the memory pool to see if the decoded data for a given image is already available. If it is, it uses that decoded data. If it isn't, the browser will go through the process of decoding the image and, eventually, storing the newly decoded data in that memory pool for later.

This decoded data is much larger in size than the disk size of the original image downloaded. Remember: a huge part of the encoding process is reducing the final size of the generated image, and the browser has just redone all of that work.

Since we know that the image is represented by an RGBA value for each pixel, we can figure out exactly how much memory that image is going to take up by multiplying the height and width of the image by 4 (an RGBA value takes up 4 bytes—one byte each for red, green, blue, and alpha). The final formula is:

```
Width × Height × 4
```

Consider a hero image that is 1,024 pixels wide and 300 pixels high. We can plug those numbers into our formula to find out how much memory it's taking up once decoded:

```
1,024 × 300 × 4 = 1,228,800 bytes
```

While the disk size of the image may not be particularly heavy, the decoded size stored in memory is a whopping 1.23 MB. As of 2015, 25% of all new Android phones were shipping with only 512 MB of RAM.[1] Factor in that the average page today uses around 30 images or so, and that memory gets eaten up pretty quickly. Generally speaking, the browser is nearly always going to need to use more memory than it has access to.

That's where the image memory pool mentioned earlier comes back into play. A browser can offer memory back to the operating system for it to reclaim, if needed.

What happens is that as you scroll down a page, the browser may choose to offer some of the memory currently being used on images back to the operating system. A great example would be a large hero image at the top of the page. The farther you scroll down, the less likely the browser is to need that decoded image (and the more memory the browser is likely to be using as it decodes images scrolling into view).

At some point, the browser may decide that it's safe to offer that memory back to the operating system. If the operating system does indeed reclaim the extra memory, the

---

1 *https://www.youtube.com/watch?v=7V-fIGMDsmE#t=81m30s*

browser will discard the decoded data for the image. If you were to now scroll that image back into view, the browser would once more need to decode that image because it would no longer be included in the memory pool.

Image pooling is a necessary feature to ensure that the operating system is not crippled by image-heavy pages, particularly on lower-end devices. The tradeoff is that whenever decoded data is evicted from the pool, the already costly process of image decoding may be duplicated, wasting CPU cycles.

One of the interesting implications of this process is the impact on *image spriting* (discussed in Chapter 10). With spriting, you combine multiple smaller images into one large image. The idea is that you minimize the number of requests necessary to get your images down to the browser. The unfortunate side effect is that, because the sprited image is now quite large, it's going to fill up that image pool much more quickly. If and when the browser needs that memory back, it's going to evict the entire sprite. Now, if even one of those images contained in the sprite needs to be displayed again, the entire sprite will need to be decoded.

If, however, each of those images were served up individually, the browser would only evict as many images as necessary to free up the necessary memory—leaving more of the images in the memory pool and reducing the risk of heavy decodes recurring.

In addition to watching the size of your images, we can take advantage of a relatively recent improvement to how browsers handle decoding and enable GPU decoding where possible.

GPU Decoding

Given the many costs associated with displaying an image—potentially limited memory, cost of decode, and risk of having to decode the same image multiple times—it's in the best interest of the user, the browser, and you as the developer to reduce the amount of memory used by as much as possible.

With this in mind, browsers started to experiment with how they might be able to reduce the memory impact of images by changing how and where the decoding occurs. The most significant optimizations involve the JPEG format.

JPEGs are saved as YCbCr data, which provides an opportunity for reduced memory usage. Using the YCbCr color space means images are stored using three channels: one luma channel and two chroma channels. If the image is decoded and stored as YCbCr data instead of RGBA, we move from 4 bytes per pixel to 3 (one each for chroma blue, chroma red, and luma). We're kind of cheating here because we're ditching that alpha data entirely. But since JPEGs don't support alpha transparency, we can get away with it.

Traditionally, the decoding process has occurred on the CPU. Only after the image has been fully decoded does the CPU pass that decoded data over to the graphics processing unit (GPU) to be rendered. However, if browsers move the final step in the JPEG decoding process (converting from YCbCr data to RGBA) to the GPU as well, they can now store the data in YCbCR format—saving precious memory space. The GPU can handle the work.

If we look back at our hero image from earlier, when it was stored as RGBA data, it took up 1.23 MB of space:

```
1,024 × 300 × 4 = 1,228,800 bytes
```

That same image stored in the YCbCr color space takes up much less room:

```
1,024 × 300 × 3 = 921,600 bytes
```

Simply saving the decoded image in a different color space results in a 25% reduction in memory usage. It requires the GPU to do a little more work (instead of merely rendering the image, it must also convert from YCbCr to RGBA), but it reduces battery life, memory use, and precious CPU cycles—not a bad tradeoff!

The impact on memory reduction becomes even more significant depending on the level of chroma subsampling involved. Brace yourselves: it's about to get mathy again.

Let's revisit the savings in chroma data for the different levels of subsampling that we saw in Chapter 4 (see Table 9-2).

Table 9-2. Chroma data savings based on subsampling level

Subsampling level	Chroma data savings
4:4:4	0%
4:2:2	50%
4:1:1	75%
4:2:0	75%

Armed with these numbers we can come up with a new formula for memory usage when the browser uses GPU decoding:

```
(Height × Width × 3) - (Height × Width ×
    Subsample_Level × 2)
```

First, let me apologize for giving you flashbacks to ninth-grade algebra. It was sadly unavoidable.

Now, let's break this down.

The first thing we need to figure out is how much the image would consume in YCbCr using no compression. As we saw a little earlier, that's the first part of this formula:

```
Height × Width × 3
```

However, if there is subsampling involved, we aren't actually using all of those bytes. If we're using a 4:2:2 subsampling level, for example, our two chroma channels aren't using 50% of their original data to be precise. So we need to subtract that. That's the second part of our formula:

```
Height × Width × 2 (number of chroma channels) × Subsample_Level
```

Let's walk through a few examples using our hero image. If the hero image were saved using 4:2:2 subsampling, then our subsample level is 50%, or .5. Here's how we'd use it in our formula:

```
(1,024 × 300 × 3) – (1,024 × 300 × 2 × .5)
  = 614,400 bytes
```

If we encoded the same image using 4:2:0 subsampling, our subsample level is 75% or .75:

```
(1,024 × 300 × 3) – (1,024 × 300 × 2 x .75) =
  460,800 bytes
```

You can see in Table 9-3 that our memory usage really starts to add up the higher the level of subsampling used, peaking at a hefty 62.5% savings if images are saved using either the 4:1:1 or 4:2:0 subsampling levels.

Table 9-3. Memory usage for a 1024×300-pixel image, based on decoding method used

Decode method	Memory use (in bytes)	Memory savings
CPU (RGBA)	1,228,800	0%
GPU (4:4:4)	921,600	25%
GPU (4:2:2)	614,400	50%
GPU (4:1:1)	460,800	62.5%
GPU (4:2:0)	460,800	62.5%

The memory savings for using a 4:2:0 (or the less common 4:1:1) subsampling level is huge, particularly when you consider that the average site today is loading 1.4 MB of images and 45% of those are JPEGs. There's a lot of room for improvement here. According to a study of 1 million images that was conducted by Colin Bendell,[2] only 40% of JPEGs online are currently using 4:2:0 subsampling.

---

2 *http://bit.ly/2b5Gxt5*

Triggering GPU Decoding

At the time of this writing, Chromium-based browsers, Microsoft Edge, and Microsoft Internet Explorer 11+ all support GPU decoding. For Edge and Internet Explorer, GPU decoding is the default process.

Chrome has taken a slightly different approach (for now) and only enables GPU decoding under certain situations.

- The `meta viewport` element is defined and includes `"width=device-width"`.
- There are not multiple rasterization threads available.
- The device is using Android 4.x (and later) or is a Nexus device.

This means that if you're using responsive design (and using the approaches mentioned in Chapter 11), then Chrome on mobile is already taking advantage of GPU decoding whenever it thinks it's the best approach available.

> ### Multiple What Now?
>
> Chrome is a *multithreaded* browser—it uses different threads for different dedicated tasks. This enables different kinds of work to be done in parallel—without blocking progress. *Rasterization*, the process of converting vector shapes to raster format (pixels) to be displayed onto a screen, is done on a dedicated rasterization thread. At times, Chrome may decide the device being used is best served by running multiple rasterization threads in parallel—greatly speeding up the process of getting pixels onto your screen. If it's able to do this, Chrome won't use the GPU for decoding.
>
> While you, the developer, have control over ensuring the proper `meta viewport` element is being used, you have no control over whether or not there are multiple rasterization threads. So, while you can provide Chrome what it needs to handle decoding on the GPU, ultimately it's the browser that decides if it should happen or not.

Summary

The browser has to do a lot of work to display an image on your screen. Sizing your images appropriately, taking advantage of chroma subsampling on your JPEG files, and taking advantage of GPU decoding can all help to reduce the impact on both processing and memory—both very important considerations particularly on mobile devices.

With a working knowledge of how to optimize each image format as much as possible, as well as how to enable the browser to do its job efficiently, it's now time to put it all together. How do you apply all of this knowledge into an efficient workflow? In the next chapter, we'll explore just that.

Image Consolidation (for Network and Cache Efficiencies)

Colin Bendell

If you've ever had to move from one home to another, you know that moving day is long and grueling. You quickly realize that you want to minimize the number of trips from your apartment to the moving truck. If you took one small box each trip, you'd spend more time going back and forth than actually loading the moving truck. Therefore, carrying more boxes in each load reduces the number of trips back up the stairs and brings that much-deserved beer that much closer. At the same time, there is a limit. Good luck trying to carry eight cartons of books in one load. An extra trip is better than a broken back.

This is the same challenge with loading images in a browser or app. In order to optimize the delivery we need to address either the number of requests or the payload per request. This is particularly true for small images. A useful technique is to consolidate images, thereby reducing requests and making each request more effective. This chapter explores how to achieve high performance for the smaller images using techniques like spriting, web fonts, and inlining.

What About HTTP/2?

Many of these solutions for small images have been cultivated in an HTTP/1.1 world. Some have argued that consolidation is an antipattern in an HTTP/2 world. This is not the case; at worst, it will not degrade performance. However, there are many reasons why consolidation is still relevant in an HTTP/2 Internet.

- It will be several years before the ubiquitous adoption of HTTP/2. During this time of transition, older browsers and corporate content filters (proxies) will continue to benefit from HTTP/1.1 optimizations.

- Many images means many requests to the browser cache. This is not free. Each cache request requires multiple interprocess communication (IPC) calls. Use consolidation to reduce the number of IPCs.

- Consolidation increases cache hit probability. A single image that is used once will be more likely to be dropped during cache eviction than if it were consolidated and sharing the cache hit rate of many requests. This also benefits images not yet referenced but displayed on other pages.

- Consolidation can, in some cases, save total bytes on the network as well as in the browser cache.

The Problem

Just like in our analogy of moving household goods, the browser (and apps) have two particular problems:

Round-trip time

How long does it take from the time the request is sent to the time the response is received? Using our analogy, how long does it take for you to leave the truck, go up the stairs into your apartment, and come back with a load? Do you have to prop open the doors, or are they open already?

Making every trip count

How do we make sure each response contains the most data? Taking one trip to deliver a single carton containing a lampshade is not very efficient and delays completing the job.

TCP Connections and Parallel Requests

To understand the impact of the round-trip time, let's start by examining what is happening at the TCP/IP layer. For reference, this section is particularly focused on the problems manifested in HTTP/1.1. The problems of congestion window scaling are specifically addressed in the HTTP/2 design.

To review, a typical Transmission Control Protocol (TCP) session starts with a handshake before sending and receiving data, as shown in Figure 10-1.

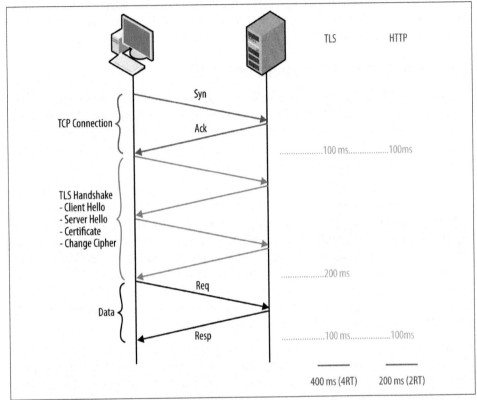

Figure 10-1. The time delay for an HTTP or TLS handshake over TCP

The biggest challenge with TCP is latency. Internet service providers (ISPs) and cellular providers have been good at selling Internet based on bandwidth—how many megabytes per second your connection can send. The dirty little secret they don't tell you is that you can have as much bandwidth as you like, but it will deliver inferior user experience if you have high latency.

Figure 10-1 shows the cost of merely establishing a TCP connection. In this illustration having just 50 ms of latency means that an unencrypted TCP connection takes 100 ms before the browser can send the first HTTP request (300 ms before the first HTTPS/TLS request). When we increase the latency to 75 ms, this problem inflates to 150 ms and 550 ms for HTTP and TLS, respectively.

To send a single small image (say 1,200 bytes), you would have the connection over-head + one packet for a request + one packet for a response. This means the total time on a 50 ms latency connection is 400 ms for just one packet of data—for just the small image.

Put another way, we are achieving 12.5% efficiency on our network connection. If we have to set up a new connection for each image, on a TLS connection only 12.5% of the total time is spent transmitting data (25% on an unencrypted connection).

Small Objects Impact the Connection Pool

Fortunately, HTTP/1.1 does provide for connection reuse with persistent connec-tions. This way, the TCP connection is negotiated once per session and the socket is reused for multiple requests. (Of course, this assumes the server behaves properly and respects the `Connection:keep-alive` header.) Despite the persistent connection, small object delivery can impact the connection pool.

The fatal flaw with HTTP/1.1 is that each image request blocks and delays other resources from being loaded. Specifically, you are limited to one request and one response at a time. Any other requests queued on the network interface must wait for the HTTP response. For this reason multiple connections are usually opened in par-allel to prevent head-of-line blocking. A browser (and operating system) imposes lim-its on the number of TCP connections. The usual limit imposed is around six connections per hostname. (Earlier versions of Android and iOS had lower global limits—as low as four.) Not just images are impacted by the connection limit; the limit affects all resources, including APIs, JavaScript, and CSS.

While a connection can be reused, it is still subject to congestion windows and TCP slow start. The situation is aggravated with small images because they won't saturate the connection. Each request may be followed by a few packets of response data fol-lowed by another request packet. For example, if an image was only four packets (assume ~1,500 bytes per packet), the cost of latency to send and then receive data becomes quite high and the effective throughput will be low. We could be sending more data on the network, but we're forced to pause and wait for the round trip for each new request.

Using our moving analogy, think of having a maximum of six movers. With small images you are only loading each worker up with one box per trip instead of many boxes per trip.

Not only are these small images blocking other requests, but they are penalized by the latency on the connection: more latency compounds the delay of page rendering.

To illustrate this, imagine a single page with 100 images of 3 KB each. The HTML is very simple: `<img src="/hpi-3k.png?v=1" width="25" height="23">`. Each image is the same, but marked with different version numbers to ensure cache busting.

Notice that even in HTTP/1.1 and HTTP/2 the network connection is never saturated (see Figures 10-2 and 10-3).

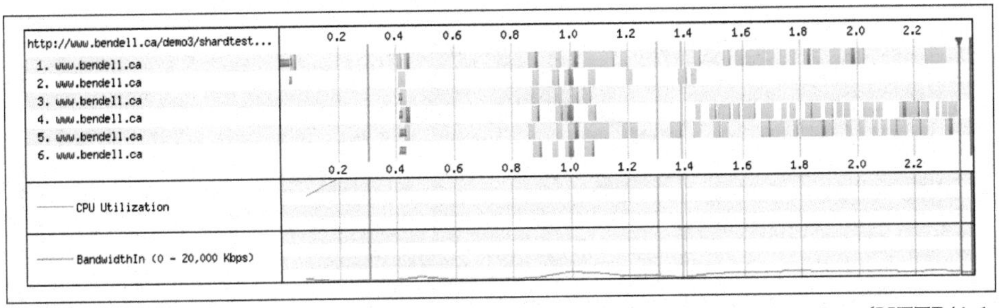

Figure 10-2. Many small images are not able to saturate the TCP connection (HTTP/1.1 unencrypted)—test with 100 3 KB images on a page

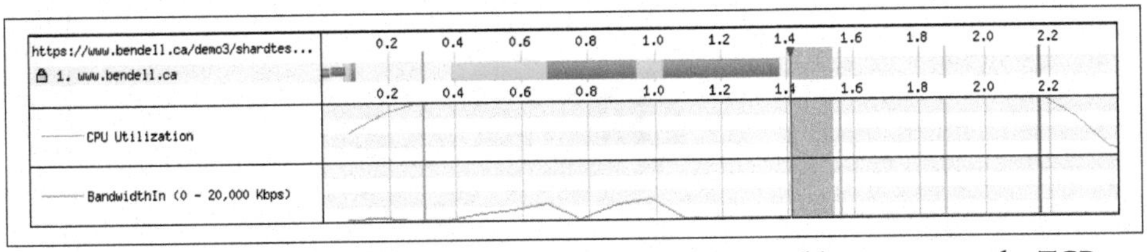

Figure 10-3. Even with HTTP/2, many small images are not able to saturate the TCP connection—test with 100 3K images on a page

Efficient Use of the Connection

HTTP/2 does improve the situation by effectively increasing the number of parallel requests. You will incur the cost of a TLS handshake, but will be able to make many requests on a single connection without the penalty of head-of-line blocking. Requests and responses occur simultaneously, maximizing the connection throughput. Still, there is a finite data capacity. Using our analogy of moving, the doorway still restricts how many boxes can actually be transported from the house to the truck. If we are transmitting images ahead of critical content, we will still delay the experience of the waiting user.

Fortunately, the browser (and the protocol) can prioritize requests: images after XHR/AJAX, JavaScript, and CSS. This is an attempt to minimize the impact of delayed requests. Increasingly, however, these resources are loaded using JavaScript and other complex mechanisms, making it easier for the preloader/speculative parser to discover and queue images but less likely to discover critical JavaScript and XHR calls. Early CSS request and parsing will also quickly populate the request queue. The net result is that small images will block resources needed for user interaction.

Take, for example, Lottee.com, a South Korean online shopping mall (Figure 10-4). On the home page (*http://global.lotte.com*), the images in the network queue delay the loading of other critical CSS and JavaScript resources. Also note the use of the network bandwidth.

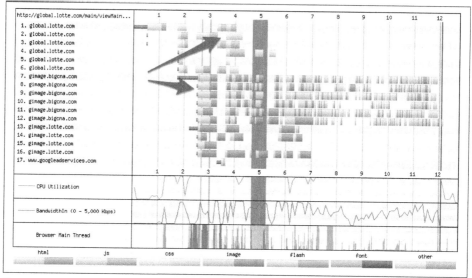

Figure 10-4. Lotte.com request waterfall

Impact on Browser Cache: Metadata and Small Images

One last challenge with small images is the overhead of maintaining the images in the cache and sending them over the wire. While the actual bytes of the image might be small, there is always overhead metadata associated with the image that is sent along with the HTTP response in the form of HTTP headers and browser/device cache. This may seem to be a trivial issue, but when you compound it with many small images, it becomes a larger problem.

There are three areas where this metadata exists: the datacenter, transit, and client. We'll ignore the cost of maintaining the images at the datacenter for now. In transit to the client, this metadata manifests itself as the HTTP response headers being sent to the client. Once received, this image must be stored and indexed on the user's operating system for future reference.

Chrome uses block files to store images and other small content that is less than 16 KB (see Table 10-1). This reduces the overhead of sector waste on the filesystem. Each block file uses different sizes of blocks and is limited to ~64,000 entries each. A cached entry will include the hashed key, HTTP headers, rankings, and pointers to payload blocks. The payload is stored using all the same block sizes, which will likely yield at least one partially filled block.

Table 10-1. Chrome's disk cache file organization with different cache block sizes for each file

File	Block size
data_0	36 bytes
data_1	256 bytes
data_2	1 KB
data_3	4 KB

Let's assume for a moment that the client has requested a 3.2 KB image and has 300 bytes of HTTP response headers. Not a big deal, right? This image will be indexed and stored in one of the cache block files; in this case, it will be *data_2* and will require five blocks: one for the headers, four for the payload. Thus we have used ~512 bytes for the cache entry records along with an additional ~100 bytes for the rank and index plus 4 KB for the HTTP response. In total we have used 5.6 KB of storage for a 3.2 KB image. That 75% increase in file size (2.4 KB) is all overhead! Worse yet, the 64,000 entries in the *data_1* block file are reduced by 4 just for a single cached file.

Modern browsers employ a fixed cache pressure to reduce IO overhead. While the use of data files optimizes the utilization of the cache for small files, the popularity of similar sized files can create cached entries to be dropped. The least-recently-used cache is a complex algorithm that takes many factors into account, including block utilization. The risk of having many small images on a page is that it will increase the probability of some or all of those images being evicted from the cache before a repeat visit from a user.

For example, if you consolidated 10 images into 1 consolidated file and request each subimage only one time, you would have effectively increased the cache popularity of the single consolidated image. As separate images they would have a cache hit of 1, whereas now the consolidated image has a hit of 10. Thus, the aggregated resource is less likely to be evicted compared to the many resources.

There is also the impact of IPC in the browser when making a request from the cache or the network. At a high level each tab in a browser has its own thread, but must communicate via IPC to the browser threads, which in turn dispatch multiple requests over the network or even fetch resources from the cache. This architecture allows isolation and parallel processing but at the cost of additional memory. IPC calls are not free and have synchronization overhead. The more we can reduce IPCs, the more efficiently the browser will behave.

Small Objects Observed

Surprisingly, a large portion of the images downloaded on the Web are small images. Of the top 1 million most popular images, 24% of all JPEGs requested by end users are less than 6 KB in size. Likewise, 80% of GIFs and 64% of PNGs are less than 6 KB. In aggregate, 44% of images requested by end users are below 6 KB, or approximately four packets wide (see Figure 10-5).

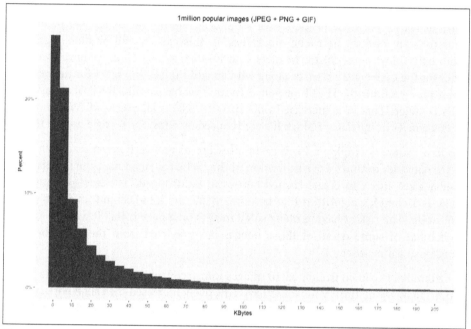

Figure 10-5. Histogram of 1 million JPEGs, GIFs, and PNGs

As we have already discussed, images make up most of the bytes downloaded on a web page. Unfortunately, this byte volume also corresponds to an average of 54 images per page, according to httparchive.org. This is despite over a decade of web performance optimization education showing the necessity of optimizing for these small images.

Logographic Pages

Unfortunately, HTTP and HTML are biased in favor of English and the Latin-based languages. Logographic-based languages have many complexities—from character encoding to text flows. Many of the early browsers, proxies, and web servers had challenges differentiating ASCII and Unicode encodings like UTF-8. As a result, many websites to this day still depend on images for logographic words to ensure styling, formatting, and aesthetics are preserved across browsers. The result is much higher volume of images since much of the text content is embedded in images.

What Is Logography?

Logography refers to writing systems where each character represents a word or phrase. Examples include Chinese characters and Japanese kanji. In contrast, English uses an alphabet.

Korean is technically an alphabet system, but because it is non-Latin-based it has the same challenges as other Asian logogram systems.

For example, compare the number of small images used on rakutan.co.jp to rakutan.co.uk (a popular online retailer in Japan), shown in Figure 10-6. The majority of this difference is to address the shortcomings of browser rendering discrepancies by using small images for words and text (see Figure 10-7).

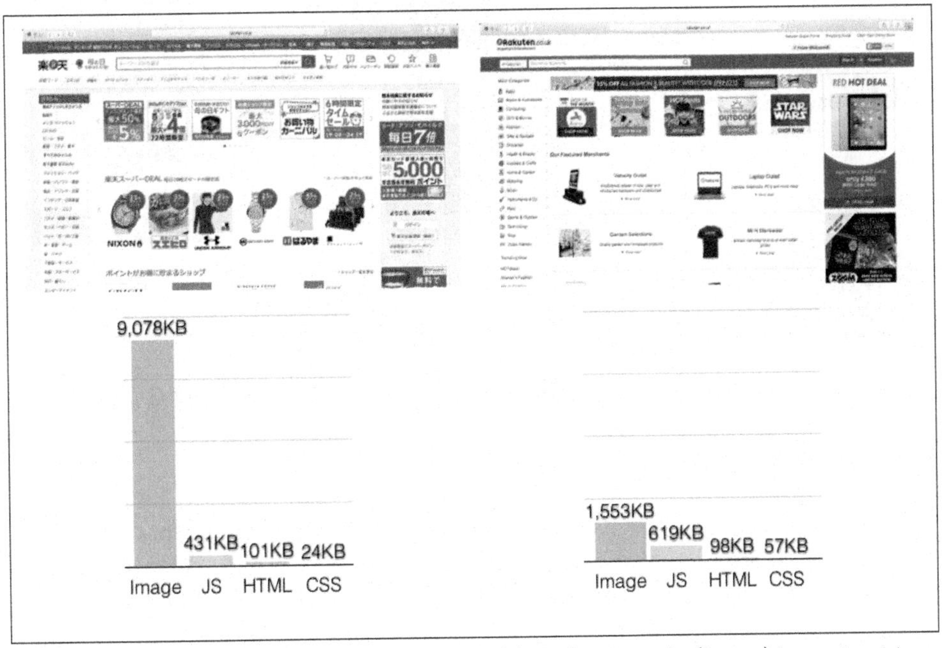

Figure 10-6. Compare the image bytes required for rakutan.co.jp (Japan) in contrast to rakutan.co.uk (UK)—nearly 6x the number of image bytes

Figure 10-7. Most of the images contain Japanese text to solve layout and font issues

Raster Consolidation

Consolidating techniques focuses on maximizing I/O—whether network or cache—by using one data stream to represent multiple images. Raster and vector images have slightly different options (see "Raster Versus Vector" on page 23 for more discussion).

CSS Spriting

The most common, and likely the most effective, way to reduce the number of small images is to utilize CSS sprites. Sprites are a robust technique that have a history stretching back to the early days of video games. A single image can contain multiple images that are sliced up and reused throughout the page. Better still: CSS sprites are supported by nearly all browsers.

Using CSS sprites accomplishes the following goals:

- Multiple images combined into a single image
- 1 HTTP request
- 1 cache entry
- Reduced file size for combined images

Consider the logos for the most popular browsers (see the following images). Including each icon as a separate file would result in the bytes downloaded and disk cache size (see "Impact on Browser Cache: Metadata and Small Images" on page 162) shown in Table 10-2.

Table 10-2. Small icons file byte size and size in cache

Logo	Pixels	Bytes	Browser disk cache size
MS Edge	128×128	1.39 KB	3.6 KB
Chrome	128×128	3.34 KB	5.6 KB
Firefox	128×128	6.55 KB	9.6 KB
Safari	128×128	5.42 KB	9.6 KB
Total		16.7 KB	28.4 KB

In total, these icons occupy 16.7 KB. Combining the four images into one results in a single 12.8 KB image, requiring only one IPC and occupying 16.6 KB of cache disk (four blocks of *data_3*). Not only is this now an HTTP request, but it also reduces the cache footprint to 3.6 KB.

Creating CSS sprites

Creating and using CSS sprites is straightforward:

1. Merge images into a single image.
2. Create CSS styles that reference the appropriate sprite location.
3. Add HTML markup placeholders for the images.

Merging images

You can use your favorite image editor, such as GIMP or Photoshop, to merge images. Create a canvas large enough to house all the sprites, copy and paste each image, lay out the images in a logical order, and save. You'll likely save the resulting image as a PNG (see Chapter 3 for selecting the right format).

```
$ convert edge.png chrome.gif firefox.png safari.png
  -append PNG8:browsers-sprite.png
```

Change sprite direction with ImageMagick

Use ImageMagick to create a sprite with -append to append vertically or +append to append horizontally.

Creating CSS styles

Once you have the single image created, the next step is to create the appropriate CSS styles. CSS sprites use the background-image and background-position properties to move the image out of the viewable area. These attributes have existed since 1996 in CSS1 and have nearly ubiquitous browser support.

```
a.icon {
  display:inline-block;
  text-indent: -9999px;
}
.icon {
  background-image: url('/images/browsers-sprite.png[]');
  background-repeat: no-repeat;
  height: 128px;
  width: 128px;
}
.icon-facebook {
  background-position: 0px 0px;
}

.icon-twitter {
  background-position: 0px -128px;
}

.icon-linkedin {
  background-position: 0px -256px;
}

.icon-googleplus {
  background-position: 0px -384px;
}
```

A quick checklist for the styles:

- Keep track of the relative position (-x, -y) of each sprite on the canvas.
- Specify the width and height of the viewable sprite to avoid visual gaffes.
- Use one style per sprite to avoid overlap.
- Update all the relative positions if you change the sprite.

Adding HTML markup

For each location where you will use the sprite you will need a corresponding HTML element that supports background styling. You'll have to use a blocking element, which in most cases means you'll use a <div> or <span> instead of <img>. The HTML markup is usually the part that grates on most purists because it requires you to mix presentation with content.

```
<a class="icon icon-edge"
href="https://www.microsoft.com/en-ca/windows/microsoft-edge">
    Microsoft Edge
</a>
<a class="icon icon-chrome" href="https://www.google.com/chrome/">
    Chrome
</a>
<a class="icon icon-firefox" href="https://www.mozilla.org/en-US/firefox/new/">
    Firefox
</a>
<a class="icon icon-safari" href="http://www.apple.com/safari/">
    Safari
</a>
```

In this example we have made the social media links clickable while also making them accessible for anyone using a screen reader.

Automating to avoid image and link rot

Clearly, creating sprites by hand isn't ideal. In fact, the biggest risk of manually creating sprites is *image rot*—images that are no longer being used but are still included in the sprite. The worst case is when the same image is included multiple times but at slightly different sizes.

If you are manually creating the sprite, then you will either need to revisit all the old references, or just blindly add a new image to the bottom of the existing sprite. The latter is the path of least resistance. Unfortunately, this will result in an ever-growing sprite canvas. Consider the pain and suffering of having to refactor all your CSS after your CEO discovers that the site is slow because of a 1 MB sprite (... not that this has actually happened to anyone I know).

Fortunately, there are many tools available to help automate the creation and referencing of sprites. Usually, the first approach is to do a global search and replace on HTML and CSS files. Don't do that. It is painful and will be fraught with problems. You shouldn't underestimate the creativity of your marketing team.

The better approach is to automate the creation of sprites and CSS styles. Clearly define the style-naming convention with your creative teams. Follow this up by removing all GIF/PNG/JPG files during your deployment process and monitor for broken links to find offenders.

Many frameworks now have automated mechanisms to create sprites. If you are starting from scratch, I suggest using Sprity (*https://github.com/sprity/sprity*). Sprity is very extensible and can plug into your existing styling frameworks (SCSS/Less) and build automation systems (Grunt/Gulp), but can also be plumbed into an existing deployment script.

For example, we can simplify our output with this command line to create both *out/ sprite.png* and *out/browsers.css* files:

```
$ sprity out/ images/*.png -s browsers.css
```

The Sprity default creates styles prefixed with *icon-* which, fortuitously, matches our preceding example.

Advanced Topics

CSS spriting has been around for a long time and is covered extensively in many blog posts and books. Some of the more advanced topics that should also be considered include:

Responsive sprites
> Using different icons and images based on viewport width

Adaptive sprites
> Selecting different icon sets based on DPR

Rollover and hover
> Simulating mouse hover effects by switching icons

Animations
> Using CSS sprites to do video spriting

Games and JavaScript
> Making a website feel more like a mobile app

A comprehensive review of the different techniques and usages can be found at *Smashing Magazine*'s post *The Mystery of CSS Sprites* (*http://bit.ly/2bt1P3K*).

Drawbacks and shortcomings

While CSS sprites do provide broad browser support and are well understood, it isn't all unicorns and rainbows. There are many rough edges in this technique.

Operationally:

- Global sprites versus local sprites: should you create one global sprite but have many of the icons unused in a page, or have one sprite per page but have duplication?

- Large sprites need to partitioned. Sprites shouldn't be larger than 10 packets (~40 KB). Use partitioning schemes to manage growth.

- Cache invalidation—any change will cause the sprite to be invalid and render downstream caches moot. You will certainly need to version your sprites and force the end user to download the new sprite, even if 90% of the icons haven't changed.

- You must be vigilant about ensuring that unsprited references to small images don't creep into the system.

- Chicken and egg: sprite first or style first? Sprites must be created first before creative teams can style a page and decide if the sprite is good enough. Iterating on an icon is burdensome.

Stylistically:

- Images can't be styled. You must manually implement CSS properties, like shadows, coloring, and underlining, by creating yet another image and sprite.

- Different sizes and layouts also require different image sprite sets.

- Animated PNG/GIF/WebP files can't be included in a sprite (though arguably they are likely not *small images*).

- Sprites mix presentation and content by injecting HTML.

Data URIs

Another technique that shares roots with CSS spriting is inlining images. This approach moves images not into a separate consolidated image, but into the referencing document, and encodes the binary into base64 text. In this way you can include the images in the HTML or CSS by using the `data:` prefix whenever a `src` attribute or property is used.

Inlining images with data URIs has benefits because it eliminates the need for yet another HTTP request and cache entry. The page becomes intrinsically consistent; there's no need for versioning. What you sent is what was expected to be rendered.

The structure of a data URI is:

```
data:[<media type>][;charset=<character set>][;base64],<data>
```

For images you can ignore the `;charset` attribute, but be sure to include the `;base64` attribute. For example, the 35-byte universal transparent 1×1 GIF is rendered as:

```
<img
  src="data:image/gif;base64,R0lGODlhAQABAIAAAP///wAAACwAAAAAAQABAAACAkQBADs=" />
```

You can use this in HTML and CSS like so:

```
<img
  src="data:image/png;base64,iVBORw0KGgoAAAANSUhEUgAAAAUAAAAFCAYA
AACNbyblAAAAHElEQVQI12P4//8/w38GIAXDIBKE0DHxgljNBAAO9TXL0Y4OHwA
AAABJRU5ErkJggg==" alt="Red dot" />

<style>
  .dot {
    background: url('data:image/png;base64,
```

iVBORw0KGgoAAAANSUhEUgAAAAUAAAAFCAYAAACNbyblAAAAHElEQVQI12P4/
/8/w38GIAXDIBKE0DHxgljNBAAO9TXL0Y4OHwAAAABJRU5ErkJggg==')

```
    }
<style>
```

There are many tools available to generate the base64 output, including Grunt tasks like `grunt-data-uri`. You can also implement this yourself using the `base64` command in Linux or OS X.

Inline SVG Using Data URI

SVGs can also be used in a data URIs. Of course, you don't need to base64 the text, but you will need to URL-encode the string. You can also safely omit translating spaces (' ') into %20 to get additional readability; the difference after Gzip compression is negligible.

If you are concerned with getting the smallest 1×1 pixel image, you can use SVG with a data URI. This is useful when you want to lazy-load images and need the `onload` event to fire, or if you need an empty image for art direction.

```
<picture>
    <source media="(min-width: 600px)" srcset="/browsers.jpg">
    <source media="(max-width: 600px) and (orientation: portrait)"
        srcset="data:image/svg+xml;charset=utf-8,%3Csvg
        xmlns%3D%22http%3A%2F%2Fwww.w3.org%2F2000%2Fsvg%22%2F%3E">
</picture>
```

This is effectively an empty SVG and the URL decoded is `<svg xmlns="http://www.w3.org/2000/svg"/>`. This example combines both common use cases: ensuring that the `onload` event fires for every media query match and that we don't cause a download of an otherwise hidden image.

Considerations

As you would expect, there are caveats to consider when you are utilizing a data URI.

Increased size

The biggest objection to using data URIs is the bloat from base64-encoding the binary. Base64 will increase the raw byte size by \~35%. Fortunately, Gzip will reduce the contents between 3% and 37%. (Using Brotli you could get this down even further.) Overall most images will have no larger net size when transferred. (Though note that really small images can see some increases in size because of the headers required.)

Figures 10-8 and 10-9 again utilize the study of the top 1 million images, this time converted using Base64 and then Base64 with Gzip, respectively. The locus of the results shows a net decrease in byte size after inlining.

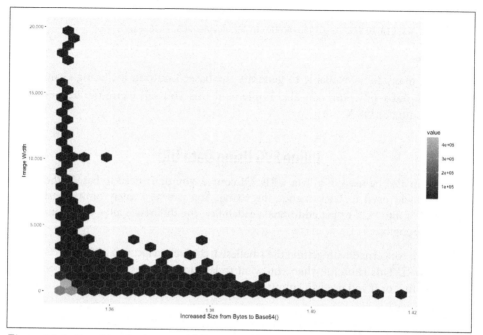

Figure 10-8. Base64 only: image width versus % increase size from base64

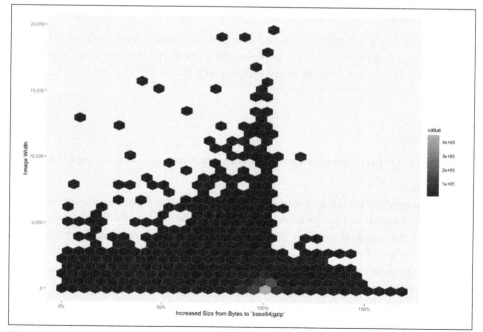

Figure 10-9. Base64 then Gzip: image width versus % increase size from base64/Gzip

Browser support

Unfortunately, data URIs are an advent of modern browsers. For those prior to IE8 you'll need to have a non-inlined version of your CSS that references the images directly. IE8 also has an artificial limit of 32 K of encoded URIs. You can use the Internet Explorer conditional comment to add the correct CSS:

```
<!--[if lte IE 8]>
<style href="ie-noinlining.css />
<![endif]-->
```

Request blocking

The real problem with inlining is that the images have effectively moved up in priority and the transfer of the image is now blocking the transfer of other critical resources. As we have previously discussed, images are generally low priority, so by inlining them with data URIs we give the image an effective high priority because it is transferred at the time of the HTML or CSS.

Processing time

Further complicating the issue is that the decode process takes additional CPU and memory. One study by Peter McLachlan (*http://www.mobify.com/blog/data-uris-are-slow-on-mobile/*) at Mobify found that "when measuring the performance of hundreds of thousands of mobile page views, loading images using a data URI is on average 6x slower than using a binary source link such as an <img> tag with an src attribute!"

While this is something that can be optimized over time in modern browsers, the use of data URIs can slow the loading and processing of the file. If you embedded all images in the HTML, resulting in an uncompressed doubling, it would impact the time to compute the DOM or calculate styles.

Caching and CSP

As with sprites, changes to images require caches to be invalidated. Unlike with spriting, though, the impact isn't localized to a single image; it now requires the encapsulating CSS and HTML to be versioned or invalidated from the cache. If only an icon changes, then the entire page must be redownloaded.

Likewise, if your site employs a content security policy (CSP), the base64 or digest hash will need to be updated. Using inline images creates an ecosystem change.

Better: Deferred data URI stylesheet

If you are concerned about blocking the critical rendering path by inlining images in the HTML and CSS, another approach is to use an asynchronous CSS stylesheet.

1. Replace CSS `background` properties to remove the `url()` reference. You can replace it with a solid color `#ffffff` or even with a 1×1 inline pixel so as not to minimize the stylesheet differences:

```
.myclass {
  width: 123px;
  height: 456px;
  background: #ffffff no-repeat
}
```

2. Create a new CSS stylesheet (we will call it *images.css*) with just the CSS selector and real `background` properties that include `url('data:images/ ...')` with inline source for the actual content:

```
.myclass {
  background-image: url('data:image/gif;base64, ... ')
}
```

3. Defer the loading of *images.css* with the following JavaScript (courtesy of Scott Jehl's *loadCSS.js* (*https://github.com/filamentgroup/loadCSS*):

```
<script>
  // include loadCSS here...
(function(w){
      "use strict";
      var loadCSS = function( href, media ){
            var doc = w.document;
            var ss = doc.createElement( "link" );
            var refs = ( doc.body || doc.getElementsByTagName( "head"
                        )[ 0 ] ).childNodes;
            var ref = refs[ refs.length - 1];

            var sheets = doc.styleSheets;
            ss.rel = "stylesheet";
            ss.href = href;
            // temporarily set media to something inapplicable to ensure
            // it'll fetch without blocking render
            ss.media = "only x";

            var onloadcssdefined = function( cb ){
                  var resolvedHref = ss.href;
                  var i = sheets.length;
                  while( i-- ){
                        if( sheets[ i ].href === resolvedHref ){
                              return cb();
                        }
                  }
                  setTimeout(function() {
                        onloadcssdefined( cb );
                  });
            };
```

```
                // once loaded, set link's media back to `all` so that the
                // stylesheet applies once it loads
                ss.onloadcssdefined = onloadcssdefined;
                onloadcssdefined(function() {
                        ss.media ="all";
                });
                return ss;
        };
        // commonjs
        if( typeof module !== "undefined" ){
                module.exports = loadCSS;
        }
        else {
                w.loadCSS = loadCSS;
        }
}( typeof global !== "undefined" ? global : this ));

  // load a file
  loadCSS( "/images.css" );
</script>

<noscript><link href="/images.css" rel="stylesheet"></noscript>

<!--[if lte IE 8]>
<style href="ie-noinlining-images.css />
<![endif]-->
```

The net result will be a combined CSS with just the inlined images. This combined CSS is loaded asynchronously (don't forget to include the legacy fallback for IE 5–8). All of the inlined images will have two distinct benefits:

- Total bytes are reduced via Gzip to 1–3% less than even the original total bytes.
- Images will avoid being manipulated by intermediate proxies that can recompress images and distort images for mobile users (we will discuss this in Chapter 13).

Tools

There are many tools options to help you create inline images with different approaches.

- You can use automated frontend optimization services, such as PageSpeed for Apache, NginX, and IIS. Many content delivery networks (CDNs) also include this service as part of their value-add delivery.
- Build tools into your development workflow. Compass can automate the creation in your SCSS/SASS stylesheets. Grunt tasks, like grunt-data-uri, can also exam-

ine existing CSS and transform the content automatically ahead of deployment to production.

- Roll your own tools. You can use the `base64` command on most Linux systems or use the `base64()` equivalent function in most languages.

Vector Image Consolidation

Using raster graphics for icons and layout styling support is not ideal. This is especially true for logographic and non-Latin-based content (hiragana, katakana, kanji, zhōngwén, hangul, etc.) and also can be problematic for responsive layouts. Either you are sending down very large raster images and forcing the client to resize down, or doing the opposite and scaling up small images. Both are undesirable from a performance and aesthetics perspective. It gets worse if you are trying to align CSS styling with these bitmap images. A better solution is to implement these small images in vector format to allow clean scaling on all resolution of displays.

Icon Fonts

Vector images can be merged into a custom web font. This approach replaces literal characters with a custom icon or graphic.

There are many downsides to this approach, and it should be used only in a few situations, particularly:

FOIT
> Flash of Invisible Text (Chrome/Safari/Firefox). Text styled by web fonts is hidden until the font is loaded.

FOUT
> Flash of Unstyled Text (Internet Explorer/Edge). Text is presented unstyled initially, then changed after the custom font is loaded.

Proxy browsers
> Many browsers, particularly those on low-powered mobile devices, don't support custom web fonts.

Accessibility
> Visually impaired and dyslexic users often override default fonts. Using custom fonts will make your website look like gibberish.

However, web fonts can make sense in some situations:

- Accents or enhancements to existing text or icons (there are already many icons presented in Unicode, including emojis)

- Ligatures where words are replaced with enhanced text
- Logographic content where standard
- Native app web views where you can limit which platforms utilize the web fonts

Overview

There are two approaches to utilizing web fonts:

- Single-character replacement: Create the new HTML entity &#broccoli; with the image seen in Figure 10-10.

Figure 10-10. Image to create new HTML entity

These images can be referenced by decimal position or defined colloquial name. Existing characters can also be replaced.

- Typographic ligatures: this is essentially the same as a single-character replacement but has some additional usability benefits. Instead of a single-character replacement, you can do multiple-character replacement to replace a whole word with an icon. For example, the word *love* can be replaced with the ♥ character. In this way, "I love broccoli" will be rendered "I ♥ broccoli."

Additionally, icon fonts can be styled with CSS just like any other text. This includes color adjustments, shading, shape, rotation, and even font styles like bold and italic. Adding CSS styles to font icons provides you with flexibility and eliminates the need to regenerate from source when applying subtle aesthetic changes.

Creating and using icon web fonts

Assembling an icon font is fairly straightforward. You can assemble a new icon font by using existing web fonts or, using SVG images as source, by defining character mapping and converting to the various web font formats. The trickier part is ensuring cross-browser support, fallback, and accessibility.

Fortunately, you don't have to build your icon web font from scratch. There are many font libraries ready for use, many of which can be reassembled into purpose-built web fonts. IcoMoo, SymbolSet, Font Squirrel, and Pictos are just some of the many sites that can assemble, create, and host icon fonts. (We'll discuss hosting and performance shortly.)

If you're using images for Asian characters, this is the best place to start to build a logographic typeface.

There are many tools for type designers and typographic experts to create custom web fonts. This includes FontLab Studio, FontForge, and many others. However, for custom icon web fonts this may involve a lot more complication and is not necessarily scalable for use with your creative teams.

There are also a number of tools that can help you automate the process of creating web fonts and avoid the manual design process. Typically these tools start with SVG images, transform them into the custom font, and provide the appropriate character mapping. The typical workflow starts with SVG images, converts to an SVG font, and then converts that font to the other web font formats, such as TTF, EOT, WOFF, and WOFF2. Alternatively, there are also Grunt and Gulp tasks (such as `grunt-webfont` (*https://github.com/sapegin/grunt-webfont*) or `gulp-iconfont` (*https://github.com/nfroi dure/gulp-iconfont*)) that wrap up these individual steps into a single task, making it easier to automate the process.

Web Fonts are Monochromatic

It is important to remember that web fonts are monochromatic. Color detail represented in SVGs will be lost when embedded in a font.

To demonstrate this workflow we will use the following libraries:

1. SVG images >> SVG font (*https://github.com/fontello/svg2ttf*)
2. SVG font >> TTF font (*https://github.com/fontello/svg2ttf*)
3. TTF font >> EOT font (*https://github.com/fontello/ttf2eot*)
4. TTF font >> WOFF (*https://github.com/fontello/ttf2woff*)
5. TTF font >> WOFF2 (*https://github.com/nfroidure/ttf2woff2*)

There are a number of other libraries that are also useful for this process that we won't explore, specifically:

- SVG Optimizer (*https://github.com/svg/svgo*), which reduces the redundant information and helps collapse the code paths.

- TTFAutoHint (*http://www.freetype.org/ttfautohint/*), which can help improve rendering of fonts, particularly in Windows, for maximum readability (*https://www.typotheque.com/articles/hinting*).

Using the same browser logos we used when creating the CSS sprite we can combine them into a web font. This time we will start with SVG representations. Our folder */images* contains the following SVGs, as shown in Figure 10-11.

- *images/safari.svg*
- *images/firefox.svg*
- *images/u0065-edge.svg*
- *images/u0063,u0063u0068u0072u006fu006du0065-chrome.svg*

Figure 10-11. SVG browser icons

Invoking the conversion to create the SVG font (*fonts/browsers.svg*) is fairly straightforward. This will create the root font we will use to convert to the other web font formats. It is also the step where the character mapping, ligature creation, and colloquial glyph naming occurs. In this example, the filename will also provide hints for character mapping for the Edge and Chrome logo. The letter *e* will be replaced with the Edge logo or the ligature *chrome* will be replaced with the Chrome logo.

```
$ svgicons2svgfont --fontname=browsersfont -s uEA01 \
  -o fonts/browsers.svg images/*.svg
```

Character Mapping with Fonts

There are many nuances with character mapping. First there is the consideration for fallback support. If there is a less ideal, but representative existing character already present in Unicode, then overriding this character might be preferred. For example, you might have an hours of operation section with a nice clock image. You can use the character ⌚ (⌚) and replace it with your nicely styled clock (see Figure 10-12 for an example).

Figure 10-12. An example of a nicely styled clock

As previously mentioned, the icons used in web fonts replace mapped characters. Using existing character mapping provides a certain level of fallback if the web font failed to load or there was another operational problem. Of course, if the replaced character is not related, you could be giving your user a very jarring experience.

The Unicode spec does provide a private user area (PUA) for mapping characters for private use. In theory this provides you a place where only your icons will exist. In practice, some platforms utilize this space and potentially cause other visual gaffes. Most notable was the emoji mapping in PUA prior to formally being included in the Unicode spec (see iOS SoftBank mapping (*http://bit.ly/2aTdL1w*)). If you are exclusively using your icon font for icons and not mixing it in with an existing web font, then PUA overlap is not a concern.

Likewise, converting to TTF, EOT, WOFF, and WOFF2 can be accomplished thusly:

```
$ svg2ttf fonts/browsers.svg fonts/browsers.ttf
$ ttf2eot fonts/browsers.ttf fonts/browsers.eot
$ ttf2woff fonts/browsers.ttf fonts/browsers.woff
$ ttf2woff2 fonts/browsers.ttf fonts/browsers.woff2
```

Utilizing the newly created web font is now as easy as adding the font declaration and associated HTML:

```
<span class="icon icon-safari"></span>
<span class="icon icon-firefox"></span>
<span class="icon icon-edge"></span>
<span class="icon icon-chrome">chrome</span>

@font-face {
  font-family: 'socialmediafont';
  src: url('browsers.eot'); /* IE9 Compat Modes */
  src: url('browsers.eot?#iefix') format('embedded-opentype'), /* IE6-IE8 */
       url('browsers.woff2') format('woff2'), /* Super Modern Browsers */
       url('browsers.woff') format('woff'), /* Pretty Modern Browsers */
       url('browsers.ttf')  format('truetype'), /* Safari, Android, iOS */
       url('browsers.svg#socialmediafont') format('svg'); /* Legacy iOS */
}
```

```css
.icon {
    font-family: 'browsersfont' !important;

    font-feature-settings: "liga"; /* enable ligatures */
}

.icon-safari:before {
    content: "\ea01";
}
.icon-firefox:before {
    content: "\ea02";
}
.icon-edge:before {
    content: "\65";
}
.icon-chrome:before {
    content: "\63";
}
```

Since we have created an icon font with only the icons, only a limited number of characters can be rendered. Any additional text that is caught in the CSS style that is not defined may render oddly with different browsers. For example, if you have the text *edge*, only the letter *e* will display and the following characters may have empty boxes. Be careful to scope icon fonts appropriately.

In this example we have enabled ligatures using the CSS property. However, a more comprehensive style would include:

```css
.icon {
    font-family: 'browsersfont' !important;

    /* Ligature support */
    letter-spacing: 0;
    -webkit-font-feature-settings: "liga";
    -moz-font-feature-settings: "liga=1";
    -moz-font-feature-settings: "liga";
    -ms-font-feature-settings: "liga" 1;
    -o-font-feature-settings: "liga";
    font-feature-settings: "liga";
}
```

As previously mentioned, using Gulp or Grunt tasks can simplify these steps and combine them into a single action. Both tasks will also generate the necessary CSS and mapping to further reduce rendering errors.

Compatibility

Unfortunately, web font support across the browser spectrum is very fragmented (see Figure 10-13). There isn't a single universal format that is supported by all browsers. While modern browsers have rallied around WOFF and WOFF2, older browsers support a myriad of formats, including EOT, TTF, and SVG. Worse yet, most proxy browsers, including Opera Mini, do not support any web fonts, so fallback is always important.

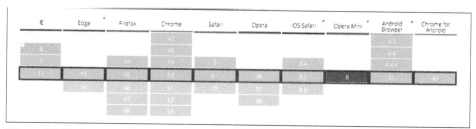

Figure 10-13. Browser support for @font-face with web fonts from CanIUse.com (2016)

Safari Support for SVG Fonts

While the SVG font container is supported by Safari, modern versions also support WOFF. Only early versions of Safari supported SVG Web fonts. It is relatively safe to omit SVG in your CSS declaration.

Each browser also loads fonts differently, resulting in a variety of rendering experiences for users. Of particular note is the dreaded Flash of Unstyled Text (FOUT). For example, Internet Explorer will display the text in an alternate font until the web font is available. This is OK if you have appropriate fallback characters, but it will display empty boxes if you're using PUA character mapping.

In contrast, Safari will hide the text until the custom font is available and display it only after the font is loaded. Finally, Chrome and Firefox will wait up to 3 seconds and use the fallback font, repainting after the font is available. This Flash of Invisible Text (FOIT) is probably worse from a user experience perspective—especially if the user is on a poor network connection.

Most browsers also load fonts asynchronously with the exception of Internet Explorer. The result is that the icon images can be displayed later and prolong the FOUT period while the fonts are loaded. For smaller icon fonts, inlining the font with a data URI can be more efficient. Unfortunately, because of the multiple font formats, you will also need to inline the different font files even if they aren't being used.

To work around this, you can use adaptive delivery for your CSS and detect, server side, the browser and version and deliver a specific CSS file with the appropriate inlined font file. (For more details, see Chapter 13.)

While the hoops to generate font files for vector images might seem arduous, the real benefit is bringing accessibility for your website and images, as well as a convenient encapsulation to bring vector images to legacy browsers.

Web font pros and cons

While icon fonts are a convenient and durable mechanism to consolidate small vector images, there are many drawbacks. Most notable is the outright lack of support by some browsers—specifically, the lack of support by proxy browsers like Opera Mini. There are also various CSS and rendering nuances in different browsers and operating systems that need to be accounted for and tested. This includes CSS tricks like including !important to avoid browser extension issues and explicitly enabling font smoothing using -webkit-font-smoothing: antialiased and -moz-osx-font-smoothing: grayscale—not to mention issues of alignment, spacing, and churning.

On the other hand, web icon fonts can be good for text, specifically to augment existing text (using ligatures) or logographic content.

SVG Sprites

While SVGs are text and highly compressible, they are not immune to the challenges of small image delivery. In fact, SVGs have nearly the same kind of file size distribution—the majority being less than a single packet wide.

If you have vector images (in SVG) you aren't limited to web fonts to consolidate. You can create SVG sprites just as you would GIF/PNG sprites. As with raster sprites, you would arrange your icons on a canvas in a grid. Most vector image editors, from Adobe Illustrator to PixelImator, make this a quick task.

For Convenience, Set SVG viewBox Equal to viewport Dimensions

When using SVG for sprites, setting the viewport and viewBox to different values can have odd results. Remember the viewport is the viewable size (i.e., how large your monitor is), and the viewBox is the portion of the SVG canvas that should be stretched or shrunk to fit the viewport. For simplicity it is best to set the viewBox and viewport to the same dimensions.

For example, for our browser icons we might have an SVG sprite such as:

```
<svg version="1.1" xmlns="http://www.w3.org/2000/svg"
     xmlns:xlink="http://www.w3.org/1999/xlink"
     width="800" height="1080"
     viewBox="0 0 800 1080" >
  <g>
   <path d="..." />
   <!-- graphics arranged in rows and columns -->
  </g>
</svg>
```

Then, as usual you can reference each icon via CSS background:

```
.icon-safari {
  width: 20px;
  height: 20px;
  background-image: url('images/chrome.svg');
  background-repeat: no-repeat;
  background-position: -110px -630px;
  position: absolute;
}
```

This approach makes it easy for your creative team since it is a very familiar process. Better yet, this approach works in all browsers that support SVG—reaching back to IE9. Unfortunately, like raster image CSS sprites, the sprite must be manually maintained, and deprecated icon usage is nearly impossible to track. Without careful change management processes it is difficult to remove old icons for fear of creating a negative user experience.

There are other drawbacks. Using SVG has the appeal of custom styling using CSS and even animations. However, if you are using an SVG in a background-image you lose this flexibility. If you don't intend to style the SVG differently on the page, use :onhover, or apply any other customization of the image, then you could stop here. But we could do better.

SVG fragment identifier links

Often it's easier to use a common, colloquial name, instead of remembering the coordinates on the canvas. Since SVG is XML, most elements can be marked with a fragment identifier or id attribute. For example, we could define our icon in a <symbol> (which won't be visible until it is displayed):

```
<svg>
    <symbol id="chrome-logo"> <!-- ... --> </symbol>
</svg>
```

You can use fragment identifiers in SVG in many ways. Just as in HTML you can apply specific CSS styling to different nodes by referencing the id. You can also use it as a template for repeat use: you can reference the id in a use block multiple times (for example, drawing leaves on a tree). The identifier link can reference whole other files or a definition in the same file. You name the identifier at the end of the URL after the hash symbol, just as you would with HTML fragment identifiers:

```
<svg viewBox="0 0 100 200">
    <defs>
        <g id="firefox-logo"> <!-- ... --> </g>
    </defs>

    <use xlink:href="#firefox-logo"></use>
    <use xlink:href="images/browsers.svg#edge-logo"></use>
</svg>
```

In this example we place two SVG images on our canvas: one internally referenced symbol and another external. For completeness you can see how we reference both a symbol and a group (`<g>`). The group is wrapped in a `defs` block to ensure that it doesn't display until referenced. Hiding the fragment isn't required; it is convenient. We could always reference the first use of a template. However, it is better practice to define your templates separately. Doing so also solves a particular bug in some browsers (noteably Safari) where references must be defined before they're used.

Using `symbol` has the advantage of being able to define the template's `viewBox` and `preserveaspectratio`. It is also more clearly identified as a template rather than just another grouping layer.

For SVG spriting, we can use the fragment identifier to reference a specific image in a single consolidated SVG. This way we can ignore the location on the canvas:

```
<img src="images/browsers.svg#firefox-logo" />
```

It would be tempting to wrap all of our SVGs in `<symbol>` elements and add the `id` attribute. Boom. Done. Unfortunately, we would have two problems:

- `<symbol>` and `<defs>` aren't visible. Externally referencing them in your HTML or CSS would likewise draw nothing since the canvas is empty.
- Browser support for referencing fragment identifiers inside an SVG is spotty—but we can work around these issues.

Fragment identifiers and viewBox

To use SVG sprites, we need to provide instruction on how to draw the vector on a canvas. Adding a `viewBox` attribute provides this detail. Just as we need to consider the `viewBox` in relation to the viewport when we display the entire SVG, we also need to specify how much of the fragment is displayed so that it can be stretched appropriately inside the referencing HTML node.

You can define the `viewBox` a few ways:

- Add `viewBox` in the URL as you would a fragment identifier: `brows ers.svg#svgView(viewBox(0, 0, 256, 256))`. Unfortunately, while Firefox, Internet Explorer, and Edge get it right, Chrome (until 40) and Safari have problems with this approach. It is also only slightly better than using the traditional CSS approach because you need to maintain the coordinate references.
- Use an inline SVG block with a reference to the fragment identifier as follows:

```
<svg viewBox="0 0 100 200">
  <use xlink:href="images/browsers.svg#safari-logo"></use>
</svg>
```

This is better but it is odd to require an SVG in order to reference an SVG sprite.

- Define a `<view>` in the SVG and use that reference. As we mentioned, `<g>` does not support viewBox and `<symbol>` is hidden, but a `<view>` can merge use cases and expose a fragment identifier:

```
<svg>
    <view viewBox="0 0 100 200" id="firefox-logo">
        <!-- ... -->
    </view>
</svg>
```

Now referencing the fragment in your HTML will behave as you expect and you'll be able to style not only the HTML container, but also the SVG elements inside. The only remaining challenge is browser support. Again, not all browsers are created equally and using an `<img>` with a reference to the SVG + fragment identifier poses problems for Safari. We can more universally get around this by using an `<object>` tag instead:

```
<object data="images/browsers.svg#safari-logo" type="image/svg+xml"/>
```

Using this approach will allow you to use both fragment identifiers and consolidate SVGs to all browsers that support SVG. We still need to support older browsers by using raster sprites as a fallback.

Other SVG Consolidation Techniques

There are a couple of other SVG techniques for consolidation that have been proposed but we haven't covered here, specifically:

SVG stacks

This approach layers all the images on top of each other and depends on CSS styling to hide/reveal the relevant layer. As you have come to expect, there are nuances to this approach and it has challenges in browser support.

CSS stylesheets with inlined SVG

This is useful for images used only in one style definition and where you don't need to style the inner SVG elements. This is the same approach we discussed in "Data URIs" on page 172. Fallback does require a parallel stylesheet that is loaded by legacy browsers.

Automating SVG consolidation and fallback

Just as with raster sprites, we can automate the creation of SVG sprites to avoid image rot and duplication. There are several libraries that can be used with Grunt and Gulp wrappers. For example, Joschi Kuphal's svg-sprite (*https://github.com/jkphl/svg-sprite*) works well:

```
$ svg-sprite --view -D out/ images/*.svg
```

This will generate a consolidated SVG as we would expect with a <view> wrapper and a fragment identifier using the filename:

```
<svg>
    <view viewBox="0 0 100 200" id="browsers-firefox-logo">
        ...
    </view>
</svg>
```

You can also use this tool if you want to generate an SVG that uses conventional CSS spriting. This will produce a stylesheet with the coordinates on the consolidated SVG:

```
$ svg-sprite -css --ccss -D out/ images/*.svg
```

Legacy support is nearly not an issue. However, there are still many users trapped on devices and browsers with IE <9, Android <5, or iOS <7. You can support them in a few ways:

- If you use the CSS style spriting, you can use device detection and return different stylesheets based on the browser support. (Unfortunately, you can't use detection examining the Accepts: header.) In this way you would serve */sprites.css* to almost all browsers, with the exception that you use a raster-sprited view in */sprites-raster.css*. This would require generating raster images and spriting them as well. Wrapper tools like Iconizr (*https://github.com/jkphl/iconizr*) can make this easy.

- If you are using <object>, add a fallback to CSS spriting and use a <div> tag inside:
    ```
    <object data="images/browsers.svg#safari-logo" type="image/svg+xml">
        <div style="no-svg icon-safari-logo"/>
    </object>
    ```

- Do nothing; let the browser show or hide the output. This isn't a terrible solution because these legacy browsers are usually running low-powered hardware. Displaying nothing will improve the experience without forcing more overhead.

Summary

Consolidating small graphics, icons, and images will improve the user experience. There are different techniques that can be employed whether the sources are raster or vector based. Spriting is the most common technique for both because it typically uses lossless formats for raster images and is fairly well understood by most web developers. The same approach can be used for SVGs but requires consideration as to what features are needed and to browser support. Other techniques, such as inlining with data URIs, can also be useful but forgo the ability for the sprite to be cached if any of the surrounding HTML/CSS is modified between code releases. Finally, web fonts can be used, but because of the many shortcomings in ecosystem support, it is generally advisable to keep their usage targeted to specific use cases.

A few considerations for content that is eligible for consolidation:

- Any file < 1,500 bytes (1 packet).
- Four or more *like* files whose total bytes <24 KB for raster or <40 KB for vector (~16 packets).
- Consolidated images shouldn't exceed 48 KB (raster) or 80 KB (vector).
- Group candidates based on probability to change. Each change will cause the client's cache to be invalid.

To help select the right consolidation technique, try the flow diagram in Figure 10-14.

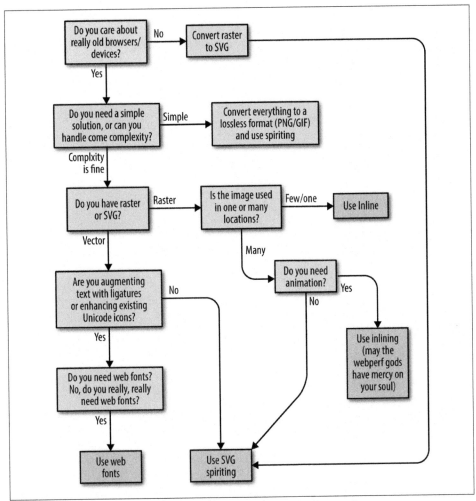

Figure 10-14. Flow diagram for selecting correct consolidation technique

It is easy to focus all of our attention on the large images that dominate the user's field of view: the hero image, the product images, the latest social media posts that get most of our attention. Yet, the presentation of our websites and apps is just as dependent on the subtle details, the small images. We can improve the performance of these small images primarily through reducing the number of requests, and reducing the overall size of the requests. The odd nuance of high performance small images is that if we do them right, no one will notice. However, if we do them incorrectly, everyone will notice.

Responsive Images

Yoav Weiss

There's no doubt that Responsive Web Design (RWD) has had a huge impact on the way we build websites nowadays. If you are operating a website, chances are that it's either responsive already, or it will be soon enough. There is no other way to serve websites while coping with the diversity of devices your users are using to access your site, and providing these users a pleasant experience.

But it's not all sunshine and rainbows. The issue of responsive images has been a thorn in RWD's side for a long while and a huge source of pain for developers trying to implement performant responsive websites.

How RWD Started

Early on, when RWD was coined in Ethan Marcotte's seminal article (*http://alista part.com/article/responsive-web-design*), the approach to images was fairly simple, if not to say naive: just send the browser the largest possible image and let it resize it on the client side to match the responsive layout.

While that approach works when testing the simpler use cases over the local network or even on a high-speed broadband network, it fails miserably when we take into account the reason RWD was needed in the first place: mobile devices over cellular networks. With the earlier approach we're sending unnecessarily large images to mobile devices, often over poor connectivity.

The immediate result of that approach was that RWD got a reputation for being slow, and it became obvious to many that a responsive website meant a bloated one.

The web developer community realized that RWD is the only scalable future for building websites that can address the myriad devices out there. At the same time, it also realized that users cannot afford to download 85 MB (*http://hawksworx.com/blog/oakleys-monster-page-of-baubles/*) (!!!) of data on their potentially limited data plans when looking up sunglasses. As a result, the community decided to take action.

And, as often happens on the Web, the first course of action was to hack around the problem.

Early Hacks

There were multiple attempts to resolve the responsive images issue using JavaScript or server-side logic. These attempts included:

- Serving images limited to the viewport dimensions based on the user agent string (e.g., sencha.io (*https://www.smashingmagazine.com/2013/07/choosing-a-responsive-image-solution/#sencha-io-src*))

- Serving images limited to the viewport dimensions based on a cookie set by the website (e.g., adaptive images (*http://adaptive-images.com/*))

- Adding the actual `src` attribute to images via script

- Overriding the page's `<base href>` via script (*https://gist.github.com/anselmh/1037666*)

- Rewriting the entire page's HTML via script after modifying the image URLs (e.g., mobify.js (*http://dev.mobify.com/blog/inside-mobify-performance-suite-responsive-images/*))

- Serving oversized yet highly compressed images, to avoid retina-related blurriness (aka compressive images (*https://www.filamentgroup.com/lab/compressive-images.html*))

Heroic and fearless as some of these attempts were, it was obvious pretty early on (*http://blog.yoav.ws/responsive_images_hacks_wont_cut_it/*) that all of them were lacking either in accuracy or performance.

The server-side approach didn't handle cases where the browser viewport was not identical to the device's dimensions (desktop and some tablets) or didn't work on first load. At the same time, the client-side methods were adding a non-negligible latency to the browser's resource loading process, by adding the images fairly late, and preventing the browser's preloader (which we discussed in Chapter 7) from loading them earlier on.

So, the Responsive Image Community Group (*https://responsiveimages.org/*) (RICG) was formed to find native in-browser solutions to this pressing issue, and after a long struggle, managed to do so.

But before we dive into the solutions, let's take a look at the various use cases that needed addressing.

Use Cases

The first step of solving the responsive images problem was to define the various use cases that developers face when using images on the Web today. The result was a document (*https://usecases.responsiveimages.org/*) that covered many different aspects of the problem. We'll cover the major ones.

Fixed-Dimensions Images

In order to frame this use case, think of a layout that resembles Figures 11-1 and 11-2.

Figure 11-1. Sample fixed-dimensions image in a responsive layout—wide viewport

Figure 11-2. Sample fixed-dimensions image in a responsive layout—narrow viewport

As you may have noticed, the image in these layouts remains in the same dimensions regardless of the layout changes that result from the responsive design, the same as images in nonresponsive designs. So why would we consider this image "responsive"?

Well, the problem starts when you're browsing that site over a high-resolution screen, and notice significant blur.

Retina screens "need" images that are twice (or more) the resolution of traditional resolution screens. If the image we provide the browser in that case is of lower dimensions, the browser will upscale the image, resulting in blurriness.

So, how do we resolve it? The first reaction from web developers was to upgrade their images, and serve larger images to their entire audience. The problem with this was that they were now serving larger images to all devices, including the ones that have absolutely no need for images that are twice as large.

For these devices, the result of the larger images was, besides the bandwidth costs and delay, increased CPU costs and higher memory consumption, as larger images had to be decoded and then stored in memory. See Chapter 9 for more details.

Variable-Dimensions Images

The variable-dimensions image use case is slightly different from the previous one, since it's tightly related to responsive websites. Consider the layouts shown in Figures 11-3 and 11-4.

Figure 11-3. Sample variable-dimensions images in a responsive layout—wide viewport of a desktop breakpoint

Figure 11-4. Sample variable-dimensions images in a responsive layout—narrower viewport of a desktop breakpoint

In this case, larger viewports need larger images; otherwise, the images will be blurry. But, similarly to the previous use case, higher-resolution screens also need larger images. Again, the initial developer response was to send the largest possible image, but that's hardly scalable. In a world with 28-inch high-resolution screens, the largest possible image can be pretty big. That's not something that you want to send down a mobile connection to your average user. That case is sometimes referred to as "download and shrink": you're downloading bytes that users don't necessarily need, burdening their mobile data plan and slowing down their experience.

Art Direction

What happens when your images are materially different in the various responsive breakpoints? When you want to adapt the images to the different breakpoints so that they will be clearer in the context of the different layout?

Well, that's a different use case from what we've seen before. A few examples of this use case are shown in Figures 11-5 and 11-6.

Figure 11-5. Crop-based art direction example (image taken from Google developers (http://bit.ly/2aV4rpr))

Figure 11-6. Art direction that changes the position and size of images between small and large viewports (image is a screenshot from http://kobe-marathon-qbb.com/)

What we see in these examples is that serving the intended images is essential in order for the user to fully understand the page and for the page to be properly laid out. The different proportions of the images mean that if we were to serve images that don't fit the layout, the layout would break.

In a way, this use case is less about "performance optimization" and more about "content optimization." The problem here is not so much about the image's quality as it is about getting the image's message accross to users, regardless of viewport restrictions. With that said, when large parts of the image are being cropped away when served to mobile devices, that certainly doesn't help the site's performance.

Art Direction Versus Resolution Switching

The fixed and variable dimensions use cases are often referred to together as *resolution switching*. The main difference between resolution switching and art direction is an issue of control. In the resolution switching cases, the issue at hand is quality. We want the user to get the best experience, where experience is a combination of visual quality and speed (and one might claim that the eventual bandwidth costs and battery life are also part of the experience). These aspects of the user's experience are not something that the web developer knows in advance, and any attempts to predict the user's "context" are bound to fail.

Therefore, for the resolution switching case, we want to give the browser the final word. Our solutions enable the developer to declare multiple resources and enable the browser to pick the one that best fits the user's current situation.

On the other hand, for the art direction case, the issue is one of fidelity. If the browser shows a different image than the one the developer intended, users may get a distorted image or a broken layout, hurting their experience as well as their ability to use the site properly. In this case, the browser doesn't know more about the user's context than the site's developer did when creating the site. So, we want the browser to be "bound" to obey the developer's instructions and download the specific image that the developer had in mind for particular viewport dimensions or other environmental constraints.

We need two distinct mechanisms to handle each one of these cases, one where the control is in the browser's hands, with the guidance of developers, and another where the control is in the developer's hands.

Image Formats

Another use case, which isn't directly related to responsive images but is very relevant to content images in general, is that of serving different image formats according to browser support. Traditionally, the answer to that has been content negotiation: have the browser advertise its capabilities using the `Accept` request header, and then the server can dynamically serve it the right image.

While that approach certainly works (as we will discuss in Chapter 13), it doesn't work for everyone. There are scenarios where the images are served from a static host (e.g., gh-pages or S3), where you have no control on the server-side logic and cannot dynamically adapt the image to the headers the browser advertises.

Avoiding "Download and Hide"

The "download and hide" scenario often happens when desktop sites are retrofitted to be responsive and some parts of the page are just not needed on mobile.

A common mistake in such a scenario is to hide the unnecessary parts with CSS and hope for the best. The problem with that approach (as you probably guessed from the scenario's name) is that even if the end user does not see these parts of the page, the resources they require—and content images in particular—are downloaded nonetheless.

You could think of this scenario as a form of art direction, where in some viewport sizes, the required image is a zero-sized one. We'll later see how to address this use case properly.

Use Cases Are Not Mutually Exclusive

There can be cases where a certain image does not strictly fall into a single use case, but combines a little bit of both art direction and resolution switching, depending on the breakpoint we see it in. For example, consider Figure 11-7.

Wildlife news

Home   About   Contact   Stories▾

A fox was walking through the forest. You won't believe what happened next!!1

Lorem ipsum dolor sit amet, cu graeci quaestio mei, et nonumy aliquam sea. Ius ad decore civibus, discere pertinacia in ius. Eos iriure detraxit tacimates at, sale saperet epicurei ex pri. An sed habeo pericula adipiscing. Id nam convenire democritum.

Purto eruditi imperdiet no nam, esse facete id quo. An duo nonumes accusam, ei verterem accusamus adversarium eum. Fastidii legendos urbanitas sed ex, erat meis iuvaret usu an. In fugit atqui quo. Nec inimicus laboramus ne, libris minimum ea mel.

Has inani cetero electram te. Movet adipiscing in mea, labores lucilius euripidis id pro. Te nec case choro ocurreret. Pro simul civibus deleniti ad, in qui justo tempor, quo bonorum patrioque conclusionemque te.

Liber dissentiunt duo at. Cu eam saepe iisque, ei eum vocibus imperdiet democritum, ut mel diam eripuit. Tempor voluptua no vim, nostrud verterem periculis ei cum. Probo putant interpretaris an has, ut his modus mazim aliquando.

Ad per wisi ullum delicata, vix te omnes expetendis. Sed ne odio modus, conceptam percipitur eam ne. Vix an prompta consequat, sea euismod scriptorem eu. An cum nostro hendrerit, eos an stet adipisci electram, eam vide constituam ei. An diceret fierent vim, pri eu alii intellegat referrentur. Sed mediocrem ocurreret maiestatis ut, vis

Wildlife news ☰

A fox was walking through the forest. You won't believe what happened next!!1

Lorem ipsum dolor sit amet, cu graeci quaestio mei, et nonumy aliquam .sea. Ius ad decore civibus, discere pertinacia in ius. Eos iriure detraxit

Wildlife news ☰

A fox was walking through the forest. You won't believe what happened next!!1

Lorem ipsum dolor sit amet, cu graeci quaestio mei, et nonumy aliquam sea. Ius ad decore civibus, discere pertinacia in ius. Eos iriure detraxit tacimates at, sale saperet epicurei ex pri. An sed habeo pericula adipiscing. Id nam convenire democritum.

Figure 11-7. An image that fits into the variable width use case up to a certain breakpoint, then gets cropped

We could also mix the image formats use case here to further optimize the delivery when content negotiation is not an option.

So when we're looking into making a certain image responsive, the question we should ask ourselves is not "what *is* the use case this image fits into?" but "what *are* the use cases?"

Standard Responsive Images

We've detailed the various use cases that need addressing, but how do we address them in practice? That is exactly what we'll explore next.

We have seen that the use cases are split into two major cases: art direction and resolution switching. Because of the fundamental difference between these two cases, we also need two different syntax machanisms in order to tackle them.

Since these are new additions to HTML that have made some noise recently, you may have heard about them: the picture element and the srcset attribute. In general the picture element is designed to handle the art direction use case, and srcset is designed to handle resolution switching.

With that background in place, we're ready to dive into the details of each syntax part.

srcset x Descriptor

So, you have an image of a cat that you want to display on your site, where said image would have the same dimensions regardless of responsive breakpoints. So, you start out writing something like:

```
<img src="cat.jpg" alt="A funky cat">
```

But, when viewing that work from a retina screen, you notice a blur. Each image pixel is displayed over 4 physical pixels, and it just doesn't look sharp. You want to provide the browser with a 2x image, twice the width and twice the height, which would get rid of the blurriness, but without sending that over to browsers that don't need it. The following syntax will do just that:

```
<img src="cat.jpg" srcset="cat_2x.jpg 2x" alt="A funky cat">
```

That is not extremely different than what we've seen earlier. All we added is the srcset attribute, providing the browser an alternative resource to fetch for the same image. That attribute enables the browser to create a list of available resources, so it can pick which one to download and display.

As you probably noticed, that syntax enables us to tackle the fixed-dimensions use case we discussed earlier.

But what if we wanted to provide multiple alternative resources? Well, `srcset` is actually a comma-delimited list, so you can provide as many resources as you want!

```
<img src="cat.jpg" srcset="cat_2x.jpg 2x, cat_2.8x.jpg 2.8x" alt="A funky cat">
```

Simple, right? The value of `srcset` in the preceding example is a list of the resources for the browser to choose from. Each resource has a descriptor attached to it, which tells the browser something about this resource to make its job of picking the right one easier. In this case, the descriptor in question is the *x descriptor*, which describes the resource's density. That gives the browser the knowledge to pick the resource that best fits the user's screen.

Image density is the ratio between the image pixels that you provide the browser and the area (in CSS pixels) that the image is displayed on. Let's say you have a 400×400 CSS pixels space in which to fit an image and you provide the browser a 600×600 pixel image to fit that space. That image would be displayed with a density of 1.5, and would look perfectly sharp on screens with up to similar density, but not necessarily on screens with higher density.

Now, different browsers may do different things when picking the best resource, and they are entitled to do that. The specification is purposely vague about the selection process inside `srcset`, in order to enable browsers to innovate in that space. Therefore, browsers can take not only the screen density into account, but also the user's cache state, network conditions, user preference, and more.

Already today there are differences between browsers regarding which image they fetch when the screen is not an exact match to any of the resources, or differences when some of the resources in the list are already in the browser's cache. These differences are likely to increase over time as browsers get smarter about resource downloads, so you should not rely on the browser picking one specific resource over another.

srcset w Descriptor

Now the fixed-dimensions case is great when this is what you need, but in responsive designs the variable-dimensions case is often more common. Your image changes its size as the viewport changes, either due to the fluid layout that contains it or due to a breakpoint change that impacted it.

The syntax to achieve that would be:

```
<img src="cat.jpg" srcset="cat_200w.jpg 200w, cat_400w.jpg 400w" sizes="100vw"
     alt="A funky cat">
```

That's very similar to what we've seen before, but with different descriptors. The *w descriptor* is there to describe the width of the image, in pixels.

And what's that `sizes` attribute that I sneaked in there, you ask? Nice catch—I hoped I could get that by you. It's there to tell the browser what the image's display width would be. The browser needs that in order to figure out which resource it should download, and it really doesn't know that at the time it starts downloading images.

In order to know the dimensions in which images will be displayed, the browser needs to perform layout, and in order to do *that* it needs to download *all* the CSS in your page, process it, and calculate which rules apply. Only then can it calculate the layout of all the elements in the page, and it's pretty late in the game. To make things worse, the downloaded image resources can also impact the layout, as the image's intrinsic dimensions are used to lay it out in case neither HTML nor CSS knows better. So, waiting for layout information to decide which image to download is just not an option.

This is the reason we need the `sizes` attribute to tell the browser what the image dimensions would be. In the preceding case we told the browser that the images will be displayed at `100vw` or 100% of the viewport width (see Figure 11-8).

Figure 11-8. An image that takes the full width of the viewport

`100vw` is also the image width that the browser would assume when calculating density if we didn't include a `sizes` attribute at all (even though we probably should include it, as our markup would be invalid if we didn't).

But often in responsive layouts, images take a smaller chunk of the viewport, and assuming they are 100% of the viewport width would mean downloading images that are just too large. For these cases, we can define a different CSS length as the value of `sizes`—for example, `70vw` (see Figure 11-9).

Figure 11-9. An image that takes only part of the viewport

See? That wasn't so hard, was it?

Variable width images often require viewport-dependent CSS lengths (e.g., the vw units), but if we want to, we could satisfy the fixed-dimensions case by using w descriptors and setting `sizes` to a non-viewport-dependent length—500px.

In other types of layout it can get more complicated than that. How can we tackle images that "shrink" inside the page's responsive breakpoints, but change dimensions entirely between breakpoints, as in Figure 11-10?

Figure 11-10. A two-column layout that turns into a single-column layout; such cases result in a nonlinear relationship between viewport dimensions and image dimensions

We can handle that case by extending the `sizes` value beyond the simple CSS length, including the various breakpoints. The syntax to implement that would be:

```
<img src="cat.jpg" srcset="cat_200w.jpg 200w, cat_400w.jpg 400w"
sizes="(max-width: 460px) 50vw, (max-width: 1200px) 25vw, 300px"
alt="A funky cat">
```

How does that work? The browser takes the entire value of the sizes attribute, and breaks it up into pairs of a media condition and a CSS length. A media condition is very similar to a media query, only it doesn't specify a media type and is optional. The browser goes over the media condition and length pairs, and checks if the media condition matches or is missing. If so, the CSS length is picked to be the element's *source size*. The browser uses the source size in order to translate all the w descriptors into internal density values, and then applies the same algorithm that it applies on x descriptors, so again, it takes into account the screen density and other factors when picking the appropriate resources from srcset.

It's important to emphasize that sizes is an optimization and even if you define a rough sizes value (e.g., 100vw), it is still in many cases better than simply sending the same image to tiny devices and retina 28-inch displays. But sizes enables you to get as close as you'd like to the actual display dimensions, and enables the browser to pick the right image resource accordingly.

<picture>

The previous srcset descriptors all assume that all the image resources represent the "same" image and are interchangeable, only in differing qualities and dimensions. While that's enough to cover the fixed-dimensions and variable-dimensions use cases, when it comes to art direction, we need more control than that. We need to be able to tell the browser "download this image resource in this particular breakpoint" and be fairly confident that it will. Otherwise, layout may break and our site may become unusable.

So, how do we define the image resources for Figure 11-11?

Figure 11-11. An art direction example

How does that work? The important bit to understand is that even though `<picture>` gets a lot of attention, `<img>` is still the element that drives image loading and display. Among other things, this means that if `<img>` were missing from the preceding example, nothing would be displayed. So, `<img>` gets created by the parser, and then the element checks to see if it has a `<picture>` parent before it starts loading an image. If a `<picture>` parent is present, the `<img>` element walks that parent's `<source>` children until it reaches itself, and picks the first one that matches as the source of image resources. In our case, "matches" means that the media query inside the `media` attribute matches. If no `<source>` element matches, `<img>` will be its own resource source.

Once a source is picked, its `srcset` attribute will be used to pick the right resource, in a similar process to what we've seen earlier.

And while we need strict control in order to get art direction right between our responsive breakpoints, we may also need to be able to mix that with the other use cases *inside* the breakpoints.

That can be achieved with syntax like the following (see Figure 11-12):

```
<picture>
    <source media="(max-width: 600px)"
    srcset="narrow_viewport_200.jpg 200w,
    narrow_viewport_400.jpg 400w">
    <img srcset="wide_viewport_200.jpg 200w,
    wide_viewport_400.jpg 400w" alt="probably a cat">
</picture>
```

Figure 11-12. An image that fits into the variable width use case up to a certain breakpoint, then gets cropped

Another use case we talked about earlier is the "download and hide" case. We can resolve that using <picture> by adding a "spacer GIF" data URI as the source for the images that are not supposed to be there. The reason this is neccessary is that the selection algorithm skips a <source> without any srcset attribute. So we need our <source> to have a valid srcset, only with a meaningless small image.

So, if we want our image to "disappear" at viewports smaller than 600 pixels, we could do:

```
<picture>
    <source media="(max-width: 600px)"
    srcset="data:image/gif;base64,R0lGODlhAQABAIAAAAAAAP///yH5BAEAAA
    AALAAAAAABAAEAAAIBRAA7">
    <img srcset="image_only_needed_for_wide_viewports.jpg">
</picture>
```

Serving Different Image Formats

The main reason the RICG came up with <picture> was to tackle the art direction use case, but that's not the only thing it is good for. Serving different image formats to browsers that support them while having a common-ground image format as a fallback is another use case it tackles.

If we look at font, video, or audio files, the web platform supports many different formats and enables client-side fallback for them right from the moment that these media types are added to the Web. Contrary to that, images always lacked such a client-side fallback mechanism. As <img> stabilized support on the three major file formats before the first browser wars were over, there were no compatibility issues related to image format support, so no one worked on a mechanism to enable them. When new file formats such as WebP or JPEG XR were introduced, the answer to people trying to use them was content negotiation, and modifying the server's logic so that it would return the newly supported types only to browsers that supported them.

 There was one major compatibility issue related to image formats between the big browsers at the end of the first browser wars. It was the matter of PNG alpha channel support, which was lacking in IE6. Since the MIME type for transparent PNGs was no different than nontransparent ones, content negotiation did not help there, and various specific hacks were created to tackle the issue instead, until IE6's market share became low enough for this to be a nonissue.

That is, until responsive images became a thing. While the RICG was working on new markup solutions to load responsive images, it became clear that the same constructs (with slight additions) could be used to create a client-side fallback, and help introduce new image formats to browsers that supported them, even if you had no control over the server's logic.

How can we do that, you ask? By using the `type` attribute!

```
<picture>
    <source type="image/webp" srcset="rad_wolf.webp">
    <source type="image/jxr" srcset="rad_wolf.jxr">
    <img src="rad_wolf.jpg" alt="A rad wolf">
</picture>
```

Here again, the browser will go over the list of `<source>` elements and pick the first that matches, only this time, "matches" means that the `type` attribute contains a MIME type the browser supports.

Practical Advice

Up until now we have talked about the basic syntax, but there are a few further considerations that you probably want to take into account when addressing responsive images in your real-life project.

To Picturefill or Not to Picturefill, That Is the Question

The first question that often comes up when discussing these features is: "do we need to polyfill it for legacy browsers?" The answer, like many things in computer science, is: "it depends."

The features were built with an inherent fallback in mind. As `<img>` must always be present in the markup, it is sufficient to add a `src` attribute to it with a fallback image, and nonsupporting browsers will have something to display. In many cases, that's good enough.

Until recently browser support for the entire set of responsive images features was not complete, and therefore if you needed art direction, for example, you had to use a polyfill, whereas if you needed fixed-width resources, you could have gone with a reasonable fallback instead.

But since then, support was added to all major browsers, and nowadays the only reason to use a polyfill is if you need to support older browsers, such as IE, and such support cannot be accomplished with a simple fallback image, since the image is art-directed.

If you do need to use a polyfill, the official and standard-compliant polyfill would be Picturefill (*http://scottjehl.github.io/picturefill/*).

Intrinsic Dimensions

Every image has intrinsic dimensions that are defined by the image file itself and composed of the image's width and height in "physical" pixels. The browser then takes these intrinsic dimensions into account when it decides how to lay out the image. If there are no HTML- or CSS-based instructions that tell the browser what the image's display dimensions should be, it is the intrinsic dimensions that dictate that.

However, when we're talking about responsive images, we don't want them to be displayed according to their "physical" intrinsic dimensions, but according to dimensions adjusted to the image's density. That helps us get properly dimensioned and sharp images, rather than oversized blurry ones—for example, when sending 2x images to the browser.

How does the browser accomplish that? When picking image resources as part of srcset's selection algorithm, the browser calculates the image density. If the image has an x descriptor, that's easy. The descriptor's value is the value of the image's density. If the image has a w descriptor, we also need to know which dimensions the image will be displayed in. As we've seen earlier, that's where the sizes attribute comes into play. The browser takes the sizes attribute, figures out the CSS length that applies to the current breakpoint, and uses that and the resource's w descriptor in order to conclude the image's density. The image density is then used by the browser to compensate and correct the "physical" dimensions when it calculates intrinsic dimensions.

OK, but why do I think that this long and complicated story is of interest here? Isn't that the problem of the people working on the browser implementation?

Well, it has real-life implications because if you give the browser the wrong details, the outcome may surprise you. I've seen many examples where people put in approximate w descriptor values or incorrect sizes attribute values *while relying on the image's intrinsic dimensions*, and end up surprised that the image is displayed in the wrong dimensions.

The point is, if you feed the browser the wrong data about the images you give it, you're likely to have a bad time debugging why your images are too big or too small. So don't.

Selection Algorithms

We already talked about the ways that the browser selects the right <source>, the right sizes length, and the image resource in srcset, but it's worth repeating in order to avoid confusion.

`<source>` elements are picked using a "first-match" algorithm. The first `<source>` element that matches both `media` and `type` (where a missing attribute is considered as matched) is the one that gets picked.

For `sizes`, it is very similar. The browser goes over the list of media conditions and CSS length pairs, and picks the first length with a matching media condition, or one with no media condition at all. This is why we often leave the last length value in `sizes` as a standalone value, to be used as a fallback.

`srcset`, on the other hand, doesn't use a "first-match" algorithm, so the order doesn't matter unless you have resources with the same density. That means that as long as your descriptors are correct, you don't need to worry about the order of the resources inside `srcset`.

srcset Resource Selection May Change

`srcset` was designed so that its selection algorithm can evolve over time to make smarter decisions about the tradeoff between image quality and download speeds. We want `srcset` to be able to respond to many things beyond simple screen density: browser cache, bandwidth conditions, user preferences, network costs, and other user conditions. Therefore, and since `srcset` only covers cases that are not related to art direction, the browser has a great deal of liberty when it comes to picking resources.

That's the reason you shouldn't rely on what you think the browser should load in different conditions when using `srcset`. That can and will differ between browsers and between browser versions. As browsers improve and get smarter, your assumptions regarding their behavior will not remain accurate for long. So make no assumptions and let the browser do its thing.

Feature Detection

Since the responsive images features were recently introduced to the web platform, there is a chance that you'll need to be able to tell if your user's current browser supports these features or not. The classic use case for this is when creating a polyfill (which you don't really need to do, as Picturefill is well maintained and fully supports the syntax), but there could be other occasions where you find yourself trying to figure out browser support for the responsive images features.

For these cases, you can use the presence of `HTMLPictureElement` in `window` to detect support for `<picture>` and use the presence of `sizes` and `srcset` in an `HTMLImageEle ment` node to figure out if they are supported.

More concretely, here's how Picturefill detects that support:

```
var image = document.createElement( "img" );
var srcsetSupport = "srcset" in image;
var sizes support = "sizes" in image;
var pictureSupport = !!window.HTMLPictureElement;
```

currentSrc

One more tool you can use when working with responsive images is the `currentSrc`
property on `HTMLImageElement`, which enables you to see which resource is currently
loaded and displayed on a specific `<img>` element.

You can use this if, say, your JS interaction with an art-directed image should differ in
case a different resource is picked.

Client Hints

Up until now, we have discussed the various markup solutions for delivering responsive images. But that's not the only type of solution we have up our metaphorical
sleeves. For some cases, it might be significantly easier to modify a server configuration than to modify HTML. For these cases, *content negotiation* could be a better
option than markup.

Content negotiation is an HTTP-based mechanism in which the client (in our case,
the browser) sends HTTP headers indicating its support or preference regarding the
content, and the server responds with the desired content. There are multiple examples for that method in the HTTP protocol, the most prevalent of which is the
`Accept-Encoding` request header, to which the server couples a `Content-Encoding`
response header, indicating if Gzip or any other encoding method was applied to the
returned response.

To offer a content negotiation–based responsive images solution, a new set of HTTP
request and response headers was created, under the banner of "Client Hints." We will
discuss those further in Chapter 12.

Are Responsive Images "Done"?

We have definitely made a lot of progress in recent years to tackle the use cases of
responsive images, but everything related to software is rarely "done." In this section
we will discuss some potential future improvements.

Background Images

In the early days of responsive images, the subject of background images wasn't considered important, and the focus was on content images. After all, background images
could be controlled through media queries, and on top of that, WebKit-based brows-

ers (so, Safari and Chrome) supported the `-webkit-image-set` CSS property, which enables the browser to load based on device pixel ratio (DPR). That was considered a handy shortcut to spelling out separate rules based on the `resolution` or `-webkit-device-pixel-ratio` media queries.

So we continued to resolve content images, leaving background images as they were. Only now, with the hindsight of the solutions for content images, do we see the deficiencies that still need to be resolved in background images.

So, let's take a look at how each one of the use cases can be resolved for background images.

The fixed-width images can be resolved with a fairly simple markup (which resembles, and in fact inspired, the markup for `srcset`'s x descriptor):

```
.fixed-dimensions-image {
    background-image: -webkit-image-set(url(1x.jpg) 1x, url(2x.jpg) 2x);
}
```

The standard form of that is the unprefixed `image-set`. Unfortunately, that is not implemented anywhere at the time of this writing.

The art direction use case is easy to solve with media queries:

```
.art-directed-image {
    background-image: url(narrow.jpg);
}
@media screen and (min-width: 800px) {
    .art-directed-image {
        background-image: url(wide.jpg);
    }
}
```

But there's no way today to define a background image that loads an efficient, variable-width image. One could imagine an extension to `image-set` that includes something like the w descriptor `srcset` has, but that's not yet specified or implemented.

Height Descriptors

You may have noticed that when discussing the use cases, we've used the term *variable dimensions*, yet the only resource descriptor we have for this case is the w descriptor, describing the resource's width. Images are *two*-dimensional! That's not fair!

While we were working on the responsive images solutions, we noticed the same injustice, yet the major use case to tackle was solving width-constrained layouts. We had significantly fewer examples for height-constrained layouts, so we preferred to wait with that use case until there's more experience with it "in the wild."

Nevertheless, the processing algorithms take the future existance of an h descriptor into account, and ensure that the introduction of such a descriptor will go over smoothly.

After having the basic set of features out there, with developers using them in production, we now see some demand for height-constrained layouts, mainly for image galleries. So, hopefully work on that front can continue and h descriptors will eventually be part of the srcset.

Responsive Image File Formats

When we talk about responsive images, the question "why not solve it using a file format?" often comes up.

While solving the responsive images problem using a file format is certainly feasible (at least for some of the use cases), there are some caveats. The browser would have to download a first chunk of the image in order to know its dimensions and the fitting byte range for the image dimensions and breakpoints it needs. That would require coming up with a loading scheme where a few initial bytes are downloaded from all images in order for the browser to know what ranges need downloading. In HTTP/1, that will most likely result in performance regressions, as there's a limit to the number of resources that can be fetched in parallel. In HTTP/2 that is less of an issue, but would still be less then ideal for the first images, especially if they don't end up being of a responsive format.

With that being said, there have been attempts to create formats that may fit the "responsive image format" label. Although none of them is of practical value today, the curious among you may find these attempts interesting.

Progressive JPEG

As we've seen earlier in the book, progressive JPEG is, well, progressive. The browser can decode it as it is being downloaded, and the result is a full image, with its details filling in as more chunks of image data are downloaded.

Therefore, we could emulate a lower-resolution image (or a smaller image) by truncating a high-resolution, large image and scaling it appropriately. Assuming we have multiple JPEG scans, we could use something like SSIM to determine the appropriate size and resolution for each one of the scans, and then communicate that information to the browser (e.g., using special JPEG markers at the start of the file), and have it download only the scans that it needs.

Such a concept (*https://blog.yoav.ws/responsive_image_format/*) has been experimented with in the past. It seems like something that might work for the fixed- and variable-dimensions cases, but not for the art direction use case.

Additionally, from experimentation, if the images that you're trying to serve need to fit both a very small space (e.g., on low-end devices) and a very large one (e.g., retina 28-inch screens), quality will suffer or bytes will be wasted. There's a limit to the range of quality that can be communicated using progressive JPEG scans.

JPEG 2000

JPEG 2000 (which we discussed in Chapter 5) is a progressive format by nature, and therefore, at least in theory, could be an ideal candidate for progressive loading.

Unfortunately, previous experiments (*http://bit.ly/2aDhlsL*) that were conducted on that front proved it to be less promising in practice.

Responsive Image Container

There have also been attempts (by yours truly) to create a responsive image container (*https://www.smashingmagazine.com/2013/09/responsive-image-container*)—an image-format-agnostic container that would encode the image using different layers, where the first layer is a thumbnail of the image, and each consecutive layer adds more information to the image, enabling it to target higher-resolution screens, larger display dimensions, and even crop-based art direction. The intent behind creating a container rather than a full-fledged new format was to avoid patent and political issues often surrounding file formats, likely increasing its chances for adoption.

FLIF

More recently, a lossless progressive file format named FLIF (*http://flif.info/*) was introduced. The name stands for Free Lossless Image Format, and it shows very good results when compared to other lossless formats.

One of its most touted advantages is its progressive nature, which could make it a candidate for a responsive format. However, it's still very early days for the format, so it's hard to be certain of the direction in which it will evolve. Its lack of a true lossy mode makes it less applicable to real-life imagery than other formats.

Summary

In this chapter, we have reviewed the various responsive images use cases and markup solutions. It is important to remember that while these solutions were contentious for a long while, they are now supported by all modern browsers, which means you can safely use them in your markup.

Client Hints

Colin Bendell

Responsive images solve the problem of art direction, variable widths (including DPR changes), and alternate formats. While they provide a lot of flexibility, following all the best practices can result in very large amount of boilerplate HTML. (See "2014 Responsive Images HTML Spec" on page 317 to see how this plays out in practice.) This approach is prone to error and exposes details on how you generate your images that can be exploited by bots.

Additionally, responsive images don't help to address websites where we can't control the HTML (such as many CMS platforms) or help with native applications that request images over HTTP but don't use HTML for the UI.

Client Hints takes responsive images to the next level using content negotiation. This helps separate the delivery from the presentation. Client Hints is a standard that utilizes HTTP to negotiate between the browser and the server—just as we do for Gzip compression. With Gzip compression, the client tells the server that it is smart enough to decompress content (`Accept-Encoding: gzip`) and the server responds, with compressed content (`Content-Encoding: Gzip`). For example, the server could decide to compress CSS, but not Gzip WOFF (because WOFF is already Gzipped internally). It's a nod and a wink between the browser and server to get bits across the network faster. The web developer and end user don't have to worry about these details; they just know it results in a better user experience.

For images it is more complex: what could we be negotiating? Academically we know we want to send a smaller image dimension to a smaller display. The problem is, the browser doesn't really know how large an image needs to be until way too late in the render process. With modern preloaders and speculative parsers, the network queue is quickly populated with resource requests long before any layout or styling has been computed. Bottom line: the browser itself doesn't know what image sizes should be sent.

This is partially true. The browser does know a few things this early in the rendering. For example, it knows what kinds of image formats it can support, information about the display (orientation, viewport dimensions, DPR), and the current network environment. Imagine moving into a new apartment: you might not immediately know how you will arrange the furniture, but you do know that your pet elephant just won't fit in your 500-square-foot New York apartment.

This is where device characteristics engines can help the backend application server select the best image for the requester. Of course, the device characteristic databases need to be up-to-date. Still, a device database only provides the generic capabilities of a device, such as viewport size. Going beyond the basic capabilities is critical to more effectively delivering images.

Bots and Scrapers Can Impact Your Performance and Steal Your Content

If you are using `?resize=400` to dynamically resize your image, what is to stop a malicious site from changing the parameters to `?resize=9999` in order to get the original-sized image? This could have implications on your cache effectiveness and put more stress on your image resize engine. While we can't always stop bots from scraping images from our websites, we shouldn't allow bots to scrape the highest resolution of images.

Overview

The object of Client Hints is to enable the client to communicate the current environment such that the server could tailor the response. At the time of writing, there are five key *hints* that the client can provide:

- DPR
- Viewport-Width
- Width
- Downlink
- Save-Data

Additionally, there are two headers that the server uses to inform the client about what it can do and has done with Client Hints. These headers are:

- `Accept-CH`
- `Content-DPR`

iOS/Android Apps Need Client Hints Too

Client Hints are important not only for browsers and web pages but also for native apps. More on this shortly.

By default, Client Hints are not transmitted. This is for privacy and other security concerns. Therefore, the server needs to inform the client that it is capable of utilizing the Client Hints. This will result in every subsequent request initiated by the web page also including these hints on the request.

Step 1: Initiate the Client Hints Exchange

To start the exchange, the client would send the `Accept-CH` header followed by the Client Hints that should be sent. Not all the hints need to be listed here. For the sake of comprehensiveness, the following example includes all of the values. There is a general assumption that the `Accept-CH` is sent on the apex HTML request. This doesn't necessarily need to be the case; it could be sent on another request. Generally that doesn't make sense, since you could run into race conditions where the hints are not enabled for some images. That said, it may make sense for offline, service-worker-based apps, or single-page apps with different application contexts.

```
GET /index.html

...

HTTP/1.1 200 OK
Accept-CH: DPR, Viewport-Width, Width, Downlink, Save-Data
```

Step 2: Opt-in and Subsequent Requests

If the browser is aware of Client Hints, from this point on every request related to the web page could include the relevant headers—assuming the client opts-in to the exchange. This includes resources requested on third-party domains. If the page initiates a request to a third-party resource, that resource can leverage this header. This can be extremely useful for advertising content, but the onus is on the first domain to enable the exchange.

```
GET /ilovebroccoli.jpg
DRP: 2
Viewport-Width: 320
Width: 600
```

```
Save-Data: on
Downlink: 0.384
```

The Client Hints response headers are not limited to images. These headers will be sent on every request related to the site.

Step 3: Informed Response

The final step is to inform the browser what happened, if anything. This includes returning the actual DPR of the image (in contrast to the DPR requested). In many ways this is very similar to the use of Content-Type header, which indicates the image format.

As well, it should include Vary and Cache-Control directives to tell the client and any middle-box proxies (like those found in coffee shops, hotels, and airports) and surrogate proxies how to cache and avoid cache collisions. While these instructions, strictly speaking, aren't required, they do make for good practice. The last thing you would want is to reach into your sock drawer in the morning only to discover that you have your toddler's socks.

```
200 OK
Content-Type: image/jpeg
ETag: "a824f;dpr0.5;width=150;q=0.5"
Content-DPR: 0.5
Vary: DPR
Cache-Control: private, no-transform
```

We will discuss the use of Vary and Cache-Control headers in the next chapter.

Client Hint Components

Client Hints has a small but important lexicon. There are two groups of HTTP headers used: those sent from the browser or client, and those sent from the server. Viewport-Width, DPR, Width, Downlink, and Save-Data are all sent from the browser to the server. In contrast, Accept-CH and Content-DPR are sent from the server to the client.

Viewport-Width

The Viewport-Width header returns the *CSS pixel width* of the browser's current viewport (see Figure 12-1). If the browser is full-screen, this will be the width of the display. It might be tempting to assume then that you can treat Viewport-Width as synonymous with the width in a device characteristics database. It's important to emphasize that this is not the pixel width, but the CSS width. Further, images inside an iFrame will have a different Viewport-Width than the parent HTML. This makes it all the more important to include the appropriate Vary and Content-DPR headers.

For Client Hints–enabled clients (who have opted in), there should not be a case where `Viewport-Width` is unavailable; that is, if the server initiated the interaction with `Accept-CH: Viewport-Width`, it is safe to assume that the browser will return this on all requests.

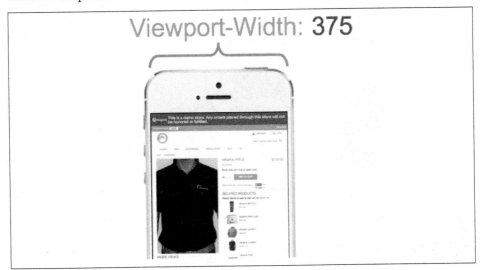

Figure 12-1. Client Hints: Viewport-Width

Device Pixel Ratio

As you probably guessed, the `DPR` Client Hint header (Figure 12-2) returns the client's device pixel ratio. Multiplying the `Viewport-Width` by the `DPR` will return the absolute pixel width of the display. Likewise, dividing the `Width` by `DPR` will provide you the CSS width of the image container.

Devices with DPR > 1 regularly upscale images. For this reason your server can choose to ignore the DPR when selecting based on `Viewport-Width`. This can give flexibility and a performance gain by adjusting the image delivery based on the type of image (logo versus product detail), the use case, and other environmental conditions like network performance.

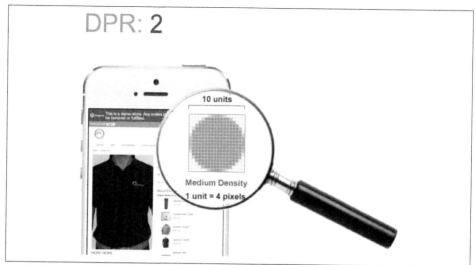

Figure 12-2. Client Hints: DPR

Width

In contrast to `Viewport-Width`, `Width` reports the container width where the image will be rendered (see Figure 12-3). And, unlike `Viewport-Width`, it is reported in absolute pixels instead of CSS. The challenge to the browser or any client is how to calculate the container width at the time of the image request.

Figure 12-3. Client Hints: Width

Remember from Chapter 7 that images in the browser are queued in the network request buffers ahead of rendering on the page. This means that the image context is largely unknown at the time the request is made to the server. Great, so why not lazy-load the images after the CSS is computed? This too is dicey because if the CSS is using relative positioning, the presence of one image might change the viewable dimensions of another image. It's really hard for the browser to figure this out a priori.

Don't lament! Responsive images are here to help. You can help the browser by giving the browser a hint of the visible context. A hint for a hint, if you will. In order for the Width header to be present you must include the sizes attribute in your <img> tag. This will give the preloader enough context to understand and compute the Width Client Hint:

```
<img src="/images/i-love-broccoli.jpg" sizes="(min-width: 500px) 33.3vw, 100vw">
```

That's it! By providing the sizes hint you give the browser enough context to provide a Width Client Hint. The good news is that you don't have to be absolutely precise and match all the specific media queries in your CSS. Of course this would be ideal, but you can get away with a few generalizations: about one-third of the viewable width. The browser's rendering engine will take care of the rest and actually lay out the image properly—despite the sizes hint.

What if your CSS changes dramatically and you didn't update the sizes? Not to worry. The Client Hint does not influence the layout. While the negotiations might be off, the stylesheet instructions still have control. The only possible downside could be a smaller image in a larger context causing upscaling.

Downlink

The client may also include information regarding the network conditions in the form of the Downlink. Unfortunately, network conditions are difficult to calculate, and there is debate on how best to communicate this environmental situation. Should it be effective bandwidth over the last five minutes or one minute? The ms latency on the connection?

For this reason, the current version of the Client Hints specification utilizes the Network Information (*http://wicg.github.io/netinfo/*) maximum downlink speed. This provides the easiest path for implementing a service worker by calling the NetInfo API and using the existing data. Alternatively, the client application could interrogate the device (if available) and return the theoretical downlink speed.

For reference, Table 12-1 shows a common set of values.

Table 12-1. Common set of Downlink values

Network type	Downlink Mbps
GPRS	0.237
EDGE	0.384
UMTS	2
HSPA	3.6
HSDPA	14.3
LTE	100
Ethernet	10
Wifi (802.11g)	54
Unknown	+Infinity

As you can expect, the utility value of the downlink is mostly to infer the type of network conditions the user might be experiencing, so you can, for example, distinguish between an LTE and EDGE cellular connection and include this in your delivery decision tree.

Be careful: the value should not be expected to be an int or float. It could be a string in the form of +Infinity for unknown network conditions.

At the time of writing, this Client Hint has not been implemented but is still part of the specification.

Save-Data

Leveraging the Save-Data hint can further help the image selection algorithm. If a client returns Save-Data: on this is an indication that there is a preference to reduce data usage. There are many reasons this may be desirable, such as cost of cellular, available data caps, or even as a proxy for network conditions beyond Downlink.

The Chrome browser has long offered a data saver service for Android and iOS versions of Chrome. This sends image requests through a remote proxy to automatically transcode the image to other formats and attempt to reduce data. However, this is not always desirable by the content owners and further does not make any claims on performance.

Several browsers now have mechanisms to allow the user to opt in to data saving services. For Transport Layer Security (TLS) connections this will mean the addition of the Save-Data: on hint. Be careful not to make the assumption that the absence of this hint should give you permission to deliver a larger image! At the time of writing, the following browsers support Save-Data: on:

- Chrome 49+: For mobile, if the user enables the Data Saver; for desktop, using the Data Saver extension.
- Opera 35+: When Opera Turbo is enabled or Data savings on Android browsers.

Accept-CH

As previously mentioned, the `Accept-CH` header or meta tag is critical when negotiating to the browser to opt in to Client Hints. Of course, there is no requirement that the client honor this contract. Consider it purely informational. It informs the client that subsequent content *could* differ if it were provided Client Hints.

There are two ways it can be sent: via HTML or HTTP header:

```
<body>
    <head>
        <title>Client Hints Demo!</title>
        <meta http-equiv="Accept-CH" content="Viewport-Width, DPR, Width">
    </head>
    ...
</body>
```

or

```
HTTP/1.1 200 OK
Accept-CH: Viewport-Width, DPR, Width
```

The easiest way is to add the response header since you could accomplish this at multiple layers in your infrastructure without changing your markup. Best practices would suggest advertising the `Accept-CH` header for `text/html` content. However, there is no strict rule for this.

For example, you could do this with Apache:

```
SetEnvIf (mime text/.*) is_html
Header set Accept-CH "Viewport-Width, DPR, Width" env=is_html
```

Content-DPR

In addition to the `Vary`, `Cache-Control`, and `Key` headers used for caching, the server can also send the `Content-DPR` header. This helps the browser interpret how to render the image content. This is especially important when relative box models are used in CSS. Without the `Content-DPR` header the image may push out the content in the layout.

A wide image might push content to the left or right if the browser doesn't have more specific instructions about the DPR. Likewise, the height of the box might also have different results.

This is more of an issue if your server decides to reduce the DPR in the interests of the user experience—for example, if the server indicates that it is currently in hostile network conditions and wants to reduce bandwidth further. Instead of just blindly sending the resized dimensions, this allows the server to communicate this in terms of DPR, helping the browser to understand how to use this image in the display.

Sending the Content-DPR header with the modified value allows the browser to preserve the intended experience. In Example 12-1 the original image of the Romenesco broccoli, at 1,400 pixels, fills the <div> element. (In the example, the X-Width header is used to demonstrate the width of the image sent from the server. See Figure 12-4.) If the server decided to reduced the size to 300 pixels, as in Example 12-2, the browser would shrink the image and the experience would differ from what was intended. In order to preserve the experience, the server should communicate the Content-DPR header. In this example we could use Content-DPR: 0.21, which is 300/1400. If the browser sent the Width Client Hint, you could also calculate the Content-DPR relative to the image width. In Example 12-2, we are using Content-DPR: 0.5, or 300/600. Both result in the preserved user experience.

Example 12-1. Original image fills the width

```
GET /romenesco-broccoli.jpg
DPR: 1
Viewport-Width: 1280
Width: 600


...


HTTP/1.1 200 OK
Content-Length: 279999
X-Width: 1400
```

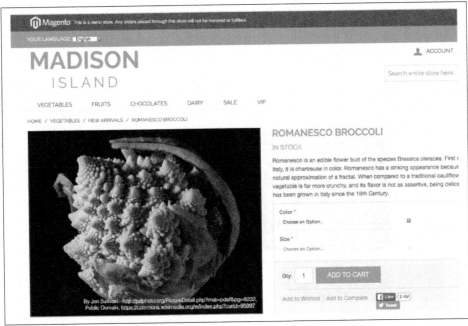

Figure 12-4. Result of Example 12-1

Example 12-2. Resized image smaller than CSS dimensions

```
GET /romenesco-broccoli.jpg
DPR: 1
Viewport-Width: 1280
Width: 600

...

HTTP/1.1 200 OK
Content-Length: 13000
X-Width: 300
```

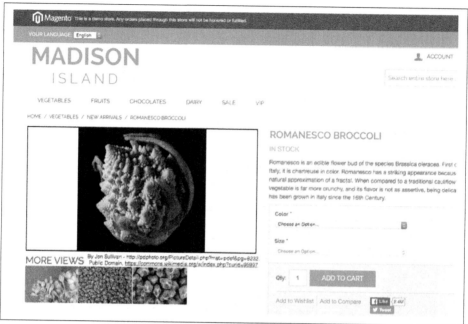

Figure 12-5. Result of Example 12-2

Example 12-3. Include Content-DPR to fit smaller image to CSS box

```
GET /romenesco-broccoli.jpg
DPR: 1
Viewport-Width: 1280
Width: 600

...

HTTP/1.1 200 OK
Content-Length: 13000
Content-DPR: 0.5
X-Width: 300
```

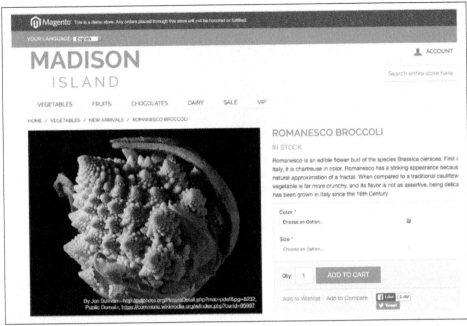

Figure 12-6. Result of Example 12-3

Mobile Apps

Not only can browsers take advantage of Client Hints, but native apps (mobile or desktop) can utilize them as well. In fact, any application that uses HTTP for transferring images could utilize Client Hints.

Many mobile apps use WebView components to render HTML inside the app. Other apps make API and image requests natively in the app and render the content. This eliminates the need for CSS and other layout controls since the app knows precisely how to interpret the content. (See an example in Figure 12-7.)

Figure 12-7. CNN app with images

But apps suffer the same problems with engagement and experiences as websites. Mobile apps have to deal with the plethora of display dimensions and resolutions. Just like websites, most mobile apps will use just one size of images for all Android or iOS users. Mobile apps need responsive images too. Fortunately, Client Hints can help them improve the user experience here as well.

Unlike a browser, a native app will likely not utilize an apex request—there isn't a starting HTML request to initiate the `Accept-CH` handshake. However, because you can control your native app behavior, you can implicitly opt in and support Client Hints on all image requests.

Adding Client Hints can enable a level of flexibility in your server infrastructure and move the selection logic from the client to the server. This way, you can launch an application with no concern for image resizing. Then later on, enable the server to respond to Client Hints. In this way you won't need to wait for customers to get the latest update of the app.

Adding Client Hints to an iOS or Android app is as simple as adding the hints to the outgoing HTTP request. Inspecting the UI control will reveal the width of the image being displayed.

```
///
/// Add Client Hints to the HTTP request for images to populate the UIImageView.
/// This will interrogate the screen and UIView to determine the hint values.
///
func clientHints(imageUrl: String, targetImage:UIImageView) {

    let nsURL = NSURL(string: imageUrl)
    let config = NSURLSessionConfiguration.defaultSessionConfiguration()
    let screen = UIScreen.mainScreen()
```

```
/// use the main screen for size and scale; UIView frame for
/// target dimensions
let viewportWidthPx = screen.bounds.size.width
let dpr = screen.scale
let width = targetImage.frame.size.width

/// convert to CSS Pixels
let viewportWidth = Int(Double(viewportWidthPx) / Double(dpr))

config.HTTPAdditionalHeaders = ["Viewport-Width" : viewportWidth]
config.HTTPAdditionalHeaders = ["DPR" : dpr]
config.HTTPAdditionalHeaders = ["Width" : width]
config.HTTPAdditionalHeaders = ["Save-Data" : "on"]

/// usual NSURLSession to UIImage work from here
/// Accept-CH likely won't make sense since your app
/// controls the UIView dimensions
let session = NSURLSession(configuration: config)

let task = session.dataTaskWithURL(nsURL) {
    (data, response, error) in
    if !error {
        /// make sure that the image is drawn on screen
        var image:UIImage = UIImage(data: data)
        dispatch_async(dispatch_get_main_queue(), {
            targetImage.image = image
        })
    }
}

task.resume()
}
```

The logic is very similar for Android. It could be taken even further to also include other information like network conditions.

Legacy Support and Device Characteristics

Client Hints is a good solution, but what about the other browsers that don't yet support this standard? Currently the adoption is limited to Blink-based browsers (Chrome and Opera). As with any technology, there is always a long tail of adoption that can take many years before it becomes ubiquitous. It is always important to consider the older browsers.

There are two ways to address the problem of browser support. First is to adopt a cookie or device characteristics approach. This has the least impact on your codebase but does depend on a few other moving pieces. The other is to use a default "best for performance" image profile. In this approach your server will utilize a default that targets your 75th percentile mobile user.

Fallback: "Precise Mode" with Device Characteristics + Cookies

In this approach you use device characteristics as a proxy equivalent for Viewport-Width. A device characteristics database uses the User-Agent to look up information about the browser and hardware the user is utilizing. Usually these datasets will include the device screen pixels as well as the DPR. Using just the device characteristics would provide you the equivalent information as the Viewport-Width.

Unfortunately, device detection is limited in many situations. For example, all variations of the iPhone use the same User-Agent. You can certainly infer based on versions of Safari which generation of the iPhone it is *not* (e.g., if the user is using Safari 9, it is certainly not an iPhone 4). This way, you know at least it is the 4" display of the iPhone 5, but it could also be the iPhone 6, 6+, and so on. The implication is that you will need to pick a lowest common denominator for all iPhone/Safari users. You will either assume iPhone 6s Plus dimensions for all users to make sure the best quality image is sent to all users. Or you will assume iPhone 5 dimensions to help optimize for the lower processing power of the iPhone 5.

To overcome this, you can use client-side JavaScript and interrogate the browser for a more accurate Viewport-Width and DPR. Make no mistake: this has all the makings of a race condition. The challenge is to execute this JavaScript early, before any image requests are made by the browser.

For example, using the TeraWurlf device characteristics database, we could set the initial Viewport-Width with a cookie:

```php
<?php

// only do this logic if the cookie isn't set
if (!isset($_COOKIE["CH"]))
{
    // load and use the wurfl device characteristics database
    require_once("TeraWurfl.php");
    $wurflObj = new TeraWurfl();
    $wurflObj->GetDeviceCapabilitiesFromAgent();

    // determine css, and px width then dpr
    // image_width returns css width of the display; resolution width is the
    // pixel width
    // Use width=100 and DPR=1 as a safety if the device capabilities
    // database draws a blank
    $width_css = max($wurflObj->capabilities['display']['max_image_width'], 150);
    $width_px = max($wurflObj->capabilities['display']['resolution_width'], 150);
    $dpr = max(int($display_width / $browser_width), 1);

    setcookie("CH", "Viewport-Width"+$browser_width + ",DPR=" $dpr);
    setcookie("CH-Verify", "1" $dpr);
}
?>
```

Then complement the backend logic with client logic to "refine" the fallback cookie values. This will provide increased resolution for devices that have multiple values for the same User-Agent such as the iPhone. It will also act as a safety if the device characteristics database draws a blank. (It happens to all of us.)

In JavaScript we would check for the cookie and update the value with the actual width and actual DPR:

```
<html>
<head>
    <script type="application/javascript">
        // place JavaScript at top of the page to prevent race condition
        // reset the CH (ClientHint) cookie values with actual display
        // width and pr
        if (document.cookie.match(/(^|;)\s*CH-Verify=/))
        {
            var width = (screen.availWidth || screen.width);
            var dpr = (window.devicePixelRatio || 1);

            document.cookie = 'CH=Viewport-Width=' + width
                + ',DPR=' + dpr
                + ';expires=Fri, 31 Dec 9999 23:59:59 GMT;path=/';
            document.cookie ='CH-Set=; expires=Thu, 01 Jan 1970 00:00:01 GMT;';
        }
    </script>
    ...
```

To be clear, this approach is a best effort, but it will do the job of informing your backend application server how to address non-Client Hint-supporting browsers.

Fallback: Good-Enough Approach

The other approach is to instead find a *good enough* image resolution set (Figure 12-8). This would be a best-effort resolution that tips the balance of performance and display toward the performance side. Client Hints and RWD try to get the best user experience for the display. Using a good-enough approach, you would select images of the minimum quality.

Finding "good enough" is a difficult strategy to negotiate with your business. The best approach is to divide your problem into two: mobile default and desktop default. This assumes that your desktop users are likely on WiFi or DSL links. In contrast, your mobile default assumes a slower processor with a cellular network.

With these two profiles (mobile and desktop), look at your RUM dataset and look up the 75th or even 90th percentile user. What screen resolution, network, and GPU/CPU does the user at the 90th percentile performance have? Use this for your image budget to help you determine what the best fallback image should be.

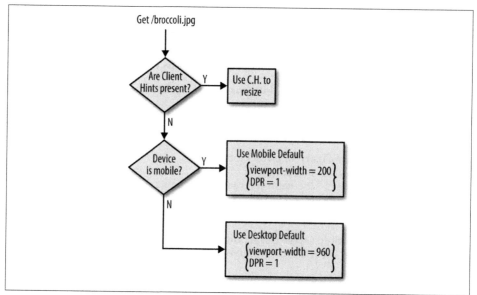

Figure 12-8. Example fallback workflow

You can further refine this decision tree by capturing large demographics that have higher-resolution devices but don't support Client Hints. Just as with option 1, we would use a device characteristics database to refine the selection. The key difference is that we don't expect JavaScript to run at the client, nor do we set cookies. Our objective is to be "good enough" without overengineering the solution.

Selecting the Right Image Width

Now that we have Client Hints negotiated between the user and the server, what should we do with it? Should we just provide resizes of an image for every possible `Width` or `Viewport-Width` available? Moreover, how do we select the right image: should we maximize the creative experience or performance?

Providing an image for nearly every resolution is not a viable solution because it would fragment your caches and put an undue burden on your image processing engine. With responsive images, whether you are using the `<img srcset>` attribute or using Client Hints, you want to find the balance of use cases.

Based on our discussion of mobile image processing, we should bucket image widths more frequently the larger the image. That is, the larger the image, the more memory is used and each pixel will have a linear growth in memory pressure and file size. Based on this information, the following bucket widths are a good starting point for selection:

- 150x
- 300x
- 600x
- 800x
- 1,000x
- 1,200x
- 2,000x
- 4,000x

Once you have defined your bucket widths, it is a straightforward process of image selection. The general algorithm is to select the nearest image breakpoint based on the smaller of Width or Viewport-Width. Then layer into the selection the "best effort" image as default:

```
image width = Width || Viewport-Width * DPR
  || Cookie.Viewport-Width * Cookie.DPR || DefaultWidth
```

This example, of course, assumes a design first approach. If the display can handle the image, send it. If the display is 3 DPR capable, send a 3x image. Unfortunately, as mobile and laptop displays increase in pixels, we will increasingly prefer the higher-resolution images; the problem of image performance will once again be upon us.

Two approaches to address this are to (1) evaluate the Save-Data Client Hint, and/or (2) use the Downlink Client Hint. Using the Save-Data Client Hint could be as simple as ignoring the DPR value and using the CSS pixel width for responsive images. This will effectively send a lower-resolution image and depend on the client to upscale the image:

```
if (Save-Data = 'on') then DPR = 1
```

Customizing the selection based on network conditions is also a useful technique. Unfortunately, as mentioned before, the Downlink header is not currently implemented, and if you were to use a service worker to populate this header on image requests, it would only report the theoretical maximum. As we are all intimately aware, just because the little icon indicates we are on LTE doesn't mean we have anything close to the theoretical maximum on LTE:

```
if (Downlink < 2) then DPR = 1
```

The other two options we have to complement pixel selection are to leverage the different image formats and use dynamic compression based on network performance to squeeze more bytes.

Don't forget to report the `Content-DPR: 1` header in the response to inform the client that you have selected a different DPR than what was requested. Also, be sure to include the necessary caching headers.

Summary

Client Hints are a great way to support the adaptive delivery of your images. This can especially help in cases where you can't easily change the source for your HTML or for applications that don't use HTML but would benefit from responsive images.

Image Delivery

Colin Bendell

Optimizing image delivery is just as important as using the right capabilities for each format and leveraging the best practices of the browser. In this chapter we will explore the practical aspects of leveraging all the best practices and the impact on operations.

Image Dimensions

As we have now discussed multiple times in Chapters 9, 11, and 12, reducing image dimensions can improve not only network performance but also memory performance. Small images for small devices on slow networks or low memory is better than using one large image for all situations—desktop and mobile alike.

In the section "Selecting the Right Image Width" on page 238 we discussed allocating buckets for different viewports. Looking at a sample of 1 million JPEG images we can examine the impact of image dimensions on file size. Figures 13-1 and 13-2 compare images at different breakpoints (assuming at least a 2:1 ratio) again by sizes—broken out by 25th, 50th, and 75th percentiles. Of course, every image has its own distribution and this should be used for illustration only.

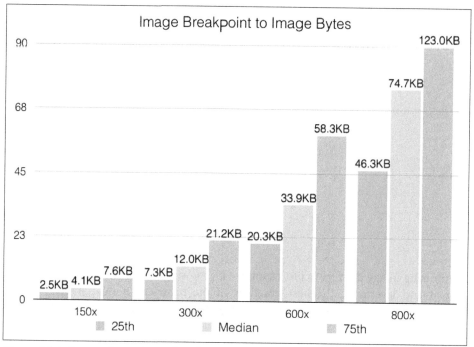

Figure 13-1. Image size to image breakpoints (150–800)

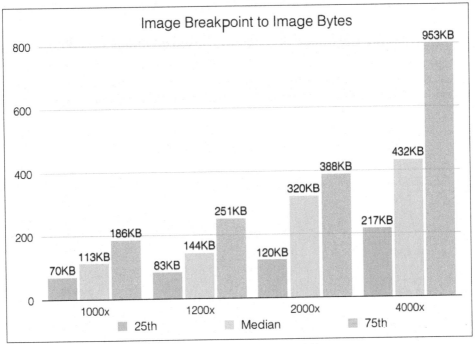

Figure 13-2. Image size to image breakpoints (1,000–4,000)

This makes sense: the larger the dimensions, the larger the file, and the longer the image takes to download. On slower links this will also impact the performance of the page. For the best performance for responsive images or Client Hints, we should be making many different dimensions available for our products.

The proposed breakpoints are a good rule of thumb and a good place to start as a default. Of course, every image might have a different variation based on its complexity. Jason Grigsby has proposed (*http://bit.ly/2alf5KC*) applying the *performance budget* to image delivery. To do this you set a goal of 16 packets (~24 KB) for each breakpoint. In this way you can reduce the number of breakpoints per image and better optimize your cache footprint.

Of course, every image could have its own set of breakpoints. This technique is most ideal for entry pages, campaign sites, and other parts of your app or website that you can examine with high intensity.

What Are the Image Breakpoints Based on Image Budgets?

Applying the budget approach to the same million images yields breakpoints that match the recommended set from earlier. Figure 13-3 represents the median width based on 16-packet increments, generally yielding a standard deviation of about 30%.

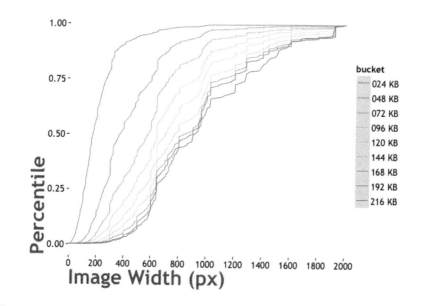

Figure 13-3. Image breakpoints cumulative distribution function in 16-packet (24 KB) increments

Image Format Selection: Accept, WebP, JPEG 2000, and JPEG XR

As we have already discussed, there are many competing image formats available. Generally for lossless compression, we can make our selection based on the features desired and be comfortable knowing that 99% of all clients have support for GIF or PNG.

The problem is lossy formats: JPEG is virtually ubiquitous. In contrast, the advanced formats—WebP, JPEG 2000, JPEG XR—are fragmented in support across platforms. One solution is to utilize responsive images' `<picture>` element and duplicate your HTML to specify the same image resolutions but with different formats. It is like buying one of every size of light bulb, and bringing them all home, just to figure out which size fits your particular lamp. This is not a scalable solution.

```
<picture>
    <source type="image/webp"
            srcset="/fido_in_dc_100.webp 100w,
                    /fido_in_dc_400.webp 400w,
                    /fido_in_dc_800.webp 800w,
                    /fido_in_dc_1000.webp 1000w,
                    /fido_in_dc_1200.webp 1200w,
                    /fido_in_dc_1400.webp 1400w" />
    <source type="image/vnd.ms-photo"
            srcset="/fido_in_dc_100.jxr 100w,
                    /fido_in_dc_400.jxr 400w,
                    /fido_in_dc_800.jxr 800w,
                    /fido_in_dc_1000.jxr 1000w,
                    /fido_in_dc_1200.jxr 1200w,
                    /fido_in_dc_1400.jxr 1400w" />
    <source type="image/jp2"
            srcset="/fido_in_dc_100.jp2 100w,
                    /fido_in_dc_400.jp2 400w,
                    /fido_in_dc_800.jp2 800w,
                    /fido_in_dc_1000.jp2 1000w,
                    /fido_in_dc_1200.jp2 1200w,
                    /fido_in_dc_1400.jp2 1400w" />
    <img src="/fido_in_dc_100.jpg"
         srcset="/fido_in_dc_100.jpg 100w,
                 /fido_in_dc_400.jpg 400w,
                 /fido_in_dc_800.jpg 800w,
                 /fido_in_dc_1000.jpg 1000w,
                 /fido_in_dc_1200.jpg 1200w,
                 /fido_in_dc_1400.jpg 1400w"
         sizes="(min-width: 500px) 33.3vw, 100vw"
    />
</picture>
```

In the same vein as Client Hints, we can negotiate and detect the formats supported by the browser—at least, we *should* be able to using the Accept: request header.

In the early days of HTTP/1.1 the Accept header was introduced as a mechanism for content negotiation. It was envisioned as a way to tell the server what kinds of media and MIME types the browser would accept. It was intended to complement the other Accept headers, such as Accept-Language, Accept-Charset, and Accept-Encoding, which focused on negotiating human languages, character encodings, and compression, respectively.

While the latter three Accept headers are still important for proper interpretation of the page, unfortunately the Accept header has become largely irrelevant with most modern browsers. Most now simply transmit Accept: */* to avoid misinterpretations by servers. Also, the sheer sophistication of a modern browser means it is capable of handling a very long list of media types. To avoid ridiculously long and verbose Accept lines, most servers all but ignore the Accept header and browsers have simplified it to the generic wildcard.

In an odd way, */* does make sense. If there is consensus in the web development community, then there is very little need to use a different Accept value. The irrelevance of the Accept header has created an opportunity for browsers to communicate new enhancements. In this way, Chrome uses Accept for situations where capabilities are diverse. For example, Android and Chrome will send Accept: image/webp, */* indicating that in addition to the standard content types, this device can also render WebP images.

Implementing the detection is then pretty straightforward. For example, the following offers a quick rewrite rule to internally rewrite *.jpg to *.webp if the requesting client indicates support:

```php
<?php
if (strstr($_SERVER['HTTP_ACCEPT'], 'image/webp') !== false) {
    # transform image to webp
    $img->setImageFormat('webp');
}
?>
```

As we cautioned in Table 5-1, Accept: image/webp can be used as shorthand to mean WebP extended or WebP animated. However, there is a small user base (Android 4.0–4.2) where only WebP standard is supported. Likewise, you should be concerned about specific Chrome versions that support animated WebP (Chrome 32+). If in doubt, consult your own user logs to determine how much traffic is from older Android and Chrome browsers and would be impacted if you delivered unsupported WebP advanced or animation formats.

You can detect JPEG XR in very much the same way by looking for Accept: image/jxr. This applies for IE 8+ and Microsoft Edge:

```php
<?php
if (strstr($_SERVER['HTTP_ACCEPT'], 'image/jxr') !== false) {
    # transform image to jpeg xr
    $img->setImageFormat('jxr');
}
?>
```

What about JPEG 2000? Alas, it doesn't use the Accept header. This means we have to resort to device characteristics in order to select the best format based on the client:

```php
<?php
    $browser = $wurflObj->capabilities['mobile_browser'];
    $browser_ver = $wurflObj->capabilities['mobile_browser_version'];
    if ((strstr($browser, 'Safari') != false) && $brwoser_ver >= 6 {
        $picture->setImageFormat('jp2');
    }
    if ((strstr($browser, 'Safari') != false) && $brwoser_ver >= 6 {
        $picture->setImageFormat('jp2');
    }
?>
```

If you do decide to use device detection to leverage specific image formats (or specific features in other formats), you can refer to Appendix A for a list of supported operating systems and browsers for each format.

Finally, device detection can be accomplished with client-side JavaScript, such as Modernizr (*https://modernizr.com/*), which detects WebP (lossy, lossless, alpha, and animated variants), JPEG 2000, and JPEG XR. This is a great option, especially if the images on your site are loaded lazily, or use another JavaScript harness to load images. The downside is that this creates a race condition and the detection only happens after the JavaScript has loaded. The result is that either your images are loaded after the JavaScript execution, or the first collection of images is downloaded as JPEG (or another unoptimized format) until the libraries are loaded.

Image Quality

So far we have explored opportunities to select the right-sized image and the right format of image. The last dimension we can leverage to optimize the delivery of an image is quality. This is a tricky subject because the very term *quality* is used as a pejorative in the creative process. To reduce the quality of an image is to make it inferior. We must resist this association. By increasing the lossy compression (decreasing quality) we can help improve user performance in many situations. The tradeoff is balancing the comprehensive user experience (are users able to interact with the page and accomplish their goals?) with localized image experience.

Quality and Image Byte Size

There is a general understanding that adjusting the quality level in lossy formats (JPEG, JPEG 2000, JPEG XP, WebP) results in a commensurate reduction in bytes. The more compression applied, the fewer bytes there will be. There is also a point of diminishing returns. Setting compression to 100 doesn't result in a pristine lossless image, just a large image.

Figure 13-4 shows the quality graph for the different image formats compared to the relative byte savings. This does not compare the relative sizes between formats but rather the change in bytes within the format. Changing between formats will yield additional relative byte savings.

This quality graph is based on a sample set of 1,000 product detail images and is fairly representative of a typical quality scale. This also highlights the variances between different libraries. It also emphasizes that quality does not mean percentage. It is tempting to conflate quality index to image quality or even file size.

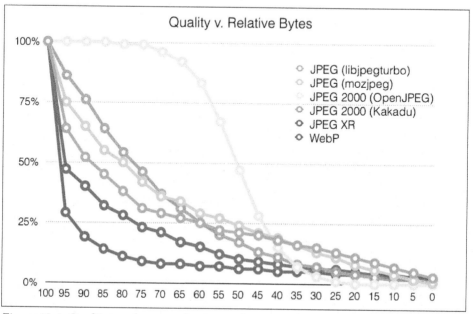

Figure 13-4. Quality graph comparing image formats to byte savings

As you can see, regardless of format, each encoding library can impact the byte size of an image differently. Specifically, there is a rapid reduction in byte size until we hit an index of around 35. Also, we can see the distortion of the highest index values on the scale. If we reset the scale and focus on an index of 90 through 35, we adjust our expectations (see Figure 13-5).

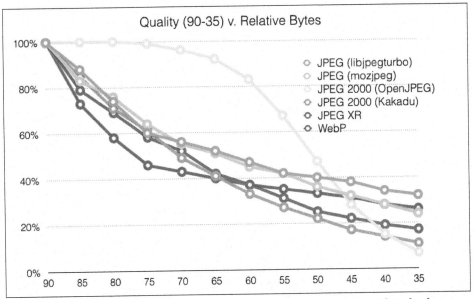

Figure 13-5. Quality graph comparing image formats to byte savings with index between 90 and 35

Nearly universally we can see that reducing the quality index can quickly reduce file sizes. Most follow a similar curve shape, but there are still noticeable differences. What we can conclude from this is that we should expect an additional 20% byte savings by moving from quality 90 to quality 80, and another 20% by moving to quality 70. From there the gains become smaller but are still impressive.

Quality Index and SSIM

But does the quality index of one encoder equal the quality index of another? Can we just assume that all quality indexes are the same? Using Structural Similarity (SSIM) calculations, we can compare the different encoding libraries and their effects. Can we assume that selecting index 80 in one library is the same as quality 80 in another? Or across formats?

Using the same dataset, we can compare the SSIM values at each index value. Using the 90th percentile value (conservative) we arrive at the curves shown in Figure 13-6. It's important to emphasize that this is a conservative view, and an individual image could well get a lower SSIM value when run through the different quality indexes. The purpose of this illustration is to provide general guidance and conclusions, so a 90th percentile was selected.

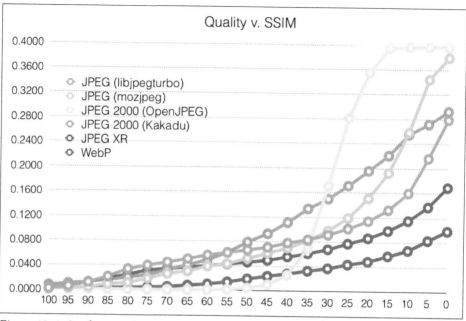

Figure 13-6. Quality graph comparing image formats to SSIM values

Clearly quality is not a consistent metric across different libraries. Each encoding library impacts the visual perception differently at the same quality index. If you set libjpeg-turbo to quality 80, you would expect the same SSIM of a MozJPEG set at quality 65.

Just as before, the top and bottom indexes heavily skew the graph. Zooming in on index 90 through 40 yields the charts shown in Figures 13-7 and 13-8.

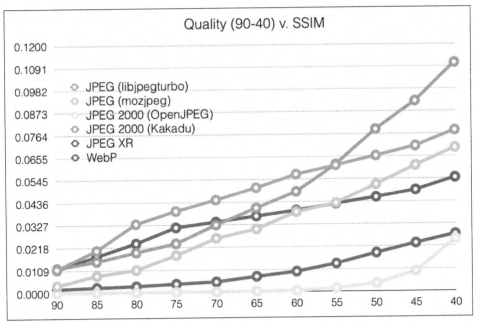

Figure 13-7. Quality graph comparing image formats to SSIM values with index between 90 and 40

Quality	JPEG (libjpegturbo)	JPEG (mozjpeg)	JPEG 2000 (OpenJPEG)	JPEG 2000 (Kakadu)	JPEG XR	WebP
1000	0.0007	0.0009	0.0000	0.0066	0.0010	0.0000
950	0.0048	0.0020	0.0000	0.0092	0.0014	0.0056
900	0.0113	0.0035	0.0000	0.0118	0.0017	0.0112
850	0.0204	0.0082	0.0000	0.0150	0.0023	0.0175
800	0.0332	0.0109	0.0000	0.0194	0.0030	0.0238
750	0.0393	0.0180	0.0000	0.0237	0.0040	0.0314
700	0.0447	0.0262	0.0001	0.0325	0.0049	0.0340
650	0.0505	0.0305	0.0003	0.0407	0.0074	0.0368
600	0.0569	0.0387	0.0005	0.0485	0.0097	0.0394
550	0.0612	0.0429	0.0015	0.0616	0.0134	0.0425
500	0.0657	0.0519	0.0038	0.0785	0.0186	0.0456
450	0.0704	0.0610	0.0096	0.0922	0.0232	0.0490
400	0.0779	0.0695	0.0252	0.1106	0.0275	0.0550
350	0.0832	0.0819	0.0689	0.1332	0.0323	0.0606
300	0.0910	0.0981	0.1705	0.1493	0.0366	0.0676
250	0.1014	0.1187	0.2805	0.1708	0.0429	0.0770
200	0.1139	0.1508	0.3544	0.1953	0.0481	0.0862
150	0.1320	0.1925	0.3941	0.2203	0.0573	0.0985
100	0.1594	0.2580	0.3963	0.2546	0.0667	0.1148
50	0.2162	0.3442	0.3963	0.2713	0.0829	0.1372
0	0.2790	0.3795	0.3963	0.2926	0.0985	0.1692

Figure 13-8. Quality index graph comparing JPEGs to other formats

One thing this does not take into account is DPR. There is anecdotal evidence that suggests that the perception of higher SSIM values goes down based on pixel density as well as form factor; that is, humans can accept a higher SSIM value when it is on a smartphone versus on a desktop. Research is early and inconclusive on the impact of visual perception based on display form factor.

How do we select a quality index and apply it across the different encoders and expect the same results? Fortunately for you, I have run the regressions and derived the charts in Figures 13-9 and 13-10 to help with our conversions.

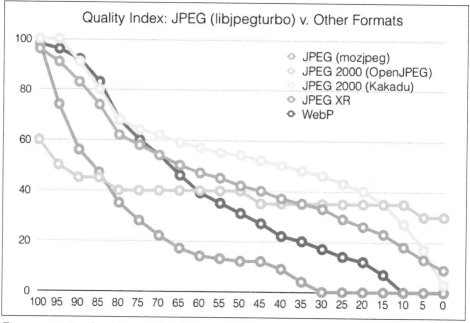

Figure 13-9. Quality index: JPEG (libjpegturbo) versus other formats

JPEG (libjpegturbo)	JPEG (mozjpeg)	JPEG 2000 (OpenJPEG)	JPEG 2000 (Kakadu)	JPEG XR	WebP
100	96	60	100	98	98
95	91	50	100	74	96
90	83	45	91	56	92
85	74	45	80	47	83
80	62	40	68	35	68
75	58	40	64	28	60
70	54	40	62	22	54
65	50	40	59	17	46
60	47	40	57	14	39
55	45	40	55	13	35
50	42	40	54	12	31
45	40	35	52	12	27
40	37	35	50	9	22
35	35	35	48	4	20
30	33	35	46	0	17
25	29	35	43	0	14
20	26	35	40	0	12
15	23	35	35	0	7
10	18	35	27	0	0
5	13	30	17	0	0
0	9	30	3	0	0

Figure 13-10. Quality index: JPEG (libjpegturbo) versus other formats

Is this a chapter on image quality or image delivery? Well, both. They are tightly linked. In order for us to select the best image quality to reduce bytes, we should also keep in mind the effective equivalent in the other formats.

So, we've reached two major conclusions about how to better deliver images:

- Focus on the desired quality index for your images to maximize SSIM and reduce file sizes.
- Layer image format and responsive images after the quality index adjustment.

Selecting SSIM and Quality Use Cases

You can take this one step further and create use cases for quality:

```
High: 0.01 SSIM
Medium: 0.03 SSIM
Low: 0.05 SSIM
```

In this way you could intentionally distort the image to maximize the user experience. For example, you could use the network Client Hints to inform the quality use case. Alternatively, you could look at the HTTP socket performance (packet RTT) or instrument latency detection with service workers. By doing so, you could adjust the user experience based on the hostility of the network conditions.

This is very similar to what was suggested in Chapter 12. In fact, both can be done at the same time for maximal benefit: adjust both the image dimensions and then adjust the quality. There are many possibilities.

Of course, there is always a point of diminishing returns. Applying these use cases to a 800-byte image has little value to the user experience. However, if the image is 100 KB, then of course you would want to apply this algorithm. Remember: every packet counts—especially on poor network situations.

The bottom line is this: if you can gain a full packet in savings it is probably worth adjusting image quality. Accordingly, we might augment the previous chart as follows:

```
High:   0.01 SSIM
Medium: 0.03 SSIM and >4,500 Byte savings (~3 packets)
Low:    0.05 SSIM and >12,000 Byte savings (~8 packets)
```

Creating Consensus on Quality Index

One final word about quality. As I mentioned, this topic is often very emotive—especially among those in your organization who are the custodians of brand (i.e., your marketing teams). Their job is to ensure that the public's opinion of your brand is positive. You, in contrast, are responsible for ensuring that the site or app works for the highest number of people. These are two sides of the same coin.

In order to bring marketing and creative teams onboard with adjusting the quality index of your images, it is useful to *show* instead of explain. For example, you can gain consensus by selecting a set of images and running them through the different quality indexes, as shown in Figure 13-11.

Figure 13-11. Building consensus on image quality

Make sure you are consistent: if you are using MozJPEG as your JPEG engine, then use this to initiate the conversation—don't use libjpeg-turbo.

Consider the Contractual Obligations of Branding When Reducing Image Quality

Also recognize that there are likely situations where you don't want to reduce the quality index because of marketing or legal obligations.

Quality Index Conclusion

When applying changes to the quality index, follow these best practices (see Figure 13-12):

- Reduce the quality index based on SSIM values instead of a fixed setting.
- Apply the equivalent quality index to other formats.
- Add network awareness to select a lower-quality index.
- Use the Client Hint `Save-Data:` on to select a lower-quality index.

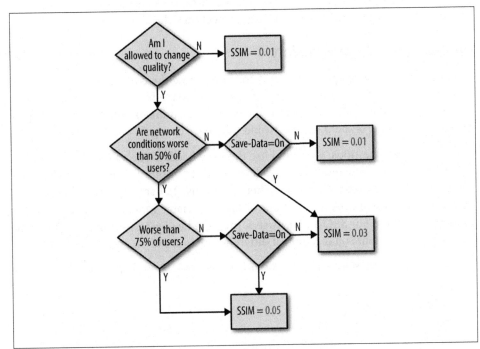

Figure 13-12. Workflow for selecting the right image quality

Achieving Cache Offload: Vary and Cache-Control

Selecting different images based on server side logic solves one problem, but can introduce new problems to downstream systems. Ultimately, we need to ensure that both the client and any middle-boxes—such as transparent proxies, surrogate caches, and Content Delivery Network (CDNs)—also follow the same selection logic. Failing to account for the ecosystem can result in clients re-downloading the same image multiple times, or worse: it could result in the user getting the wrong image. Additionally, we also need to ensure that even search-engine bots understand the logic so that SEO isn't impacted because of "clocking" penalization. If we aren't careful, changing delivery logic can have many unintended side effects downstream.

Fortunately, the authors of the HTTP spec considered this situation. The Vary header is intended to express how the content would vary from one request to another. There is also an enhancement specification proposed to help provide increased resolution with the Key header. The challenge, of course, is to ensure that all the current consumers (clients and middle boxes) also respect these headers.

Informing the Client with Vary

The first objective is to inform the end consumer how the content may change with different requests. For example, if the request were made by a mobile versus a desktop user, would the content change? If the user changed the orientation of the display to have a different Viewport-Width, would the image change?

To answer these questions, we would use the Vary header. The value of the header is *not* the value used, but the HTTP header used as an input. Some of the values you could use include Accept-Encoding (when Gzip is used), User-Agent, and Viewport-Width. We will discuss the implications of highly variable inputs such as User-Agent in the next section. For SEO and browsers, the Vary header helps properly inform the client that the content could change if different inputs are used.

If we used DPR: to select a different image, we would expect Vary: DPR in the response:

```
GET /broccoli.jpg
DPR: 1.5

...

HTTP/1.1 200 OK
Content-Type: image/jpeg
Vary: DPR
```

For changes in image dimensions using Client Hints we could use the following values: `Viewport-Width`, `Width`, `DPR`, `Downlink`, or `Save-Data`. These can also be combined; for example, if you are using both `DPR` and `Width` in your calculation you would emit:

```
Vary: Width, DPR
```

Changes in format are a bit more complex. For WebP and JPEG XR it is sufficient to use `Vary: Accept`. However, for JPEG 2000 (Safari/iOS) we have to use device detection and therefore we should send `Vary: User-Agent`.

Internet Explorer (all versions) adds an unfortunate wrinkle: `Vary` will cause a revalidation on every request instead of caching. This is because IE does not cache the requesting headers and so cannot use them to compute the internal cache key. As a result, each load of the image will, at the very least, prompt a new request with an `If-Modified-Since` (or `If-None-Match`) to revalidate. The workaround for IE is to drop the `Vary` header and mark the content as private with a `Cache-Control` header.

For Internet Explorer users only:

```
GET /broccoli.jpg
User-Agent: ...

HTTP/1.1 200 OK
Content-Type: image/jpeg
Cache-Control: private
```

Changes based on network conditions are likewise a challenge since the variation is not based on HTTP headers but on network conditions. If we have access to the `Down link` Client Hint header, that would work well in the response. Otherwise, we should treat the variation much like we do for Internet Explorer and use `Cache-Control: private` to ensure that middle boxes don't give the wrong experience to the client.

Middle Boxes, Proxies with Cache-Control (and TLS)

There are many middle boxes deployed throughout the Internet—in hotels, coffee shops, ISPs, and mobile operators. Their goal is to provide an additional layer of caching. Of course, these automatic middle boxes have to be conservative. They will only cache content that is marked as cacheable just as an end user would.

However, it would be problematic if they were to cache a WebP response and send it to a Safari user, or a smartphone response and send it to a desktop. It would be one thing to assume that the proxies and middle boxes all honor the `Vary` header as the browser does. Unfortunately, they don't.

Worse yet, many middle boxes controlled by network operators often try to apply their own image optimizations out of your control. This can be problematic if they do things like strip the color policy profile or further apply a lower-quality index.

There is a clear risk versus benefit with these middle boxes. If you are applying any logic in delivery selection, you can confuse these middle boxes and inadvertently deliver an inferior user experience despite your best intention.

To work around this problem you can do two things:

- Use Transport Layer Security (TLS) as a transport for your images. These middle boxes cannot intercept TLS connections because it would cause the client to distrust the resigned response (aka man-in-the-middle attack).

- Mark the response as private with `Cache-Control: private`. This will ensure that these proxies don't accidentally cache the content and serve it to the wrong person.

Even if you are not doing selection in resolution or format, it is still good to account for these middle boxes impacting the delivery of your images. To control your destiny, it is good to also mark the response with `Cache-Control: no-transform`. This will indicate that middle boxes shouldn't further mutate the response and possibly delay the delivery of your images. Again, using TLS will also accomplish the same goal.

CDNs and Vary and Cache-Control

It is useful to remember that the CDN acts on your behalf in the delivery solution and is under your control. While you cannot control the cache and life cycle of images sent to the end client (or intercepted by ISP proxies), you can control the CDN as you can your infrastructure.

There are two ways to invoke a CDN when delivering your images: passively or actively. In a passive setup, the CDN honors the `Vary` and `Cache-Control` headers in the same way that the client would. Unlike a transparent proxy, a CDN can often also serve TLS traffic on your behalf with a valid certificate. This makes it all the more important to ensure that you decorate your response with a properly formed `Vary` header.

The problem with CDNs in a passive mode is that while the possible values for `Vary: DPR` might be somewhat limited, the possible values of `Vary: User-Agent` or `Vary: Accept` result in a very fragmented cache. This is the equivalent of a infinite permutation and will yield a very low or no cache offload. Some CDNs, like Akamai, will treat any value of `Vary` other than `Vary: Accept-Encoding` as equivalent to no store. Be sure to configure the CDN to ignore the `Vary` header but pass it along to the end user.

To reiterate: using `Vary` has value for the end client but will have minimal to no value at the CDN. The client may have a few possibilities for `Vary: Viewport-Width`, but the CDN will have thousands upon thousands. Think about how many mobile devices have different screen dimensions. If you Vary: Viewport-Width, the CDN would have to cache for each possible value from 320 all the way up to 2,000 pixels. Similarly, with Vary: User-Agent, there are literally millions of permutations that would each need to be cached interdependently.

Active CDN configurations extend the decision logic from your origin into the CDN. In this way you can use device characteristics in the CDN to form the cache key. You should also be able to extend the cache key with multiple buckets of values to make it more succinct.

For example, you could bucket values of Width into 0–100, 100–200, 200–300 to a rationalized cache key with Width = 100, 200, and 300, respectively. This creates 3 cached versions instead of 300 possible variations.

With an active CDN configuration you will need to ensure that your server-side logic matches the CDN (see Figure 13-13).

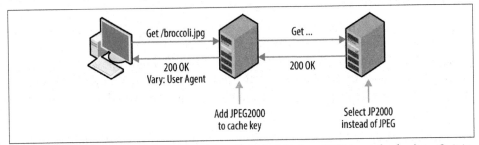

Figure 13-13. User (Vary: User-Agent) ←- CDN (add isJpeg2000 to cache-key) ←- Origin (select JPEG 2000)

In advanced solutions you can move the image selection to the domain of the CDN. This way, the CDN not only reflects the cache key but also is responsible for making the image selection and subsequently picking up the correct files from the origin or passing to an image transformation solution (see Figure 13-14).

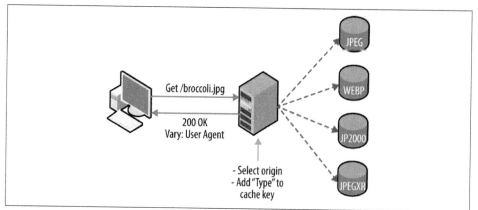

Figure 13-14. CDN selects origin file

Near Future: Key

There is a proposed standard that in the near future may help CDNs and the browser better understand the cache key partitioning of a response. The IETF httpbis working group (*https://tools.ietf.org/html/draft-ietf-httpbis-key-00*) has proposed the use of the Key HTTP response header to describe the secondary cache key. Key would complement the Vary header by providing the ranges of values that would result in the same response.

For example, using Key in a Client Hints–informed response could help describe the various breakpoints for an image, like so:

```
HTTP/1.1 200 OK
Vary: DPR, Width
Key: DPR;partition=1.5:2.5:4.0
Key: Width;div=320
```

Single URL Versus Multiple URLs

There are many metaphysical debates on whether an application should utilize one canonical URL for many derivative images or manifest each combination and permutation as a uniquely accessible URL. There are both philosophical arguments to be made as well as pragmatic.

The single URL camp usually starts with a discussion about "the forms" and quotes Socrates and Plato nine times before breakfast. The argument is to keep a canonical single URL representation exposed in order to ensure simplicity and agility. If you have one URL that has many derivations from the original, then you can partition or collapse the responsive image buckets at will without worrying about stale caches or link rot. A single URL allows regular iterations of optimization to find the best performance for the highest number of users.

```
/images/broccoli.jpg
```

On the other hand, the advocates for many URLs would argue that using one URL for each permutation avoids the unnecessary complications to address caching and proxies. (They also would likely claim Socrates was just a hack and scared of shadows.) Each derivative for responsive images, formats, and quality should likewise be manifested as a unique URL. This is in addition to the various use cases, such as "search results," "product detail," or "banner ad."

```
/images/broccoli-search-400-80.jpg
/images/broccoli-search-400-80.webp
/images/broccoli-search-400-80.jp2
/images/broccoli-search-400-80.jxr
/images/broccoli-search-800-80.jpg
/images/broccoli-search-800-80.webp
/images/broccoli-search-800-80.jp2
/images/broccoli-search-800-80.jxr
...
```

Clearly, there is no single answer. There is a need for both approaches. As user demographics change, so too will the effectiveness of image breakpoints, image formats, and quality. For this reason it is good to remain flexible. Yet at the same time there are classes of content that should be exposed independently. Generally, the image use cases are best served as a unique URL. This is practical for your content creators and will likely have positive SEO impact as well.

Regardless of the approach, all the derivative images will need to be produced at one of the layers in your architecture. Whether the images are generated and stored in a filesystem at the origin or through a cloud-based transformation service, all of the variations must be stored somewhere. The key question is what makes the simplest operational sense and what has the least impact on your catalog of images.

File Storage, Backup, and Disaster Recovery

One of the often-overlooked aspects of image delivery is the performance (and cost) of storage, backup, and disaster recovery. Content creators and web devs often forget the cost of infrastructure. Modern storage infrastructure is fast and abundant. However, this doesn't preclude operational complexity when you're dealing with a large volume of images—especially small images (in bytes) that are optimized for delivery.

This section is not intended to be exhaustive, as there are just as many variables with efficient storage and backup as there are with image delivery. A good delivery experience also requires a balance of the infrastructure requirements. Millions of small images may not pose a problem in a steady state, but in a disaster recovery scenario, they can create a significant bottleneck that could impact the operation of your business and be the root cause for a mean time to recovery of 8 hours instead of 30 minutes.

Image delivery should always consider business continuity in the infrastructure planning. While we always hope that a datacenter will be resilient, we know that nature has a way of throwing a spanner into the works. The question, then, is how quickly can we recover.

Images transferred over the Web are predominantly small—at least in comparison to databases, videos, and other key assets an organization needs to preserve for business continuity. Using the median byte size for various breakpoints (see Figure 13-1) we can attempt to estimate the impact of these derivative images.

Let's do the math:

```
100,000 base images
x 4 use cases (search, product details, hero ad ...)
x 8 widths
x 4 image formats (WebP, JPEG XR, JPEG 2000, WebP)
x 3 quality index
= 38.4 million images
```

Focusing on just the 300x breakpoint and assuming 30% savings for each format and an additional 20% for each quality:

```
10,000 base images
x 12.1KB (8.4KB, 8.4KB, 8.4KB)
= 1,200MB + 840MB + 840MB + 840MB
+ 3 quality (12.1KB/9.6/7.2, 8.4/6.7/5)
= 960MB + 672MB + 672MB + 672MB
= 720MB + 504MB + 504MB + 504MB
= 8.93 GB per use case and per breakpoint!
```

38.4 million images doesn't sound like much, nor does 9 GB. But let's look at the two factors that matter: size on disk and the cost of metadata.

Size on Disk

Most modern filesystems, from EXT4 to NTFS, use a block size of 4 KB. This ensures that the block size lines up with the physical attributes of the disk. Alignment to physical disk matters more with a spinning disk than it does for solid state. There is always inefficiency in filling every block. The assumption is that there will be more completely filled blocks than partially filled blocks.

In the previous example, rounding to the nearest block size adds an extra 25% to the total storage; that is, the 9 GB actually uses 12 GB of storage. Fortunately, as file sizes increase, the impact of size on disk decreases.

Cost of Metadata

The second issue is the cost of metadata. Every filesystem has some form of metadata to track the location on disk for a file and the block association for this file. This metadata is usually the root cause for any limits on the number of files per directory. For example, in ext4, the limit is 64,000 files. Generally speaking, each file and directory on a filesystem includes metadata (in ext4 it is an inode) to track the size of the file and the location on disk as well as its location in the hierarchy.

Different filesystems use different allocations, but it can be 2–3.2% of the total volume of a disk allocated to metadata. Even if you are storing the files in a database, the database itself will have to track the location with metadata. What can be tuned is how much metadata.

When ext4 was released, a number of tests were conducted by *Linux Magazine* (*http://www.linux-mag.com/id/7642/2/*) based on different file sizes and directory depths (see Figure 13-15). The key here is that every file written must also have metadata recorded. It is not just one write for the file, but multiple writes. These tests showed the impact of creating small images and large images with shallow or deep directory structures.

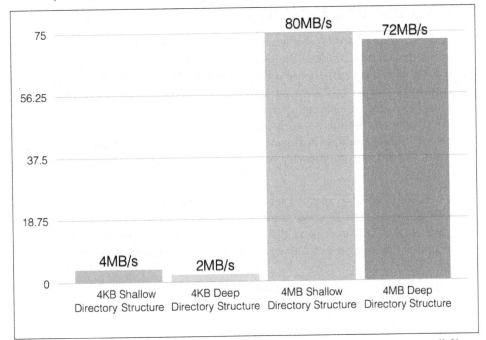

Figure 13-15. Ext4 metadata writes reduce disk performance: creating many small files is slower

As you can see, the impact of file size and metadata can be very large. The bottleneck here is now the filesystem metadata. Fast drives are no longer the bottleneck.

The cost of metadata is the bottleneck for disaster recovery. If we use the same scenario as we did for the 300x breakpoint and applied it to the eight other breakpoints, we would have a total storage of 2.5 TB. Even at 80 MB/s the expected time to recovery would be over 8 hours. In this scenario, your business would be out of commission for a full workday while we recover images.

Consider the impact of your design decisions on your infrastructure. Bottom line: you may be making decisions that your CFO might not be comfortable with in a disaster recovery event.

 To address this specific problem of many small images and the cost of metadata, Facebook has purpose-built an optimized object storage system called *Haystack (http://bit.ly/2aThJab)*. Haystack uses an in-memory index designed for single write and many reads while minimizing the overhead cost of metadata. Replication, election, clustering, and other distributed or backup functions are outside the scope of the storage system and handled by other system logic.

Domain Sharding and HTTP2

As we discussed in Chapter 7, browsers are limited by the number of connections. To overcome this, and to improve the throughput for downloading images (and other small content), many websites use *domain sharding*. The objective of domain sharding is to work around TCP slow start, congestion window scaling, and head-of-line blocking. Normally, by opening up parallel TCP connections, up to six per host, you can effectively saturate the network connection. Domain sharding takes this a step further by utilizing multiple hostnames that point to the same infrastructure. In this way you can trick out the browser to send even more parallel requests by opening more sockets.

In Figures 13-6 and 13-7, you can see how the browser opens additional socket connections with each new domain shard. The impact is a faster completed download and page render. This is because the network is more fully utilized. (This example uses a 3 Mbps connection and 200 ms of latency to emphasize the impact.)

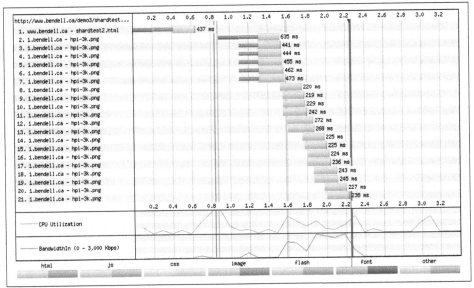

Figure 13-16. One resource domain on an HTTP/1.1 connection

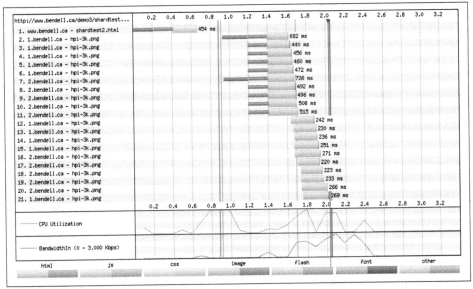

Figure 13-17. Two resource domains on an HTTP/1.1 connection

Even though TLS has a handshake tax, sharding can also have some benefits. For example, Figures 13-18 and 13-19 show the same website from before using one or two shards.

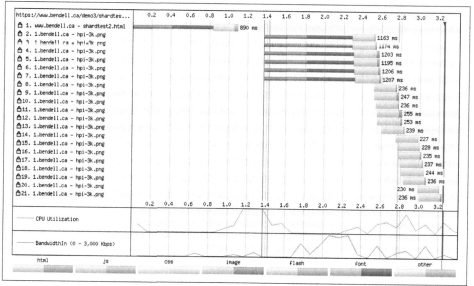

Figure 13-18. One resource domain on an HTTP/1.1 + TLS connection

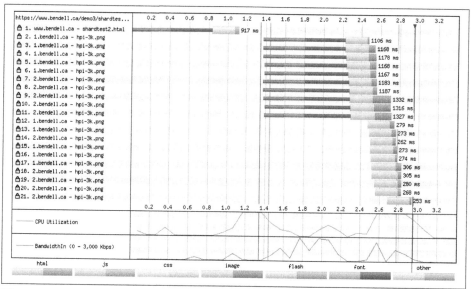

Figure 13-19. Two resource domains on an HTTP/1.1 + TLS connection

Typically you'd implement this approach by adding a different prefix, or even whole domain, to the resource request. Requesting *http://www.example.com/i-love-broccoli.jpg* now becomes *http://images1.example.com/i-love-broccoli.jpg*. These different hostnames are usually just aliases to the same content. Typically the subdomains would resolve in DNS to the same IP and depend on the virtual host mapping on the application server to serve the same content.

Using domain shards is straightforward but does have a few implementation considerations.

How Do I Avoid Cache Busting and Redownloading?

We have two objectives when using sharding: maximize the browser cache, and avoid downloading the same resource twice. However we implement domain sharding, we must ensure that *i-love-broccoli.jpg* doesn't show up using *img1.example.com* on the first page but *img2.example.com* on the second. This would effectively void the browser cache and force redownloading the content.

To avoid this, you should partition your images into groups of content. However, avoid using a counter to switch between shards. Also, it is tempting to use one shard for CSS and another for JPEG. You should avoid this temptation because you don't want all the critical resources to be bunched up on a single request queue. Instead, use a hash or an index to equally distribute filenames between available shards.

How Many Shards Should I Use?

Selecting the right number of shards is not as clear cut as you would expect. Early research suggested two to four shards per page, but this was a best practice from 2007 when browsers only made two connections per hostname. Steve Souders has provided the most recent guidance, suggesting ~20 resources per domain (*http://bit.ly/2aOGIfs*) to provide a good balance of sharding for performance.

This remains the best general guidance. However, there are other questions, such as: what is the impact on congestion control and TCP scaling? If each socket is attempting to maximize the congestion window but competing with itself, this could result in packet loss and thus decrease overall performance. The size of the resources also impacts the effectiveness of sharding. Sharding works because many small resources don't use more than a few packets to send/receive. (We discussed this more in Chapter 10.) However, this value can diminish with larger content, many more resources in parallel, or low bandwidth.

What Should I Do for HTTP/2?

Is domain sharding an anti-pattern for HTTP/2? The short answer is: no. The longer answer is: it could be, if you don't consider HTTP/2 in your implementation.

HTTP/2 has many advantages, one of which is the ability to have multiple parallel requests on a single socket connection. In this way we can avoid the HTTP/1.1 head-of-line blocking problem. Domain sharding is not necessary to saturate the network connection. By using a single socket you can also scale the congestion window more quickly and avoid packet loss and retransmission.

In 2015, the IETF finalized HTTP/2 (RFC7540), which is the successor to the HTTP/1.1 protocol. The expectations of HTTP/2 are that it will:

- In most cases, substantially and measurably improve end-user-perceived latency over HTTP/1.1 using TCP.
- Address the "head-of-line blocking" problem in HTTP.
- Not require multiple connections to a server to enable parallelism, thus improving its use of TCP, especially regarding congestion control.
- Retain the semantics of HTTP/1.1, including (but not limited to) HTTP methods, status codes, URIs, and where appropriate, header fields.

More specifically, HTTP/2 supports:

- HTTP/1.1 and is backward-compatible
- Multiplexing on a single connection
- Header compression
- Prioritization of requests
- Server push

However, there are a number of barriers to HTTP/2 adoption. Aside from the consideration of adopting TLS (because there aren't any implementations that can do HTTP/2 without TLS), there is also the factor of the user adoption curve. HTTP/2 requires recent versions of modern browsers. For native apps it also requires modern OSes (or client libraries) that can likewise use HTTP/2. Beyond user adoption there is also the challenge of corporate (and home) content filters that intentionally decrypt and resign TLS encryption. In *some* situations, Akamai has observed the interception of TLS requests to be as high as 17% in a region or demographic. There are many causes, most likely from web filters or local antivirus software. The problem is the same: these content filter proxies likely do not use HTTP/2, even if the browser behind the proxy supports HTTP/2.

As with many other web technologies, we should expect the organic adoption of HTTP/2 to take many years. Consider that between 1998 and 2016, only 10% of users were on IPv6 reachable networks. Likewise, SNI (Server Name Indicator) support in TLS has been a standard since 2003, but it wasn't until 2016 that 95% of TLS web traffic supported SNI (mostly as a result of the end-of-life of Windows XP). As of 2016, HTTP/2 adoption is between 50% and 75% depending on the demographic or segmentation. We should expect the long tail of adoption of HTTP/2 to take three to five years before we come close to 100%.

So what should we do in this interim?

Option 1 is to dynamically generate the domain sharding. If the user is connected on a HTTP/2 connection, disable domain sharding. If the user has HTTP/1.1, then utilize multiple sharding as before. This approach, of course, requires that your local caching infrastructure and your CDN be aware of the different rendered outputs and add the HTTP/2 connection as part of the cache key. Unfortunately, there isn't a corresponding `Vary:` header that can properly describe a variation based on the protocol. The best solution is to use `Vary: User-Agent` to communicate the variation (as you would with a RESS design).

Option 2 is to simply ignore the problem. Fortunately, most (if not all) HTTP/2 implementations have an optimization to address domain sharding. Specifically, if the shared domain resolves by DNS to the same IP and the shard is on the same certificate (the hostname is in the Subject-Alternate-Name list), then the HTTP/2 connection will consolidate the sockets. In this way, multiple hosts will use the same HTTP/2 connection and therefore avoid any penalty of sharding. It still remains a single connection. The only penalty is the DNS request. See Figure 13-20.

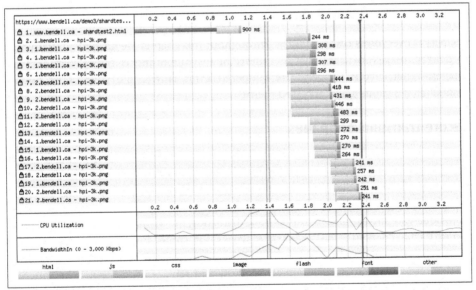

Figure 13-20. HTTP/2 with two resource domains

This is the easiest option because it simply means less work. It also allows you to continue to use sharding for the laggard adopters. And it is these laggard adopters that likely need any performance bump you can give them.

Best Practices

You should continue to use multiple domain shards for your website to maximize the connection throughput. This also helps you avoid images from blocking more critical resources like CSS and JS.

In preparation for HTTP/2 make sure that you:

- Use the same DNS for all of your shards and primary hostname.
- Use the same certificates—add them to the SAN fields of your TLS certificate.

Use Progressive JPEGs for the Best HTTP/2 User Experience

If you have access to the low-level inner workings of your HTTP/2 network stack and are able to adjust the priorities of requests, you should also use round-robin to deliver progressive JPEGs. Instead of sending the bytes for a progressive JPEG as fast as possible, weave the payloads of parallel JPEGs. Use HTTP/2 stream prioritization to deliver progressive JPEGs for a better user experience.

Secure Image Delivery

Security is everyone's responsibility. Throughout this chapter we have focused on how to deliver images to users. Just as important to your brand is the security of your images. What if your images were tampered with? How could your brand be tarnished if a nefarious agent accessed them?

Secure Transport of Images

Up until recently the majority of the Web has been delivered unencrypted. As we have all experienced, there are many locations where content can be hijacked in an unencrypted flow. Public WiFi does this intentionally to force you through a captive portal before granting you access to the Internet. ISPs, with good intentions, have notoriously applied higher compression, distorting the visual quality of your brand. Using `Cache-Control: no-transform` works for some, but not all, well-behaved image transformations (see Figure 13-21). But there are also not-so-well-intentioned transparent proxies that hijack image requests and replace the content with different advertisements or placeholders.

Figure 13-21. Use Cache-Control: no-transform to prevent degraded quality by ISP prox-ies

Securing the transport for images is straightforward. Using TLS you can ensure that the communication from user to server is trusted and that there aren't any middle boxes interfering with or mutating your content. Moving to HTTP/2 also requires the use of TLS.

> **Be Careful of Content Hijacking on Untrusted WiFi**
>
> There have been increasing reports of free WiFi hotspots found at hotels, coffee shops, and restaurants replacing web content with alternate advertising. Putting the ethical argument aside—whether service providers can generate ad revenue from offering free Wifi—there are branding implications for your own web content. Hijacking content like this is only possible with unencrypted pages and images. Moving to TLS prevents man-in-the-middle interception.

Secure Transformation of Images

Securing image delivery is about more than just the transport layer. We should also be concerned about the attack surface of our transformation engines. Whether you are using an on-premise image transformation engine or an off-premise one, there are many possible vulnerabilities. Third-party and open source libraries are extremely useful but also can introduce risk to the enterprise if not properly isolated.

An index of Common Vulnerabilities and Exposures (CVE) is maintained by Mitre (*http://cve.mitre.org*) (see Figure 13-22). It is critical to keep up-to-date with the latest known exploits on the libraries and tools used in your image transformation work-flow. Isolating and patching should be part of your regular team practices.

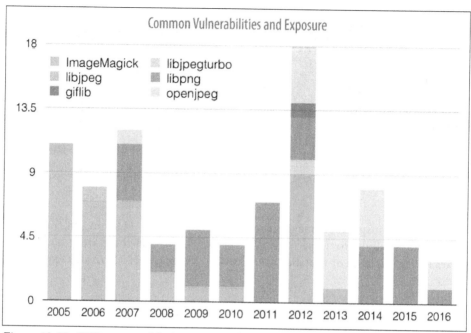

Figure 13-22. CVEs reported for ImageMagick and common image libraries

Image Exploits and Attack Vectors Common Across All Image Formats

News and blog posts of image exploits are commonplace nowadays. Most image-related attacks leverage a technique called *steganography*, which involves hiding a message or exploit code inside the image. No image format is exempt. In 2013, a security researcher found a backdoor that hid data within Exif headers in JPEG (*http://bit.ly/2axef8V*), and Trend Micro blogged about another, similar attack vector with JPEG (*http://bit.ly/2axQ4wU*). Similar attacks have used BMPs (*http://bit.ly/2aXUGck*) and PNGs (*http://bit.ly/2aTNtgj*) to accomplish their malicious activities. Not only are image libraries vulnerable, but image transformation engines as well. In the spring of 2016, ImageMagick made headlines with the remote-execution vulnerability colloquially called "imagetragic" (*http://www.imagetragic.com*).

The main concern for image transformation engines is if a contaminated image enters for processing and, through the decode or mutation process, exploits a vulnerability. This could leverage a byte alteration from the logic edge case, checksum collision, or remote code execution. Consider that the famous Jailbreakme exploit that allowed jailbreaking on iOS 3 used a flaw in the TIFF decoder in iOS. This single flaw allowed rooting of the entire operating system. Imagine the potential impact on your images. This vulnerability could impact subsequent images, possibly tagging them with brand-damaging messages. Just because the bytes of the image have left the processor doesn't mean that there isn't residual code running on the thread. The last thing you want is all of your product images graffitied with "EAT BROCCOLI" without your realizing it (see Figure 13-23).

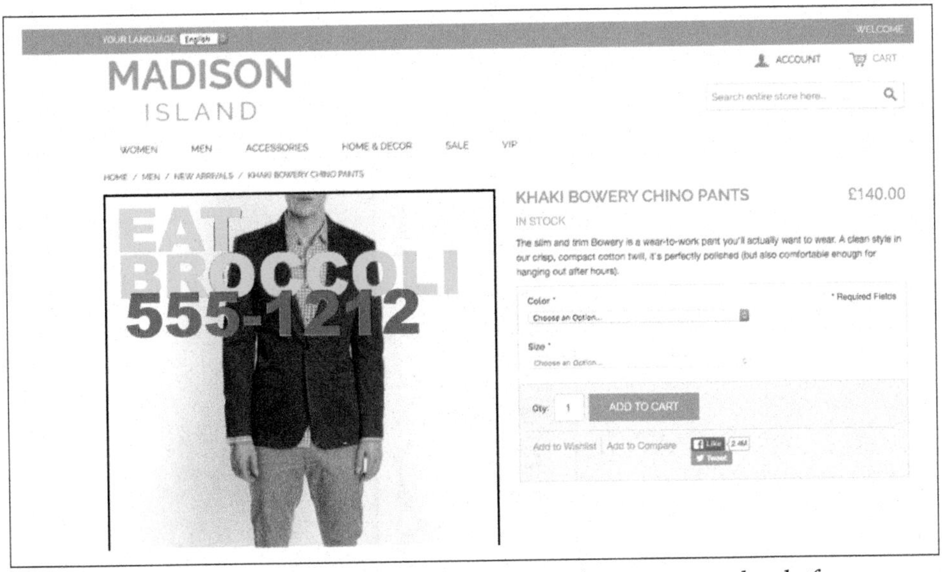

Figure 13-23. We want to avoid one image affecting other images on the platform

How could a contaminated image enter your workflow?

- User-generated images, compromised at source
- Vendor-supplied product images, compromised at source
- In-house photography, compromised by malware on the artist's laptop

It is easy to imagine how a compromised image could enter your workflow. So how can you ensure that a compromised image doesn't impact your ecosystem? How do you isolate the impact to just that compromised image? How can you minimize risk and exposure to your image transformation service?

Secure Transformation: Architecture

Whether your image transformation is on premise or with a cloud-based SaaS provider, you should evaluate the architectural security of the transformation engine. Ideally, there should be isolation at every level of processing. You want to ensure that no single compromised image can affect other parallel threads/processes/systems that are also transforming other images. You also need to ensure that there isn't any residual code that may impact the next image processed by this specific thread.

A well-secured transformation architecture should consider three major areas for isolation (see Figure 13-24):

- TCP connection pools (retrieving and storing)
- Transformation engine (e.g., ImageMagick)
- Encoding and decoding shared objects

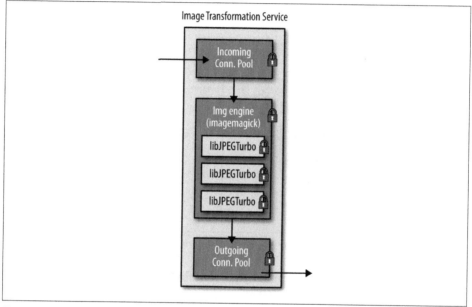

Figure 13-24. A model for secure image transformation architecture

For example:

- We need to ensure that there is no way that images being sent or received via TCP (or disk) can impact another thread or process. The initiating worker should only have access to the stream of bytes for this job.
- The transformation engine, such as ImageMagick, must not be able to store, execute, or preserve any state between image processing. The worker threads must be each isolated to exclusive scratch areas and restricted to access only certain system libraries. For example, the transformation engine should not be able to open up new TCP sockets or leave temporary files or memory state between jobs.
- The various encoding and decoding shared objects (e.g., libjpeg-turbo) also need to be isolated. Memory state should not be allowed to persist or be accessed by parallel threads or other jobs.

This is not an exhaustive list of ways to isolate and segment the architecture. Your local security team should be able to help you ensure that there is no way that a maliciously tampered image can have ecological impact on the rest of your valuable assets. If you are using a cloud solution, you should also ensure that the same level of scrutiny can be applied.

Summary

Downloading an image is no longer simple. There are many variables to consider to ensure the best performance. In order to deliver the best image we want to:

Adjust image dimensions
> Provide a set of breakpoints available for an image to reduce memory usage on the device and improve delivery performance. Use a general rule of 16 packets (24 KB) per breakpoint.

Use advanced image formats
> Newer formats support additional compression as well as more features. For mobile environments, use WebP and JPEG 2000 for Android and iOS users, respectively.

Apply different quality
> Reducing the quality index for a format can reduce byte size. Use DSSIM to find the lowest-quality index for an image. Use three different steps of quality for slower network conditions.

In addition to considering the matrix of image delivery options, you must account for impacts to infrastructure, operations, and security. Transforming images will increase your storage footprint and can impact disaster recovery. Finally, the security of transforming and transformed images is an important and oft-overlooked aspect of delivery. Delivery requires balance between the user's situation, operational complexity, and security.

Operationalizing Your Image Workflow

Mike McCall

Now that you know all about what makes fast, responsive images, let's figure out how we can get them into your workflow and onto your site.

If there's one thing that's consistent about nearly all imagery that exists on the Internet, it's that each image started as something completely inappropriate to display on the Web. We call these images our *master* images, and they're the reference image each *derivative* image—the image that actually shows up on your site—is generated from. How one gets from the master to derivative image varies from one site to the next, but there are often common workflows that exist, usually within certain market verticals.

Some Use Cases

To expand on the concepts of master and derivative images further, let's dig into a couple of use cases to see how master images are created, and how they can sometimes be a huge (in more than one sense of the word) problem for your high-performance image workflow.

The e-Commerce Site

Let's start by imagining an e-commerce site, filled with a catalog of thousands of products, each product containing shots from multiple angles with numerous color variations. We can also imagine our fictitious e-commerce site has large hero imagery that serves as a section heading, and might contain photos of the products being worn or sale items.

It's safe to assume that each and every one of these photographs was taken at a studio, with a high-end DSLR camera. While the images leaving the studio may be beautiful, high-resolution photos, they are almost certainly not the images you want on your site. The files can weigh in at tens to hundreds of megabytes in size, and they are often at 300 DPI resolution since the same imagery is frequently used for both web and print. Often, these images are processed lightly by the studios themselves before being sent off to the site's creative team for further touch-up work. The images leaving the studio are typically in a non-web format, like Photoshop PSD, Tagged Image File Format (TIFF), or occasionally RAW format. The output from the studio to the creative team will usually be well specified in terms of shot angles, background colors, output format, and any touch-up work required prior to the handoff to creative.

TIFF and Raw File Formats

While less common than other formats you may be familiar with, TIFF and RAW files are extremely important in professional photography. TIFF in particular is interesting, as it fully supports CMYK and is well suited for high-color-depth images. It also has support for transparency, as well as layers in some cases, so you may find some high-end photo retouching studios that deal in TIFFs for source imagery.

RAW files are just that—raw. They are basically data straight from the camera's sensor, and as such, are never suitable for web delivery. To make matters more complex, there is no standard for RAW images. In fact, RAW-formatted files are often proprietary to the camera manufacturer, and in some cases differ from one camera model to another, so being able to actually read a RAW image could be in some cases more trouble than it's worth. However, as with TIFF, RAW-formatted images may have other attributes that make them desirable as the source for a master image. If this is the case for you, you will almost certainly need to do some preprocessing before using them in your high performance image workflow.

Once the images are received from the studio and processed by the creative team using a digital photo editing tool like Photoshop, they are saved in a format suitable for use on the site itself, like JPEG. At this stage the images are often loaded into a *digital asset manager* (DAM) for cataloging prior to publishing to a *content management system* (CMS) for presentation. Once we've made it to this point, we have arrived at the master image, but we still don't have our derivative images yet. Before we get there, let's look at another use case.

The Social Media Site

Another class of website that tends to be extremely image-heavy is social media sites. These sites are a nice contrast to the e-commerce use case, because the images on them are almost *never* shot by professionals, let alone in a studio using a fancy camera.

Let's imagine a social media site that allows users to connect with friends and share photos with them. Since the images for our social media site are user-generated, it's the wild west: some are coming from digital point-and-shoots, others are taken with a smartphone, and still others are scans of photographs. Each of these sources could be problematic for different reasons. The point-and-shoot, depending on vintage, could output very low-quality JPEGs that require sharpening to look good; the smartphone could output JPEGs with sensitive GPS data stored in the image metadata; and the scanner could save images as BMPs. And each of these could span a wide range of file sizes, ranging from tens of kilobytes to tens of megabytes.

Malicious JPEGs!

As with just about anything else on the Internet, you should never trust user-submitted input. This holds true with user-submitted images, which could contain malware that could infect your back-end processing systems, or worse, your end users. We discussed the importance of security with images in "Secure Image Delivery" on page 270, and it's worth reviewing that section to understand the risks user-generated image content can present to your imaging workflow.

To get these images from the chaotic state they are in to a master image, we can imagine a process that runs upon user upload and normalizes the images to a standard set of dimensions, format, visual quality, and metadata to protect our users' privacy.

But wait! Due to the nonuniform nature of these images, it's very likely that the offline process will run unpredictably, since some images can be processed quickly due to their file size (small) and image format (JPEG), while others will take considerably longer due to factors like format, file size, and resolution (in terms of pixel density and dimension), and image metadata. These factors will be covered a little later in this chapter when we discuss the factors that influence how long it takes to process an image.

Once our image processor has completed its work of taming the user-generated content beast, we have once again arrived at our master image.

The News Site

While both e-commerce and social media sites have always been image-first in terms of content, news organizations haven't always been. Now they are moving in that direction, and one might find that their use cases are a bit different. For one, they often act as a hybrid of the formal Photo Shoot→Creative→Upload to DAM process we saw in the e-commerce example, and the "take a picture with your smartphone" we saw in the social media example. Let's put ourselves in the hypothetical newsroom of our news site.

While much of our site's content is going to be text, more and more frequently, news media is leading stories with large images. For featured content, it's not uncommon to see accompanying galleries of high-resolution, beautiful images. This content typically comes from many different sources: syndicated content providers, photojournalists who work for the site, freelance photographers, and social media for "eyes on the ground" coverage.

To get it on our site, we will definitely need an intermediate processing step. While occasionally less meticulous than an e-commerce store's creative department would be as far as retouching, there is often a very heavy amount of photo editing in terms of cropping images coming in from the field. In fact, cropping might be the second-most popular image transformation performed next to resizing, because the story might require particular focus on a specific part of an image to tell the story.

In a news site, since images are often catalogued for possible later use in a story that might require similar imagery, some sort of centralized DAM is required in order to facilitate image indexing. Once the final, visually correct version of the image with all of the relevant cropping has been generated, both it and the original image are uploaded to the DAM. And again, we have arrived at our master image.

Business Logic and Watermarking

Before we get to the fun part—making the images that will be displayed on your site —it's also important to discuss business logic.

In some cases, business logic for web imagery boils down to ensuring that each image displayed contains a watermark—usually a company logo—on each image delivered from the site. While this sounds easy enough, it often comes with pitfalls. For example:

- Do you want the logo to always remain the same size? If so, then you'll need to make sure that you apply it *after* you have resized the master image to the final dimensions of your derivative image.

- Do you need it to be semitransparent? Then your image toolchain would ideally support file formats that have an alpha channel, like GIF and PNG, and your imaging software would support an operation that alters the *opacity* of the watermark.

In the next section, we will discuss a method to watermark an image by performing a composition of two images using some of the great open source image tools that are available freely online.

In addition to watermarking, companies occasionally have a requirement that each image delivered on the site contains copyright or other information embedded in the image file's metadata. While invisible to end users, this information can be useful to content producers who want to demonstrate ownership of the image. Usually, this data is encoded into the IPTC (a standard created by the International Press Telecommunications Council) metadata segment of the file, but it's not uncommon to also have the data encoded into the Exif segment of the file. If it's important for your use case, most graphics libraries will copy these segments from the master image to any derivative images, but it's worth making sure yours does. In some cases, image optimizing software strips out these segments since they often add unseen "bloat" to the image; however, this might not be bloat at all for you!

Another important aspect of business logic is the dimensions of the images used on a site, since there is often a central UX department that sets standards to define what the site layout will be. Often, a single master image may need to be generated in a number of different sizes to accommodate the various uses throughout a site—for example, thumbnail, large, and high-resolution used for a zoomed-in view.

Revisiting each of the use cases described earlier, we can see where each might need one or many of these types of business logic:

- The e-commerce site almost certainly has a very specific set of sizes each product image must adhere to, to ensure visual consistency of products when they are displayed in various contexts (search page, product detail, etc.) across the site.
- The social media site will probably want some sort of unobtrusive watermark on the image to show provenance of the image in the event it's shared elsewhere on the Internet.
- The news site may have contractual obligations to its freelance photographers stipulating that their images contain embedded copyright information.

Now, with some of this business background in mind, let's make some derivative images!

Hello, Images

Now that you know what it takes to get a master image into your system and some of the things you'll need to keep in mind to ensure your images meet your business goals, let's figure out what it takes to get the derivative images created from it. The following steps are relevant regardless of whether you run an e-commerce, social media, or news site—in each of those cases, we rarely if ever want to deliver our master image to an end user.

Getting Started with a Derivative Image Workflow

At its most basic, just about every operating system nowadays comes with an image viewer that contains basic editing capability allowing one to resize, crop, and even do minor color and sharpness corrections. Adobe Photoshop is an incredibly common tool for graphic designers to use for this very purpose, and comes with even more bells and whistles than the built-in photo editor on your computer. If you have a lot of time on your hands and a small number of master images to read and a small number of derivative images to create, then this method might be fine for you. Once you get past the point of a few dozen master images, however, it would be wise to move beyond this laborious work and into a fully automated workflow.

The easiest workflow you can start out with also has a nice ability to scale quite well as your image library grows: simple scripts that orchestrate command-line programs that read in your master images and output your derivative images. Let's dig in and see how we can take a library of master images, resize them to a small number of pre-set sizes, and convert them to some of the new formats supported by browsers.

ImageMagick

Next to Adobe Photoshop, ImageMagick is one of the most well-known image manipulation software suites, and also one of the most versatile. It's an open source, Apache-licensed tool that runs on just about every operating system (Windows, MacOS, and Linux, to name a few), has interfaces for just about every programming language (Python, Ruby, Perl, C/C++, Java, among many others), and allows you to do a huge number of transformations on an input image. Covering all of its capabilities would require a book of its own, but suffice it to say, it can handle our most basic use cases of resizing and converting to different image formats quite well.

 This chapter will spend a good amount of time diving into Image-Magick's command-line utilities, but you can find a list of tools, both command-line and GUI, to suit many different image-related use cases in Appendix B.

To begin, visit the ImageMagick website (*http://www.imagemagick.org/script/binary-releases.php*) and download and install the binary version that's appropriate for your operating system. The binaries on the ImageMagick website are a good starting point, because they offer built-in support for high performance output formats like progressive JPEG and WebP, but they do have some limitations in that they don't support other high performance formats like JPEG 2000 and JPEG XR. A word to the wise: any time you download binaries from the Internet, it's worth spending some time making sure that what you downloaded is what the developer uploaded. The Image-

Magick site offers a message digest file that allows you to compare the SHA256 hash of your local file with the one that should exist on the server. If they don't match, don't use it!

Compiling ImageMagick

Support for JPEG 2000 in ImageMagick requires manually compiling the software. The steps for doing so are covered here (*https://www.imagemagick.org/script/install-source.php*). In general, it's useful to have all of your supporting libraries and binaries in place before beginning the process. In particular, installing OpenJPEG for JPEG 2000 support, libwebp for WebP support, and the JxrDecApp and JxrEncApp located somewhere in your path for JPEG XR support would be required at a minimum to add support for these formats. There are also some optimizations you can make by compiling ImageMagick with OpenMP to improve parallelization, libjpeg-turbo to speed up JPEG decoding and encoding, and OpenCL to leverage GPU processing for certain operations. Luckily, the `configure` script that comes with ImageMagick is well documented and very verbose about its operations, so you can quickly tell when you're missing a dependency, or if the script isn't able to locate it.

Let's start by creating a project directory and populating it with some sample master images. We'll use this (*https://www.flickr.com/photos/image-catalog/18502982581*) freely licensed image to start with, since it's a good representation of a high-quality master image we might see in some of the use cases we covered earlier in this chapter:

```
$ mkdir -p images/master images/derivative
$ wget "http://bit.ly/hpi-ops-sample" -O images/master/master1.jpg
```

Now we're ready to take ImageMagick for a spin. Here, we'll have ImageMagick read in our master image using the `convert` command and change the output format to a lossless WebP. We'll also have ImageMagick convert the same image to a PNG, so we can compare. We'll then use ImageMagick's `identify` command to tell us a little about the images we created:

```
$ convert images/master/master1.jpg \
         -define webp:lossless=true images/derivative/master1.webp
$ convert images/master/master1.jpg images/derivative/master1.png
```

We now have a WebP and PNG version of our master image. Easy, right?

The `identify` command that ships with ImageMagick is an indispensable tool for anyone working on images. Without any command-line arguments, it outputs basic information about an image. Let's take a look at its output for the PNG:

```
$ identify master1.png
master1.png PNG 4000x2670 4000x2670+0+0 8-bit sRGB 22.12MB 0.030u 0:00.030
```

We can see some useful information, such as its format (PNG), dimensions
(4000x2670), colorspace and depth (8-bit sRBG), size (22.12MB), and how long it
took to read the file (0.030u 0:00.030).

Doing the same for our WebP image, we see the following:

```
$ identify master1.webp
Decoded /var/tmp/magick-62187w4ZOgPPXPHwt. Dimensions: 4000 x 2670 .
       Format: lossy. Now saving...
Saved file /var/tmp/magick-62187MoIDfyfUBubq
master1.webp PAM 4000x2670 4000x2670+0+0 8-bit TrueColor sRGB 42.72MB 0.000u
   0:00.000
```

While largely similar to the output we saw for PNG, one interesting thing about the
preceding output for the WebP is that ImageMagick doesn't support extracting this
information natively from WebP images, and therefore needs to extract it to a temporary format that has a significantly larger size in bytes (42.72 MB) than the WebP it
was derived from, which was about 6.1 MB on disk.

So why do we care about identify? Well, first and foremost, it's an indispensable tool
when you're debugging issues with an image, such as corrupt file metadata, or for
understanding the actual contents of the image and its metadata segments without
opening up a hex editor. While the previous output shows identify at its most basic,
there are a huge number of command-line options available to the identify command, all of which are worth exploring. One of the most valuable is the -verbose
option, which dumps a large amount of information about an image. Running it on
the master image, we get a mouthful of interesting data:

```
$ identify -verbose images/master/master1.jpg
Image: images/master/master1.jpg
  Format: JPEG (Joint Photographic Experts Group JFIF format)
  Mime type: image/jpeg
  Class: DirectClass
  Geometry: 4000x2670+0+0
  Resolution: 300x300
  Print size: 13.3333x8.9
  Units: PixelsPerInch
  Type: TrueColor
  Endianess: Undefined
  Colorspace: sRGB
  Depth: 8-bit
  Channel depth:
    red: 8-bit
    green: 8-bit
    blue: 8-bit
  Channel statistics:
    Pixels: 10680000
```

```
Red:
  min: 0 (0)
  max: 255 (1)
  mean: 97.7792 (0.383448)
  standard deviation: 72.505 (0.284333)
  kurtosis: -0.979603
  skewness: 0.609351
  entropy: 0.97042
Green:
  min: 0 (0)
  max: 255 (1)
  mean: 112.28 (0.440314)
  standard deviation: 66.938 (0.262502)
  kurtosis: -0.934222
  skewness: 0.400476
  entropy: 0.983699
Blue:
  min: 0 (0)
  max: 255 (1)
  mean: 120.169 (0.471252)
  standard deviation: 64.9808 (0.254827)
  kurtosis: -1.05091
  skewness: 0.0985773
  entropy: 0.985951
Image statistics:
  Overall:
    min: 0 (0)
    max: 255 (1)
    mean: 110.076 (0.431671)
    standard deviation: 68.2158 (0.267513)
    kurtosis: -0.994197
    skewness: 0.359281
    entropy: 0.980024
Rendering intent: Perceptual
Gamma: 0.454545
Chromaticity:
  red primary: (0.64,0.33)
  green primary: (0.3,0.6)
  blue primary: (0.15,0.06)
  white point: (0.3127,0.329)
Background color: white
Border color: srgb(223,223,223)
Matte color: grey74
Transparent color: black
Interlace: None
Intensity: Undefined
Compose: Over
Page geometry: 4000x2670+0+0
Dispose: Undefined
Iterations: 0
Compression: JPEG
Quality: 96
```

```
Orientation: Undefined
Properties:
  date:create: 2016-04-21T10:03:16-04:00
  date:modify: 2015-06-05T17:01:42-04:00
  exif:ApertureValue: 4970854/1000000
  exif:CFAPattern: 2, 0, 2, 0, 0, 1, 1, 2
  exif:Contrast: 0
  exif:Copyright: gowildimages.com
  exif:CustomRendered: 0
  exif:DateTime: 2013:06:20 18:14:25
  exif:DateTimeDigitized: 2013:03:11 09:31:34
  exif:DateTimeOriginal: 2013:03:11 09:31:34
  exif:DigitalZoomRatio: 1/1
  exif:ExifOffset: 484
  exif:ExifVersion: 48, 50, 51, 48
  exif:ExposureBiasValue: 0/6
  exif:ExposureMode: 1
  exif:ExposureProgram: 1
  exif:ExposureTime: 1/500
  exif:FileSource: 3
  exif:Flash: 16
  exif:FNumber: 56/10
  exif:FocalLength: 500/10
  exif:FocalLengthIn35mmFilm: 50
  exif:FocalPlaneResolutionUnit: 4
  exif:FocalPlaneXResolution: 5488689/32768
  exif:FocalPlaneYResolution: 5488689/32768
  exif:GainControl: 0
  exif:GPSInfo: 1140
  exif:GPSLatitude: 27/1, 485473/10000, 0/1
  exif:GPSLatitudeRef: N
  exif:GPSLongitude: 86/1, 433530/10000, 0/1
  exif:GPSLongitudeRef: E
  exif:GPSVersionID: 2, 2, 0, 0
  exif:ImageDescription: A stupa under snow (left) on the trail to Tengboche
                        monastery (centre). Mt Everest (8850m) is making
                        clouds just left of centre, with Lhotse (8498m)
                        partly obscured just to the right. Far right is
                        Ama Dablam peak.
  exif:ISOSpeedRatings: 100
  exif:LightSource: 0
  exif:Make: NIKON CORPORATION
  exif:MaxApertureValue: 10/10
  exif:MeteringMode: 5
  exif:Model: NIKON D600
  exif:ResolutionUnit: 2
  exif:Saturation: 0
  exif:SceneCaptureType: 0
  exif:SceneType: 1
  exif:SensingMethod: 2
  exif:Sharpness: 0
  exif:ShutterSpeedValue: 8965784/1000000
```

```
exif:Software: Adobe Photoshop Lightroom 4.4 (Windows)
exif:SubjectDistanceRange: 0
exif:SubSecTimeDigitized: 40
exif:SubSecTimeOriginal: 40
exif:thumbnail:Compression: 6
exif:thumbnail:JPEGInterchangeFormat: 1348
exif:thumbnail:JPEGInterchangeFormatLength: 19066
exif:thumbnail:ResolutionUnit: 2
exif:thumbnail:XResolution: 72/1
exif:thumbnail:YResolution: 72/1
exif:WhiteBalance: 0
exif:XResolution: 300/1
exif:YResolution: 300/1
jpeg:colorspace: 2
jpeg:sampling-factor: 1x1,1x1,1x1
signature: 23a119d052552e6cc10619e2737aceaf6d455d4382eb057df4740fb6
unknown: 2
Profiles:
  Profile-8bim: 19680 bytes
  Profile-exif: 20420 bytes
  Profile-icc: 3144 bytes
  Profile-iptc: 505 bytes
    City[1,90]: 0x00000000: 254700 -%
    unknown[2,0]:
    Keyword[2,25]: Ama Dablam
    Keyword[2,25]: Lhotse
    Keyword[2,25]: Mount Everest
    Keyword[2,25]: Tengboche
    Keyword[2,25]: blue sky
    Keyword[2,25]: clouds
    Keyword[2,25]: forest
    Keyword[2,25]: monastery
    Keyword[2,25]: mountain
    Keyword[2,25]: peak
    Keyword[2,25]: ridge
    Keyword[2,25]: snow
    Keyword[2,25]: stupa
    Keyword[2,25]: summit
    Keyword[2,25]: trail
    Keyword[2,25]: trekking
    Keyword[2,25]: valley
    Created Date[2,55]: 20130311
    Created Time[2,60]: 093134
    unknown[2,62]: 20130311
    unknown[2,63]: 093134
    Copyright String[2,116]: gowildimages.com
    Caption[2,120]: A stupa under snow (left) on the trail to Tengboche
                    monastery (centre). Mt Everest (8850m) is making
                    clouds just left of centre, with Lhotse (8498m)
                    partly obscured just to the right. Far right is
                    Ama Dablam peak.
  Profile-xmp: 11162 bytes
```

```
Artifacts:
  filename: images/master/master1.jpg
  verbose: true
Tainted: False
Filesize: 7.676MB
Number pixels: 10.68M
Pixels per second: 381.43GB
User time: 0.000u
Elapsed time: 0:01.000
Version: ImageMagick 6.9.3-0 Q16 x86_64 2016-02-10 http://www.imagemagick.org
```

Many of these fields are self-explanatory and some are wildly esoteric, but there are a number of key fields we want to pay attention to because they provide us with important information that could influence how we optimize or manipulate the images.

Resolution

First, we can see that the master image has a resolution of 300 DPI. This is important, because while it may be a visually beautiful image suitable for print in a magazine, it's certainly too high for publishing on the Web, where images are often at most 72 DPI or less. Since 300 DPI images are much more dense, data-wise, than their 72 DPI brethren, they could take significantly longer to process into a derivative image, so be sure to factor that in when building your high performance image workflow if you have many 300 DPI images in your master image catalog.

Interlace

Looking next at the `Interlace` field, we can see it is set to `None`, which means it's a baseline JPEG. If the image were a progressive JPEG, which was discussed earlier in Chapter 4, this value would be set to `JPEG`.

Quality

Another important field is `Quality`, which can be somewhat misleading. The quality of the JPEG is unfortunately not deterministic since it's not encoded anywhere in file metadata or anywhere else at creation time, and so tools like `iden tify` have to make a best guess by looking at the image's quantization tables. They're generally pretty close to what was input when the image was initially created, but not always. In the case of this image, we can see that the `Quality` was determined to be 96. Again, that's great for print, but almost certainly too high for delivering over the Web, as discussed in Chapter 13.

Properties

Farther down in the output, we see the contents of the Exif metadata within the `Properties` field. In the case of our master image, there is a lot of it, containing information ranging from when and where the photo was taken, the f-stop settings used for the photo, and even the make and model of the camera. There's also a little stowaway—an Exif thumbnail image, which is nearly 19 KB in size.

Our image's Exif segment also contains GPS coordinates of where the photo was taken, which, as we discussed in our social media use case, means that you might inadvertently leak sensitive data if you didn't strip it.

Profiles

The `Profiles` field displays information about the various profiles embedded in the image. In particular, we can see that our sample file contains a Photoshop-proprietary 8 BIM profile that's nearly 20 KB; a 20 KB Exif profile; a 3 KB ICC color profile; a 500-byte IPTC profile containing scene, keyword, and copyright data; and an 11 KB XMP embedded into it. Just think, if this image were delivered over the Web, not only would it be sent at too high of a resolution and JPEG encoding quality, it would also have over 50 KB of extra metadata baggage that would be invisible and largely useless to the casual end user.

A Note About Image Metadata Segments

Some metadata segments are especially important to retain, or at least take into consideration. Take, for example, color profiles, which ensure that the image contains visually correct colors when displayed on a screen. Color profiles are particularly important for companies that sell goods that depend on accurate colors, like a clothing or paint store. Many companies in these lines of business will tell you that a number of online returns happen because the color of the actual item was different than what was shown online. Unfortunately, some color profiles are rather large, which led Facebook to develop its own ICC profile, called *TinySRGB*, which weighs in at 524 bytes and is embedded into every photo on the site. More details about it and Facebook's rationale for creating it can be found on their website (*http://bit.ly/2aTjnJ7*).

Another metadata segment worth mentioning is the orientation data contained in Exif. This is where certain manufacturers keep information about the orientation of the camera when the photo was taken. If you've ever noticed an image on the Web that was inexplicably displayed sideways, it might have had its Exif orientation information removed, or in some cases, the browser didn't correctly support Exif-based rotation. In fact, the browser world is rather torn on the subject; on desktop versions of Chrome, Safari, Firefox, and Internet Explorer/Edge, Exif orientation data is ignored when the image is wrapped in an HTML `<img>` tag. But if the image URL is on its own in a tab? In all browsers but IE and Edge, the image is rotated according to Exif. Only Safari Mobile rotates images when they're in an `<img>` tag. How you want to handle this oddly high level of inconsistency is up to you, but if you think your images might contain relevant orientation data, like we might see in the social media or news use cases, you may consider automatically rotating the images in your image workflow, rather than relying on browsers to do the right thing.

So a word to the wise: make sure you don't get too overzealous when trying to save bytes on your images!

A Simple Derivative Image Workflow Using Bash

We've covered ImageMagick and two of its utilities, convert and identify. Now we're going to put them into action as part of a simple high performance images workflow.

Let's start with the project folder structure we laid out earlier:

```
images
 |-> derivative
 |-> master
```

Imagine that we had a number of our source images in the *master* folder, and that we wanted to convert all of them into three different sizes for our responsive website, with a progressive JPEG version and a WebP version. We could write a simple bash script that takes convert through its paces to generate our derivative images:

```bash
#!/bin/bash

INPUT=images/master/*.jpg
OUTPUT=images/derivative
Q=75

mkdir -p $OUTPUT/{100,300,800}

for f in $INPUT
do
    echo "Processing: $f"
    fn_ext=$(basename "$f")
    fn="${fn_ext%.*}"
    convert $f -resize 100x100 -interlace Plane \
            -quality $Q $OUTPUT/100/$fn.jpg
    convert $f -resize 100x100 \
            -define webp:lossless=false \
            -quality $Q $OUTPUT/100/$fn.webp
    convert $f -resize 300x300 -interlace Plane \
            -quality $Q $OUTPUT/300/$fn.jpg
    convert $f -resize 300x300 \
            -define webp:lossless=false \
            -quality $Q $OUTPUT/300/$fn.webp
    convert $f -resize 800x800 -interlace Plane \
            -quality $Q $OUTPUT/800/$fn.jpg
    convert $f -resize 800x800 \
            -define webp:lossless=false \
            -quality $Q $OUTPUT/800/$fn.webp
done
```

Let's examine the output of our script:

```
images/derivative/100:
56K  master1.jpg
2.1K master1.webp

images/derivative/300:
72K master1.jpg
16K master1.webp

images/derivative/800:
total 600
183K master1.jpg
114K master1.webp
```

One thing you may notice in this output is that the JPEGs are much larger than the equivalent WebP. For example, the 100-pixel version of the image is 56 KB in JPEG format, while only 2.1 KB as a WebP. What gives? As mentioned in "Business Logic and Watermarking" on page 280, ImageMagick copies over the metadata from the original image. That means these tiny images have many times more metadata than actual image content! In the next section, we'll make sure we strip it out, as we don't need that extra weight on our sites for this particular image.

So there we have it: a very simple workflow using ImageMagick and bash. Clearly, there is a lot of room to improve the script, but it's a start, and perhaps good enough to work for sites that have a small number of images. One possible improvement to this script would be to incorporate business logic into it as we discussed earlier, for example, by adding a watermark to each image. We can easily do this by adding a composite command, like so:

```
convert images/master/master1.jpg -resize 1000x1000  \
        -interlace Plane -quality 75 images/master/logo.gif \
        -gravity NorthWest -geometry 250x250+10 \
        -composite images/derivative/master1_watermark.jpg
```

The result of this command should look something like Figure 14-1.

Figure 14-1. Image with watermark

We now have a set of derivative images that meet our responsive website layout requirements, follow some of the best practices in terms of image format, and meet our business requirements. Not bad for a few lines of `bash`.

Now that we've created a simple script to generate offline derivatives, it's time to kick things up a notch. First, one thing that's seriously lacking in the previous example is that everything is done serially. Image processing is an extremely computationally expensive operation. In this day and age, even the most basic machines have many CPU cores, so it makes sense that we'd want to leverage all of the horsepower we have at our fingertips to process our image catalog. One incredibly simple way of adding a little parallelism is to add a simple function to our script and have it run in parallel by backgrounding the function, then waiting until all tasks are complete before starting on the next. At the same time, let's also give it a couple more output sizes to crunch to accommodate high-resolution displays:

```
#!/bin/bash

INPUT=images/master/*.jpg
OUTPUT=images/derivative
Q=75

mkdir -p $OUTPUT/{100,300,800,1000,2000}

process_image() {
```

```
# $1 - input
# $2 - size
# $3 - filename

convert $1 -resize $2x$2 -interlace Plane \
            -quality $Q $OUTPUT/$2/$3.jpg
convert $1 -resize $2x$2 \
            -define webp:lossless=false \
            -quality $Q $OUTPUT/$2/$3.webp
}

for infile in $INPUT
do
    echo "Processing: $infile"
    fn_ext=$(basename "$infile")
    outfile="${fn_ext%.*}"

    for size in 100 300 800 1000 2000
    do
        process_image $infile $size $outfile &
    done
    wait
done
```

On my system, that small change improved performance by more than 30% even while adding two extra sizes—not too bad for a quick and dirty script. While there are clearly improvements that can be made here, the point is that it doesn't take much to get a little more performance out of your system. Of course, scripts like this can be quickly outgrown, which leads us to the concept of build systems.

An Image Build System

As we saw with the simple bash script examples, it's not difficult to write a bare-bones system for image processing. However, as many web developers have discovered over the years, there is a lot of complexity and repetition that comes with creating a site, so it makes sense to have a system in place that helps assemble all of the pieces into one coherent build. In fact, the concept of a build system that helps get all of the right pieces in place is almost as old as software—as old hands in C or C++ development know, a Makefile is often a source of amazement (and frustration, when it doesn't work well) at its ability to orchestrate a number of complex tasks to build a piece of software.

Some of the most popular systems to do this today in the web development world are task runners, which are often written in JavaScript and leverage the amazing infrastructure behind the Node.js project (*https://www.nodejs.org/*). The two most popular are Grunt (*http://gruntjs.com/*) and Gulp (*http://gulpjs.com/*). Both of these systems are incredibly simple to use, as well as roughly similar to one another in function and syntax. Take a look at the landscape of these build systems, and choose the one that works best for you and your project.

Taking the bare-bones `bash` system as a reference, we can translate and improve upon it using a Gulp task. To get started, you first need to install Node. The instructions to do so are well documented on the Node site, and there are installers for just about every major platform. From there, it should be as simple as invoking `npm`, Node's package manager, to install Gulp:

```
$ npm install --global gulp-cli
$ npm install --save-dev gulp
```

At this point, you should have Gulp installed on your machine. Now it's time to get a couple of plug-ins that will allow us to resize images, as well as optimize them. Before you do so, make sure that you have ImageMagick installed, since the `gulp-image-resize` plug-in uses it to modify the images. If you followed the steps earlier in this chapter, you should be good to go:

```
$ npm install --save-dev gulp-image-resize
$ npm install --save-dev gulp-imagemin
$ npm install --save mozjpeg
$ npm install --save imagemin-mozjpeg
$ npm install --global cwebp-bin
$ npm install --save imagemin-webp
$ npm install --save-dev gulp-pipes
```

Let's explore a few interesting bits about these commands.

First, two of them install binaries (`mozjpeg` and `cwebp-bin`) for mozjpeg and WebP image encoding. As mentioned earlier, there are some security implications to using binaries from nontrusted sources. However, both of these Node packages build the files from source, which is good, but much of it is done out of sight from the end user. It's up to you to trust that the binaries they create do what you expect them to. If you don't want to use them, and if there is a system-wide version of the mozjpeg and WebP tool sets already available on your machine, then you don't need to install either package.

Another thing that might stick out to those not familiar with Node is the different save commands, particularly `--save-dev`, `--save`, and `--global`. Described most simply, they are different ways you can manage package dependencies for your project. The commands listed are recommended by the developers of each package, so they should be fine defaults to start. Your Gulp workflow might require them to be different, however, so take some time to understand the various options available to you.

Let's look at our Gulp file, and see what it does:

```javascript
var gulp = require('gulp');
var imagemin = require('gulp-imagemin');
var mozjpeg = require('imagemin-mozjpeg');
var pipes = require('gulp-pipes');
var resize = require('gulp-image-resize');
var webp = require('imagemin-webp');

gulp.task('highperf_images', function() {

    var sizes = [100, 300, 800, 1000, 2000];
    var stream;

    for (size in sizes) {
        stream = gulp.src('images/master/**/*.{jpg,png,tiff}')
            .pipe(resize({
                width: sizes[size],
                height: sizes[size],
                upscale: false,
                format: 'jpg'
            }))
            .pipe(imagemin({
                use: [mozjpeg({
                    quality: 75,
                    progressive: true,
                    tune: 'ms-ssim'
                })]
            }))
            .pipe(gulp.dest('images/derivative/' + sizes[size] + '/'))
            .pipe(webp({
                quality: 75
            })())
            .pipe(gulp.dest('images/derivative/' + sizes[size] + '/'))
    }
    return stream;
});
```

As you can see, there aren't many more lines of code here than in our simple bash version of the script. If we look at it line by line, however, we can see some subtle but important differences. For instance, at the beginning of the file, you must reference the packages that actually do the heavy lifting—remember, Gulp (and the others) are just task runners, and rely on modules or plug-ins to do work. Next, we create a Gulp task. If you're familiar with JavaScript, this is just a simple JavaScript function that Gulp knows how to turn into tasks it can perform. Within the task, we create an array of output sizes, and then loop through each to create derivative images for each master. The nice thing about Gulp is that it has a lot of built-in parallelization, whereas our bash solution didn't without a little work (and even then, it left a lot to be desired), so each input and output image is processed in parallel, greatly reducing processing time and keeping all CPUs on the machine nicely busy.

Within the task, the real work is being performed by three different pipes: one to resize the master images to our desired derivative output size and convert any non-JPEG master files to JPEG (by default, the resizer will use the input format as the output); another to optimize the JPEG output using the mozjpeg encoder; and lastly another to create a WebP version of the file as we'd done with the bash script.

To execute the Gulp task, first make sure your Gulp file is saved as *gulpfile.js* to the root of your project, so that the *images* directory is immediately above it. Then, it's as simple as:

```
$ gulp highperf_images
[17:21:13] Using gulpfile ~/Desktop/tmp/book/gulpfile.js
[17:21:13] Starting 'highperf_images'...
[17:21:14] gulp-imagemin: Minified 1 image (saved 55.05 kB - 96.4%)
[17:21:14] gulp-imagemin: Minified 1 image (saved 59.8 kB - 82.4%)
[17:21:14] gulp-imagemin: Minified 1 image (saved 95.83 kB - 52.6%)
[17:21:14] gulp-imagemin: Minified 1 image (saved 120.84 kB - 47.4%)
[17:21:15] gulp-imagemin: Minified 1 image (saved 320.43 kB - 37.8%)
[17:21:16] Finished 'highperf_images' after 2.53 s
```

With that, we now have a very nice build system to use for creating high performance images for your site. What next? There are some Gulp plug-ins that allow you to process only files that have changed, which could be worth investigating if you frequently add new images to your site, since the current task will reprocess every image each time it's run. There are also a number of other plug-ins to imagemin that do things like optimize PNGs, animated GIFs, and SVGs. You may want to investigate these if you find that these plug-ins add value to the images you serve on your site.

A Build System Checklist

A system like this is particularly useful if you:

- Have a small-to-medium image catalog that is fairly static
- Have a small-to-medium number of image transformations that need to be performed on each image
- Don't mind writing a little JavaScript to orchestrate your image creation workflow
- Have a business or other requirement that all images are generated in advance:
  — There is a manual review process for each image
  — It is not cost-effective to transform the original images in any other way because they are so large (in terms of files or size), have a high information density (300 DPI), or leverage a nonstandard format (PSD, TIFF, RAW)

- Are not yet ready to build and scale a service that can convert images dynamically

If you have a large number of images on your site, or if the images on your site change frequently, then it may be worth looking into a dynamic image optimizer.

High Volume, High Performance Images

In the last couple of sections we've discussed using shell-based tools to resize and optimize images. In general, these methods can scale very nicely to an image library sized on the order of thousands of master images, and require a very low level of effort to get started. However, relying only on shell commands and task runners for your image build system has some pitfalls.

First and foremost, the tools we've discussed so far don't easily scale horizontally: the larger your image library and number of output images you create, the longer the tasks will take to run on a single machine. You can certainly speed things up by adding more CPU, memory, and disk, but there could come a time when you will outgrow the solution.

Second, there is a lot of hardcoding of attributes like image sizes—what happens if you want to change them? You'd need to reprocess your entire image library. What happens if you want to change the encoding quality of your images? You'd need to reprocess your entire image library. As the number of master and derivative images grows, the amount of storage and management overhead grows as well. For example, if you had to ensure each image had to be copied to every web server in your cluster, you might quickly run into a huge management nightmare trying to keep everything in sync. Thus, it makes sense to discuss what it would take to create a dynamic image server that processes images on demand.

A Dynamic Image Server

Before we begin this section, it's worth pointing out that actually implementing a dynamic image resizing and optimizing server is a large topic to cover, and the design or code for one would not be possible to cover in a chapter. However, we can discuss some of the key attributes you should consider when designing and implementing your own, or choosing one from a third party.

At a very high level, the typical request flow through a dynamic image server is as follows:

1. Receive request
2. Parse request parameters
3. Download master image

4. Decode master image

5. Perform transformation

6. Encode derivative image

Let's break each of these steps down further, starting with Step 2

Parsing the request

Typically, dynamic image servers are invoked via an HTTP-based API. This API is often based on adding query string parameters, or as a RESTful path-based approach. For example, it could look something like this for a query string-based API:

http://dynamic.example.com/?w=300&h=300&format=webp&src=http://your site.com/master.jpg

Or like this for a RESTful API:

http://dynamic.example.com/resize/300x300/format/webp/http://your site.com/master.jpg

One great thing about a dynamic image server is that you can reference these URLs directly in your HTML, and only have to manage the master image. From there, your CDN or caching infrastructure would be responsible for storing and serving the derivative images. In contrast to the approach outlined in the previous sections, where all images are created out-of-band once and stored and served from disk, with a dynamic server, the images are often ephemeral.

System Tuning

Depending on the operating system your image server runs on, there are a number of different kernel and system parameters you can tune to achieve good performance, since many of the defaults aren't always the best for high-throughput servers. When it comes to the client-facing side of the request, there are a few parameters worth tuning:

TCP initial congestion window

This topic was all the rage back in 2010 after a study from Google showed that the default window of 4 was too small, and is still relevant today. Most modern operating systems set their initial congestion window to 10, but there could be benefit in increasing it even higher than that if you know you have good upstream connectivity and are connecting to well-connected clients, like a CDN server. In Linux, you can set this using the `ip route change` command; in Windows, you'd need to use the `netsh interface tcp set supplemental` command. In both operating systems, similar commands (`ip route show` for Linux;

`netsh interface tcp show supplemental` for Windows) can be used to view
the current initial congestion window setting.

TCP buffers

When writing packets to the network, it may make sense to increase how much
memory you allow the kernel to allocate to doing so. In Linux, you can do this by
increasing the `net.core.rmem_max` values in *etc/sysctl.conf* on most systems.

Open file descriptors

On Linux, file descriptors are used for network connections as well as "files" in
the traditional sense. If you expect to have a large number of inbound connections to your image server, or if you plan to process a number of files concur-
rently, you may need to increase the defaults to something high, like 64,000. You
can do this by updating the `fs.file-max` value in *etc/sysctl.conf*, and changing *etc/security/limits.conf* to have `* soft nofile 64000` and `* hard nofile 64000`.

Downloading the master image

Once the request has been received and parsed, the dynamic image server would then
download the master image from the origin web server. There are a number of things
to keep in mind for this step, since it will help you understand where performance
can be improved.

- The request to fetch the image will nearly always happen over HTTP if the file
  isn't available via a local filesystem, or a remote one that presents locally, like NFS
  or SMB. When this happens, latency and bandwidth to the origin web server is
  incredibly important, since no work can be done until the master image is downloaded. It is worth spending time ensuring this part of the request happens
  quickly and is tuned well, and caching is leveraged as much as possible where relevant.

- The size of the master image should be taken into consideration. In the beginning of this chapter, we discussed some of the use cases where we might see large
  master images. If your master images are larger than several hundred kilobytes, it
  could be worthwhile to convert them to a more reasonable size; often it makes
  sense to convert them to the largest size you will ever deliver over the Web. This
  will not only help when downloading the original image, but also when decoding
  it for further processing.

Decoding the master image

Next, the dynamic image server will decode the image into memory. We'll break this
down a bit, since some of it isn't exactly intuitive.

One thing in particular that's not immediately obvious is that an image's size in terms of bytes is not entirely reflective of how large the image will be in memory. Unless your master images are raw bitmaps (which I hope they aren't!), they are often compressed in one way or another. However, the dynamic image server needs to work with the images on a pixel-by-pixel basis to perform operations like resizing and chroma subsampling, which means it must first expand the image to its full size in terms of pixels in memory, and then do work on it. The more images worked on simultaneously, the more memory needed to process the image.

The other part that may not be entirely obvious is that the amount of CPU time spent on decoding the images can be a scaling factor. Again, something highly compressed, like a JPEG or WebP, will certainly take longer to decode than a simple format like bitmap. So it's worth keeping these things in mind, especially when it comes to scaling a service like a dynamic image server.

Transform!

When all of the work to decode the image has been completed, the dynamic image server next needs to perform whichever transformations were requested. Oftentimes, this work is not particularly CPU-intensive, like resizing (since much of the time is spent getting the pixel-by-pixel representation of the image), but there are some convolutional effects that could be more intensive to process, thereby affecting scalability and/or latency of the service.

Encoding the derivative image

Finally, once the image is visually correct from a transformation perspective, the last thing the dynamic image server needs to do is encode and deliver the image. Here again is a potentially CPU-intensive operation, since many of the new high performance encoders are often extremely intensive in their efforts to squeeze every last byte out of the file. In general, JPEG is one of the fastest formats to encode, mostly because it has been around for a while and there are good encoders out there, like libjpeg-turbo (*http://www.libjpeg-turbo.org/*), which leverage CPU instructions that are optimized for doing vector operations very quickly. However, some new optimizing encoders, like MozJPEG, are actually not great candidates for real-time image manipulation, because they are much slower to encode than libjpeg-turbo. It's a good idea to benchmark a few of these yourself to understand the performance characteristics of each, and how they affect the scalability of your dynamic image resizing service. In the end, it may be worth getting slightly more hardware in order to serve and deliver smaller and more optimized images.

Summary

Colin Bendell and Tim Kadlec

People love images. We make more images than ever and we share more images than ever (22,338 uploaded per second between Facebook, Snapchat, and Whatsapp). The increasing amount of imagery available to us is reflected in user expectations for websites. Sites are expected to be visually rich and compelling, and effectively using imagery is a big part of that. Serving these images to the wide variety of devices and browsers being used, in the most performant way possible, is a big challenge—one we've tried to help steer you through in this book.

Throughout the book we've looked at why performance matters online and the huge role images play in that performance. We've discussed the foundational concepts of digital imagery and how those concepts impact performance and compression. We looked at both lossless and lossy image formats in detail, looking at the role each plays and how to shave as many bytes as possible based on the image type.

We looked at how browsers load these images. Far from being purely about file size, performance can be affected by resource loading in the browser, as well as the device's memory and CPU. We looked at the challenges presented by responsive images, and how new standards like <picture>, srcset, and Client Hints can help you provide the optimal image no matter the situation.

And we looked at how you can start to put all of this knowledge together to create a plan of attack for your organization that ensures a high level of performance and security.

So…What Do I Do Again?

If you managed to digest all of this in one read, you're cleverer than we are. These are important topics, but it's certainly a lot to absorb.

There are a lot of variables involved in determining the right approach for you and your organization to take; there's no clear formula that will lead you to image nirvana. That being said, here are a few safe strategies for you to begin the process.

Optimize for the Mobile Experience

- **Use WebP and JPEG 2000.** Android and Chrome users can benefit from WebP; iOS and Safari users can benefit from JPEG 2000. Both provide superior byte savings (and feature capabilities) over JPEG. Finally, for desktop users, use MozJPEG.

- **When using JPEG/WebP/JPEG 2000 images, take advantage of chroma subsampling.** Chroma subsampling not only leads to reduced file sizes, but if you use 4:2:0 subsampling, it also allows browsers to make clever optimizations to reduce the impact on memory and CPU drain—important considerations, particularly in our increasingly mobile world.

- **Send appropriately sized images to the browser.** Sending images that are larger than needed is one of the most common, and most troublesome, mistakes made online. It makes the browser work harder and costs your users precious time and bytes. For bonus points, use a breakpoint budget of ~24 KB (16 packets) per breakpoint.

- **Lazy-load images.** We know that users may not scroll very far and many images "below the fold" may not be seen. Delaying download of these images saves bandwidth and helps improve the web performance. Images are one of the easiest resources for the browser preloader to discover and can compete with dynamically loaded content, including JavaScript and API calls.

Optimize for the Different "Users"

There isn't just one user to consider for high performance images. It might be easy to assume that only the end consumer requirements need to be optimized. In reality, there are many "stakeholders"—each with different opinions and competing interests for high performance images. It isn't just the end user experience that we have to manage.

- **Users want fast**, so optimize for the fewest bytes on the network and the fastest browser rendering.

  — **Ideal state**: Sending the smallest possible size of image for each port view and layout, using the best image formats, and using all the format-specific optimizations.

  — **Reality**: Users are a highly fragmented browser ecosystem, with different device sizes and variable network conditions that can result in hundreds of permutations (if not thousands) for each situation.

  — **Action**: Create performance budgets using groups of like-sized viewport ranges. Use the responsive images `srcset` and `sizes` HTML5 tags to let the browser pick the smallest image for the experience.

- **Creative teams care about aesthetics**, so optimize for the highest-quality possible.

  — **Ideal state**: High-resolution, high-DPR, lossless images. A web page or app should be pixel-perfect if you walk up to a 100-inch wall mount display.

  — **Reality**: The higher the quality, the larger the file size, which will negatively impact the user experience.

  — **Action**: Use SSIM to determine the lowest-quality index you can use in an image without the human eye noticing. If lossless is required, utilize newer formats such as WebP and JPEG 2000.

- **Web and dev teams want flexibility** to make changes to responsive layouts and art direction requirements easily without having to force reprocessing of an image library.

  — **Ideal state**: One image that CSS and JavaScript crops or scales to the necessary dimensions.

  — **Reality**: Using a "one size fits all" approach will serve the lowest common denominator, which will be targeted to the desktop and large monitor experience.

  — **Action**: Use HTML5 responsive images tags to support art direction (`<picture>` and `<source>`) and eliminate the need for client-side JavaScript.

- **Operations, infrastructure, and security teams** want fewer image files to back up and are concerned about long-running reprocessing jobs. They are also concerned with how to ensure that transforming images doesn't create other security vulnerabilities.

  — **Ideal state**: No images, or just one image per product.

— **Reality**: Images need to be resized, cropped, and watermarked. Unchecked, this can create many terabytes of data to back up and security concerns as images are transformed and manipulated.

— **Action**: Eliminate raster images and use vector (SVG) images wherever possible. Plan ahead and inform infrastructure of breakpoint requirements—strike a balance of storage requirements, disaster recovery requirements, and breakpoint volume. Finally, create a secure sandbox for any image transformation service to ensure that optimizing images doesn't create an enterprise vulnerability.

Creating Consensus

Images are awesome. There is no doubt that high performance images improve usability, reputation, and brand. There are many strategies, approaches, and opinions, but there is no silver bullet.

The best way to create consensus is to experience, firsthand, the pain and the benefit of high performance images. There are two strategies:

- Re-create the experience. Start with a histogram of performance experience and create a persona representing why a user is at that part of the curve. How do these users differ? Is the variation because of mobile hardware, screen size, CPU/RAM, network latency, or bandwidth? Finally, re-create these user experiences so that stakeholders and managers can experience that user. Either use real hardware so that everyone has an authentic experience, or create side-by-side videos of the experience using tools like WebPageTest.org.

- Visualize the results: you don't necessarily have to go to the full length of acquiring hardware and slowing down browser rendering. You can also show side-by-side comparisons of the output. Show how different sizes, formats, and other optimizations do not degrade the experience. This will demonstrate that you can preserve the experience while improving operations, performance, and other metrics.

With these strategies, together, we can make high performance images.

Raster Image Formats

Nick Doyle and Colin Bendell

There are many image formats to choose from, each with various capabilities and support from different browsers and platforms. As a result, selecting the right image can be challenging. Use the chart in Figure A-1 to help you select the ideal set of images to meet your needs.

		Features										Supported Browsers					
		Indexed Color	Full Color	Binary Transparency	Full Transparency	Chroma Subsampling	Progressive Loading	Animation	Lossy Compression	Lossless Compression	Byte Savings	Chrome (non iOS)	Chrome (iOS)	Safari (all)	Firefox (all)	IE / Edge (all)	Opera (desktop)
	GIF	✔	✗	✔	✗	✗	✔	✔	✔	✗	Poor	✔	✔	✔	✔	✔	✔
	JPEG	✗	✔	✗	✗	✔	✔	✗	✔	✗	Okay	✔	✔	✔	✔	>= 7	✔
PNG	Basic	✔	✔	✔	✔	✗	✔	✗	✔	✔	Poor	✔	✔	✔	✔	✔	✔
PNG	Animated	✔	✔	✔	✔	✗	✔	✔	✔	✔	Okay	✗	iOS 8+	>= 8	>= 3	✗	✗
	JPEG 2000	✗	✔	✗	✔	✔	✔	✗	✔	✔	Good	✗	✔	>= 5	✗	✗	✗
	JPEG XR	✗	✔	✗	✔	✔	✔	✗	✔	✔	Good	✗	✗	✗	✗	>= 10	✗
WebP	Basic	✗	✔	✗	✗	4:2:0	✗	✗	✔	✗	Good	>= 9	29 to 47	✗	✗	✗	>= 11.5
WebP	Extended	✗	✔	✗	✔	4:2:0	✗	✗	✔	✔	Good	>= 23	29 to 47	✗	✗	✗	>= 12.1
WebP	Animated	✗	✔	✗	✔	4:2:0	✗	✔	✔	✔	Good	>= 32	✗	✗	✗	✗	>= 20

Figure A-1. Raster image formats

Common Tools

Mike McCall

In Chapter 14 and others, you've read a lot about ImageMagick and some of the tools in the ecosystem. It's worth taking some time to investigate other utilities that, if perhaps not quite ready for a large-scale image workflow due to their interface (GUI) or performance (slow), could still prove useful. Since tastes vary, it's not unusual for two tools to provide similar functionality but with slightly different results, so try a few to see which one suits you best!

PNG Utilities

PNG is one of the formats that gets a lot of optimization attention. There are a few reasons for this. First, since it's a lossless format, there aren't a lot of dials you can tweak to sacrifice a bit of quality at the expense of fewer bytes. Second, it's a relatively straightforward format in terms of implementation, and has a number of parts of its binary format that aren't necessary for rendering the image. Lastly, PNG uses DEFLATE compression for its pixel data, and there have been a couple of attempts to improve it over the years.

pngcrush (http://pmt.sourceforge.net/pngcrush/)
> One of the more well-known PNG optimizers, pngcrush attempts to reduce the size of PNGs by trying a number of different filtering and compression methods, as well as removing unneeded metadata.

OptiPNG (http://optipng.sourceforge.net/)
> Similar to pngcrush in terms of methodology, OptiPNG has some performance benefits over its predecessor in that the trials used during filtering and compressing are performed in-memory.

pngquant (https://pngquant.org/)

A "lossy" PNG optimizer, pngquant leverages quantization algorithms to reduce the number of colors, and therefore, the perceived quality of the image. This has the effect of reducing the amount of data in the image, and in turn the number of bytes.

ZopfliPNG (https://github.com/google/zopfli)

Google has published a few research papers describing their work on better compression algorithms, and Zopfli is an output of those exercises. One of the more interesting attributes of Zopfli is that it retained compatibility with DEFLATE encoding, which means that it can be used to compress PNGs. To highlight this, as part of the Zopfli source distribution, it includes a command-line tool called zopflipng that encodes PNGs using Zopfli.

A nice breakdown of what it takes to compress and optimize a PNG, as well as a list of a few other tools, can be found on the OptiPNG site (*http://optipng.sourceforge.net/pngtech/optipng.html*).

JPEG Utilities

Since JPEG is by far the most prevalent image format on the Internet, there are a number of tools that have been built to optimize JPEGs in various ways. Many of these try to do clever things like optimizing the compression algorithms, often taking wildly different approaches.

cjpeg and jpegtran (part of most JPEG suites, like libjpeg/libjpeg-turbo/MozJPEG)

A Swiss Army knife for JPEGs, jpegtran has a number of features that allow you to do transformations like optimize Huffman tables, convert to progressive JPEG, as well as make visual changes like cropping, rescaling, and various forms of rotation. While usually used for encoding JPEGs, the cjpeg utility has some additional command-line arguments under the "Switches for wizards" help heading, like -qtables and -qslots, which allow you to use a different set of quantization values for encoding the image and tuning the chrominance and luminance of the output image. These settings aren't for the faint of heart, so make sure you read Chapter 4 closely before tweaking them. Some more details about them can be found here: *http://uw714doc.sco.com/en/jpeg/wizard.txt*.

JPEGrescan (https://github.com/kud/jpegrescan)

Previously a standalone utility, JPEGrescan employs a technique that is now included in the MozJPEG encoder, which means it's not only faster, but you can get its benefits just by running MozJPEG. If you want to go the standalone tool route, JPEGrescan has a number of optimizations it tries to do on the compression settings, and also includes options to remove Exif and JFIF metadata.

Adept (https://github.com/technopagan/adept-jpg-compressor)
> Described as the "adaptive JPEG compressor," Adept uses a novel approach to compression by looking for parts of the image that might be more compressible than others by leveraging a saliency algorithm to detect where to attempt higher compression levels.

Animated GIF Utilities

Animated GIFs have taken the Web by storm (again!). Unfortunately, many GIF authoring tools create poorly optimized images, but there are some tools available to help you.

gifsicle (http://www.lcdf.org/gifsicle/)
> Perhaps the best-known standalone tool for creating and optimizing animated GIFs, gifsicle can perform a number of different optimizations to animated GIFs. In particular, it performs a number of color optimizations to reduce file size.

giflossy (https://kornel.ski/lossygif)
> Based on gifsicle, giflossy implements lossy LZW (Lempel–Ziv–Welch, named after its creators) compression onto the tool, which allows for significantly smaller animated GIFs while sacrificing a little quality.

gifify (https://github.com/vvo/gifify)
> In contrast to gifsicle and giflossy, gifify's authoring tools are focused on creating optimized animated GIFs from video sources. It leverages giflossy for its optimizations.

GUI Utilities

For those who feel more comfortable with a GUI than stringing together commands at the command line, there are a few options out there that can be quite useful for those who prefer to use their mouse.

ImageOptim (https://imageoptim.com/)
> One image utility to rule them all? If you prefer a single GUI tool to numerous command-line utilities and use a Mac, ImageOptim might be the tool for you. It brings the best of many of the aforementioned tools to a simple-to-use GUI interface, and supports PNG, GIF, and JPEG input. Its drag-and-drop interface makes optimizing images a breeze.

RIOT (http://luci.criosweb.ro/riot/)
> Similar to ImageOptim, RIOT too supports optimizing PNG, GIF, and JPEG input. Unlike ImageOptim, though, RIOT is a Windows-only tool. The software also has a plug-in architecture allowing its functionality to be extended, and can

itself be used as a plug-in to popular Windows image tools like IrfanView or the cross-platform GIMP.

Caesium (https://saerasoft.com/caesium/)

A cross-platform tool that optimizes JPEGs and PNGs, Caesium has a nice GUI to help you process files one at a time or as a batch. It is available in a few different forms, including desktop GUI application, command-line utility, and mobile app.

Exif Utilities

Exif is one of the more interesting metadata attributes found in images, since it can contain valuable information, like copyright and ownership data, as well as add unnecessary bloat to your images. Exif is supported by both JPEG and TIFF formats. Here are a few utilities that can help you rein in the beast:

jhead (http://www.sentex.net/~mwandel/jhead/)

An incredibly easy-to-use tool to manage Exif metadata, jhead allows you to view the contents of an image's Exif segments, as well as perform operations like copying, adding, and removing. It also supports autorotating images based on Exif data, as well as allows you to copy Exif over when modifying the image using a tool like ImageMagick.

exiv2 (http://www.exiv2.org/)

While similar in spirit to jhead, exiv2 is a very powerful tool that comes as both a standalone utility and a C++ library. If you have a need for advanced Exif management, spend some time understanding exiv2 and all it can do for you.

exiftool (http://www.sno.phy.queensu.ca/~phil/exiftool/)

exiftool is another Exif management utility that comes as both a command-line tool and a Perl library. Similar to exiv2, it's an incredibly powerful tool that contains numerous options to add, view, edit, and delete Exif. It is well documented with a number of usage examples to help you add it to your workflow.

Evolution of <img>

Colin Bendell

High performance images is a complex subject partly because of the apparent fragmentation in the browser ecosystem. It is useful to examine the history of images on the Web and specifically the history of the HTML <img> tag.

1989: Inline Images, GIFs, and Patents

Images, the way we know them on the Web, almost didn't happen. The <img> tag is nearly ubiquitous in web development, so it is no surprise that nearly all modern application platforms and documents have followed in its path—supporting the same formats and styles. It wasn't that images weren't conceived of when Sir Tim Berners-Lee invented the Web; in fact, he used images and diagrams as part of his memo, proposing hypertext and the 18 elements. Inline images, however, were not one of the elements or use cases he described. Instead, the purpose of hypertext was to provide text and then link to documents. Those documents could be other hypertext files or binary files such as PostScript. It was assumed that the user would navigate to an image and not embed it into the text.

At the time, CERN was using NeXTSTEP, so it is not too surprising that PostScript and Encapsulated PostScript (EPS) were the primary image formats that the first-generation browsers could render natively in the browser application. This was mostly because NeXTSTEP provided handy APIs to render this content. Still, the expectation was that the user would select a hyperlink and the image would load in a separate window (see Figure C-1). Images were a hyperlink destination, not part of markup language.

By the time HTML 2.0 was formalized, the Mosaic browser on Mac had become immensely popular mostly because of its ability to inline images with the introduction of the new <img> element (see Figure C-2).

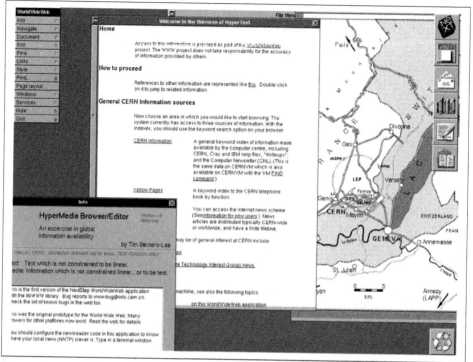

Figure C-1. World Wide Web browser on NeXTSTEP (1990); images and documents were opened in a new window

Figure C-2. Mosaic browser with inline images on Mac System 7 (~1992)

While EPS images were convenient for those on NeXTSTEP and Mac, they proved unpopular for cross-platform compatibility. Fueled partly by CompuServe's market penetration and the accessibility of documentation for the file format, GIF quickly became a universal image format on the Web. Not only did it yield smaller images, but those images were small enough to be used in web pages served over dial-up modems. It was the right format at the right time. Later, due to GIF patent issues and initial royalty demands by CompuServe, PNG was developed, but it has taken a long time to become as widely used.

Just as the now-infamous patent claims against GIF started to emerge, the community-driven image standards body (Joint Photographic Experts Group) produced a lossy image format now known as JPEG. JPEG had a lot of the advantages of GIF, such as an increased number of colors, while also producing small file sizes that were amenable to slow Internet connections. With the mainstream availability of SVGA monitors and cheap video cards that were capable of showing off 64,000 or more colors, JPEG had a strong appeal to graphic designers and web developers. Just like GIF earlier, JPEG was the right image format at the right time for a burgeoning web.

1995: HTML 2.0 and <img lowsrc>

The first HTML standard was completed by the IETF's HTML working group in early 1994, corralling all the various proposed tags and different browser implementations. (After 1996, the W3C maintained the HTML spec.) Even as the first standard was inked, Netscape continued to innovate with new tags focused on the utility of inline images and performance.

At this point, developers thought of images on the Web like this:

```
<img src="/fido_in_dc.jpg"
    title="Fido goes to Washington" />
```

Access to the Internet was just starting to take off in the US and other parts of the world. Windows being the dominant operating system for most households also meant that Netscape quickly became the dominant browser. Likewise, since most households used dial-up with the newly available 14.4 Kb and 28.8 Kb baud modems, performance was critical to both Netscape's success as well as Internet adoption.

Netscape 1.0 introduced the lowsrc attribute, which was later adopted by many of the other browsers and then eventually dropped. lowsrc allowed the browser to download a very small image (often a GIF) and then load the much larger size image. Thus, on a slow Internet connection, the user could interact with the page and get a sense of the page layout and content without having to wait for the high-resolution image. Unfortunately, we discarded this feature, only to run into the same problems again later with Responsive Web Design and Client Hints. The major downside of lowsrc was that Netscape would download both sizes, even if it was unnecessary.

At this point in time the savvy web developer would implement images in web pages like this:

```
<img src="/fido_in_dc.jpg"
    lowsrc="/dog.gif"
    alt="Fido the dog on the grass in front of the white house" />
```

2000: Dark Ages of Images—HTML 4.01, CSS, and the Status Quo

Not much changed in the intervening years. The lowsrc attribute was eventually discarded by the community. Cascading Style Sheets (CSS) and inline styles became the standard way to decorate and style images and HTML. HTML 4.01 was standardized by 2000 as the dot-com era boomed and busted.

The average consumer still used monitors with a resolution of 800×600 and 96 DPI screens. With all the excitement of dot-coms, images didn't see a lot of obvious evolution.

This was the dark ages of images on the Web.

Yet, during this time, vector graphics took on several lives that culminated with SVG (Scalable Vector Graphics). Eventually, through the adoption of Gecko-based browsers, then WebKit-based browsers, the SVG 1.1 standard became available to the mass market. Unfortunately, it wasn't until 2011, with Internet Explorer 9, that SVG was finally added to the then-most-used browser.

2007: Mobile! Mobile! Mobile!

It is cliché to say this, but the iPhone changed computing. Shortly after 2007 smartphones quickly became more and more prevalent in the hands of the consumers. This introduced a set of new problems for the Web—namely, smaller displays, touch interfaces, slower hardware, and slower network connections. Not to mention lack of Flash!

As a result of the constraints of processor power and the lack of Flash, developers increasingly deployed duplicate websites dedicated to mobile—colloquially known as mDot sites. Instead of being forced to pinch and zoom on the website, users were redirected to a website that had buttons and text at the right size for the display. These mobile websites shared a lot of similarities to WAP websites, and in fact many WAP or HTML3.2 websites were retrofitted to serve as the default mDot. The result was a very lightweight website that not only had very little JavaScript, but often very few images as well. Fortunately, Safari was a fully fledged HTML5 browser and supported all the latest image formats, including SVG.

Mobile websites had a tight connection with native apps. The original plan for apps on the iPhone was to "install" the website on the home screen. This quickly gave way to developer desire for a native app ecosystem. Despite the differences in underlying codebase and deployment, apps used many of the same design philosophies as the Web—making API calls and downloading images—to create a rich experience. Because of this shared history, mobile apps on Android and iOS treated images in much the same way. Core operating system libraries included image handling and supported all the same image formats as the Web.

Alas, not much changed in the ecosystem of images. You were expected to either use the same images for all of your websites, or regenerate them with a different filename so that you could show a smaller image or different orientation for smartphones and tablets.

2010: Responsive Web Design, Retina Displays, and Responsive Images

Images became really exciting in the second decade of the new millennium. Ethan Marcotte famously led the charge with his positional paper on how to create a Responsive Web (*http://alistapart.com/article/responsive-web-design*). Using CSS (and usually a dash of JavaScript), a single website could respond to the user's screen layout; that is, a user with a small screen and a user with a large screen could have a different website design but with one codebase. This solved a lot of problems for developers and users alike. First, it started the evolution away from separate mDot websites, which confused users and social media link sharing. More importantly, it solved the problem of feature fragmentation between the mDot, tDot, and desktop sites by unifying the codebase.

Mobile users were no longer second-class citizens on the Web. Beautiful, magnificent websites with rich images saturated our eyes. Finally!

Too bad I only had three bars of 3G cellular signal on a mobile device that was barely faster than a Pentium 3. RWD focused on design, but not necessarily on performance. Fortunately, much has been written on RWD performance. Guy Podjarny's Responsive & Fast (2014) (*http://oreil.ly/1pafMaq*) is a good resource on the subject.

Performance of images on mobile devices, specifically RWD but also native apps, can be addressed in two major ways: (1) send fewer bytes for an image, (2) resize the image dimensions to the displayed size.

Sending resized images isn't a new idea; it's what we've been doing on the Web for a long time. You would see a smaller thumbnail in the search results when searching eBay for comically large shoes, then a larger image when you clicked through to the product detail. Applying this same technique of the right size for the right context, Tim Kadlec found that you could save over 72% of the image bytes (*https://timka dlec.com/2013/06/why-we-need-responsive-images/*) (see Figure C-3). That is, if you were to send a smaller image to a device that had a smaller display, and thus shrunk the image in the layout, you could make your page faster without the user ever knowing the difference. Notably in this research, even desktops benefited from this approach: images are often not correctly sized for *any* display and whatever image is available is thus sent to desktop and mobile alike.

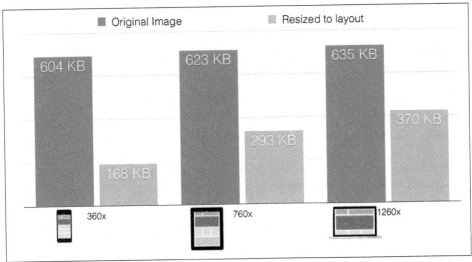

Figure C-3. Responsive images can reduce image weight by 72%

Sending the right image for the right display became the topic of responsive images. Accomplishing this was difficult: you either had to leverage JavaScript and custom HTML attributes or embed your images in CSS and use media queries.

2014 Responsive Images HTML Spec

To simplify this process and to unify the approach, the Responsive Images Community Group proposed an enhancement to the HTML5 specification. After a tumultuous couple of years filled with more drama than a high school student's dating life, a unified voice emerged. The group finalized on adding the `<picture>` element and `<img srcset>` attribute to improve responsive images in HTML. (There's more on this in Chapter 11.)

Chrome was the first browser to ship native support for `<picture>` and `<img srcset>`, and other browsers have followed suit (see Figures C-4 and C-5). For the other browsers or users that have older versions, there is a polyfill by Scott Jehl (*https://github.com/scottjehl/picturefill*).

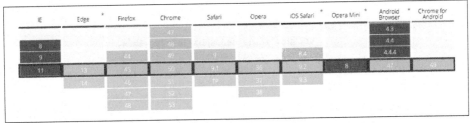

Figure C-4. Browser support for `<img srcset>` from caniuse.com (2016)

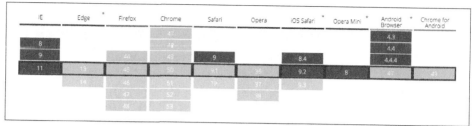

Figure C-5. Browser support for <picture> from caniuse.com (2016)

At this point, your standard RWD website could look something like this (see the discussion in Chapter 9 for selecting the best image resolutions):

```
<script type="text/javascript"
        src="/picturefill-2.1.min.js"></script>

<img src="/fido_in_dc_100.jpg"
        srcset="/fido_in_dc_100.jpg 100w,
                /fido_in_dc_400.jpg 400w,
                /fido_in_dc_800.jpg 800w,
                /fido_in_dc_1000.jpg 1000w,
                /fido_in_dc_1200.jpg 1200w,
                /fido_in_dc_1400.jpg 1400w"
        sizes="(min-width: 500px) 33.3vw, 100vw"
/>
```

This solution specifies multiple versions of the same image in different dimensions using the w notation. Additionally, the sizes attribute is used to give the browser hints.

If you're more adventurous and want to support art direction—that is, changing the orientation or context of the image based on the form factor of the displaying device —you could use the new <picture> element this way:

```
<script type="text/javascript"
        src="/picturefill-2.1.min.js"></script>
<script type="text/javascript">
    // Picture element HTML5 shiv for legacy browsers
    document.createElement( "picture" );
</script>
<picture>
    <!--[if IE 9]><video style="display: none;"><![endif]-->
    <source media="(max-width: 640px)"
            srcset="/fido_headshot_100.jpg 100w,
                    /fido_headshot_200.jpg 200w,
                    /fido_headshot_400.jpg 400w
                    /fido_headshot_800.jpg 800w,
                    /fido_headshot_1000.jpg 1000w" />
    <source media="(max-width: 1024px)"
            srcset="/fido_landscape_800.jpg 800w,
                    /fido_landscape_1000.jpg 1000w,
```

```
                                /fido_landscape_1200.jpg 1200w,
                                /fido_landscape_1400.jpg 1400w" />
   <!--[if IE 9]></video><![endif]-->
   <img src="/fido_in_dc_100.jpg"
        srcset="/fido_in_dc_100.jpg 100w,
                        /fido_in_dc_400.jpg 400w,
                        /fido_in_dc_800.jpg 800w,
                        /fido_in_dc_1000.jpg 1000w,
                        /fido_in_dc_1200.jpg 1200w,
                        /fido_in_dc_1400.jpg 1400w"
             sizes="(min-width: 500px) 33.3vw, 100vw"
     />
   </picture>
```

This is starting to get complex, but you can see the flexibility that `<picture>` provides the web designer. This is truly awesome!

Complicating matters is the introduction of retina or high-pixel-density devices. Apple's introduction of the retina display in the iPhone 4 meant that you could display even larger, richer-quality images on a smaller visual display. For web developers this meant that if you sent a larger image and resized it, the browser would now use the wasted pixels: 1 CSS pixel on a device with a 2x device pixel ratio (DPR) meant that you had 4 pixels on screen (2×2 or 2 high and 2 wide for every CSS pixel). See Figure C-6.

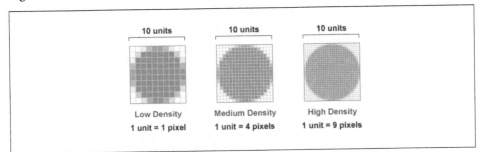

Figure C-6. *Device pixel ratio: 1 CSS pixel = 4 image pixels (2x DPR) = 9 image pixels (3x DPR)*

Fortunately, the `<img srcset>` specification handles this and lets the browser select the right size image for the display, accounting for even high DPR. In the preceding simple example, you can see that while the CSS media query specifies a `max-size` of 640 pixels, the browser can select image sizes larger than 640.

Of course, you will need to generate all these images, maintain them, and back them up. That's a problem for the infrastructure and operations teams! Fortunately for you, we cover this in more detail in Chapter 13.

New Image Formats

At the same time as the responsive images HTML specification Google introduced a new image format called WebP. This new format not only improved the compression over standard JPEG but also merged the capabilities that were only available previously in PNG, such as alpha channels. Support for this new format was quickly introduced into Chrome and Android, covering half the smartphone and desktop user base.

Just as Google was launching WebP in Chrome, Microsoft's Internet Explorer adopted the JPEG eXtended Range (JPEG XR) format, which functionally accomplished the same goals as WebP. Namely, it provided much smaller image sizes with better compression and offered some additional features that were not available in standard JPEG.

In 2013 Apple joined in by supporting a slightly older, but open standard, image format: JPEG 2000. Safari 7 and iOS 7 both introduced full JPEG 2000 support for the web and native apps.

Fortunately, `<picture>` also anticipated this use case with the support of `<source type="image/webp">`. This allows you to support all the different formats in one declaration with the elegance of an elephant in a subway:

```
<script type="text/javascript"
        src="/picturefill-2.1.min.js"></script>
<script type="text/javascript">
    // Picture element HTML5 shiv
    document.createElement( "picture" );
</script>
<picture>
    <!--[if IE 9]><video style="display: none;"><![endif]-->
    <source type="image/webp"
                    srcset="/fido_in_dc_100.webp 100w,
                            /fido_in_dc_400.webp 400w,
                            /fido_in_dc_800.webp 800w,
                            /fido_in_dc_1000.webp 1000w,
                            /fido_in_dc_1200.webp 1200w,
                            /fido_in_dc_1400.webp 1400w" />
    <source type="image/vnd.ms-photo"
                    srcset="/fido_in_dc_100.jxr 100w,
                            /fido_in_dc_400.jxr 400w,
                            /fido_in_dc_800.jxr 800w,
                            /fido_in_dc_1000.jxr 1000w,
                            /fido_in_dc_1200.jxr 1200w,
                            /fido_in_dc_1400.jxr 1400w" />
    <source type="image/jp2"
                    srcset="/fido_in_dc_100.jp2 100w,
                            /fido_in_dc_400.jp2 400w,
                            /fido_in_dc_800.jp2 800w,
```

```
                   /fido_in_dc_1000.jp2 1000w,
                   /fido_in_dc_1200.jp2 1200w,
                   /fido_in_dc_1400.jp2 1400w" />
   <!--[if IE 9]></video><![endif]-->
   <img src="/fido_in_dc_100.jpg"
      srcset="/fido_in_dc_100.jpg 100w,
                   /fido_in_dc_400.jpg 400w,
                   /fido_in_dc_800.jpg 800w,
                   /fido_in_dc_1000.jpg 1000w,
                   /fido_in_dc_1200.jpg 1200w,
                   /fido_in_dc_1400.jpg 1400w"
         sizes="(min-width: 500px) 33.3vw, 100vw"
      />
</picture>
```

How glorious! The browser can select the right size image, for the right display, and even select the right image format.

In order to save trees, I didn't extend this example to include art direction. We'll let you imagine what that looks like. What used to be a simple `<img src>` tag has now become a very unwieldy component of your web pages.

2015: Client Hints and Accepts

Luckily, the lowly `<img>` element doesn't need to be that onerous in your web pages to support all the formats and sizes. A number of techniques have evolved to help simplify the boilerplate HTML and improve image delivery. First, the `Accept` header can be used to let the server decide which format to deliver to the device or browser. Second, Client Hints allows the browser to indicate the display or resource size and the pixel density of the device.

Chrome is the first browser to support Client Hints, but it gives us a glimpse of a future that will look like this:

```
<img src="/fido_in_dc.jpg"
         sizes="(min-width: 500px) 33.3vw, 100vw"
/>

GET /fido_in_dc.jpg HTTP/1.1
HOST: www.example.com
DPR: 2.0
Width: 160
Viewport-Width: 320


HTTP/1.1 200 OK
Content-DPR: 0.5
Very: DPR
```

Of course, we have many challenges ahead to achieve broad support. There is much work to be done.

Index

A

above-the-fold debate, 127
Accept header (HTTP), 245
Accept-CH Client Hint, 229
accessibility, 115, 178, 184
adaptive delivery, 184
additive color creation, 14
Adobe Illustrator
    Effect menu, 100
    height and width attributes, 87
    reducing complexity created by, 104
    SVG Filters option, 101
alpha channels, 21, 34, 213
alt attribute (HTML), 112, 115
ancillary bits (PNG format), 36-38
animation
    animated WebP, 246
    GIF utilities, 309
    GIF89a file format, 32
application markers (JPEG format), 48
arithmetic encoding, 54
art direction, 198-200, 203, 209, 289

B

background images
    background color index (GIF format), 31
    background-image property (CSS), 113
    preload directive, 122
    responsive, 217
backups, 261-264
bash scripts, 290-293
below-the-fold debate, 127
bit depth, 18
bitmaps, 12

Blink-based browsers, 74, 235
bots, 222
BPG (Better Portable Graphics), 123
breakpoints, 244
Brotli, 102
browser image loading
    CSS Object Model (CSSOM), 122
    DOM creation, 116
    DOM preloading, 117, 133
    HTTP/2 prioritization, 121, 128, 158
    inconsistent handling, 121
    networking constraints, 119, 128
    referencing images, 111-115
    service workers and image decoding, 123
browser-specific formats
    benefits of, 73
    drawbacks of, 73
    JPEG 2000, 79-82, 220
    JPEG XR, 77-79
    WebP, 74-77
build systems, 293-297
business logic, 280
butteraugli, 27

C

caches/caching
    cache offload, 256-260
    data URIs and, 175
    domain sharding and, 267
    fixed cache pressure, 163
    IPC impact, 163
    metadata impact, 162
    raster consolidation, 166-177
canvas (SVG format), 86

canvas width/height (GIF format), 30
CDNs (content delivery networks), 258
CGI (computer-generated images), 11
character mapping, 181
chroma subsampling, 51, 80
Chrome Dev Tools
    Timeline Tab, 144
    tracing feature, 145
    USB debugging, 148
chunk data (PNG format), 36
cjpeg, 77
Client Hints Exchange
    concept of, 221
    device characteristics, 235-240
    headers used, 224-233
    informed responses, 224
    initiating, 223
    legacy support, 235-240
    mobile apps and, 233
    opting in and subsequent requests, 223
    overview of, 222
    responsive images using, 217
    vs. responsive images, 221
    selecting the right image, 238
CMS (content management systems), 278
CMYK (cyan, magenta, yellow, and key), 16
codec (coder/decoder), 20
color profiles, 20, 289
color resolution (GIF format), 31
color spaces
    absence of color, 21
    additive vs. subtractive color creation, 14
    CMYK (cyan, magenta, yellow, and key), 16
    color theory basics, 13
    RGB (red, green, blue), 14
    YCbCr model, 16, 50, 66, 152
    YCgCo model, 17, 78
color-tables (GIF format), 30
Compass, 177
compression (see also DCT (Discrete-Cosine
    Transform); image consolidation)
    browser-specific formats, 73
    constraints and considerations for, 20, 65
    encoders/decoders for, 20
    entropy encoding, 24
    generic algorithms for, 23
    image quality comparisons, 25-27, 249
    image-specific, 23
    lossy vs. lossless, 23

LZV (Lempel-Ziv-Welch), 34
    need for, 47
    precompression filtering, 38
    prediction and, 24
    of raster vs. vector images, 23
    of video formats, 25
compromised/contaminated images, 272
CompuServe, 34
cones, 13
containers (JPEG format), 48
content negotiation, 201, 217, 221, 245
Content-DPR Client Hint, 229
convert command (ImageMagick), 283
cookies, 236
copyright information, 280
CRC (Cyclic Redundancy Code), 36
critical chunks (PNG format), 36-38
CSS
    background-image property, 113
    CSS Object Model (CSSOM), 122
    "download and hide" scenario, 201
    filter effects, 98
    render-blocking, 121
    sprites, 166-172
    stylesheets with inlined SVG, 188
currentSrc property (HTML), 217
custom web fonts, 178
CVE (Common Vulnerabilities and Exposures),
    271
cwebp, 77, 294

D

DAMs (digital asset managers), 278
data URIs, 172-177
data-src attribute, 128, 172
DCT (Discrete-Cosine Transform)
    compression levels, 65
    DC and AC components, 57
    dequantization, 66
    methodology, 56
    minimal coding units, 61
    one-dimensional, 57
    quantization, 62
    two-dimensional, 58
    WebP format, 75
    zeroing out coefficients, 65
decoders
    defined, 20
    dequantization, 66

encoding process, 143
GPU (graphics processing unit), 152
image memory pools, 150
JxrDecApp, 79
prediction and, 24
service worker-based, 123
decodeToYUV task, 149
decoding
on lower-powered devices, 150
process of, 144
time in Chrome, 144-149
time in Edge, 149
deferred image loading, 129
defs element (SVG format), 96
delta encoding (filtering), 38
density, 204, 251
dequantization, 66
derivative images, 277
device detection, 216, 236, 247
digital cameras, 11
digital fold, 127
digital image formats
basics of image data representation, 12-22
browser-specific, 73-82
compression techniques, 22-27
JPEG, 47-72
lossless, 29-45
raster, 83, 305
selecting for optimal delivery, 244-247
SVG and vector images, 83-108
digital image loading
in browsers, 111-124
Client Hints Exchange, 221-240
image consolidation, 157-191
image delivery optimization, 241-275
image processing, 143-156
image workflow optimization, 277-300
lazy, 125-141
responsive images, 193-220
digital image tools
EXIF utilities, 310
GIF utilities, 309
GUI utilities, 309
JPEG utilities, 308
PNG utilities, 307
disaster recovery, 261-264
DNS resolutions, 118
DOCTYPE element, 86
documentComplete event, 125

DOM (Document Object Model)
building, 116
CSS Object Model (CSSOM), 122
HTTP/2 prioritization, 121, 128, 158
inconsistent image handling, 121
loadImages function, 132
networking constraints, 119, 128
preloading, 117, 133
service workers and image decoding, 123
domain sharding, 120, 264-270
Downlink Client Hint, 227
"download and hide" scenario, 201, 213
"download and shrink" scenario, 197
DPCM (differential pulse code modulation), 69
DPR (device pixel ratio)
Client Hint header, 225
comparing, 251
dwebp, 77
DWT (Discrete Wavelet Transform), 80
dynamic image servers, 297-300
dyslexic users, 178

E
e-commerce sites, 277, 289
encoders
arithmetic, 54
defined, 20
encoding process, 143
Huffman, 53-56, 68
image quality comparisons, 25-27, 249
JxrEncApp, 79
prediction and, 24, 69
quantization matrices and, 65
entropy encoding, 24, 53-56
event-driven image loading, 132
EXIF (Exchangeable Image File Format)
benefits of, 48
drawbacks of, 49
image-related attacks and, 272
JPEG optimization, 70
orientation data, 289
(see also art direction)
utilities for, 310
EXT4 filesystem, 262

F
Facebook
number of images shared on, 301
optimized object storage system, 264

TinySRGB color profile, 289
user engagement on, 1
FDCT (Forward Discrete-Cosine Transform), 56
feature detection, 216, 236, 247
FFmpeg tool, 33
filtering (delta encoding), 38
filters (SVG format), 97-101
fixed-dimension images, 195
FLIF (Free Lossless Image Format), 123, 220
FOIT (Flash of Invisible Text), 178, 184
foreground images, 114
formats (see digital image formats)
FOUT (Flash of Unstyled Text), 178, 184
frequency domain, 22, 56 (see also DCT (Discrete-Cosine Transform))

G

\<g> element (SVG format), 92
gamma correction, 16, 19
gamut, definition of, 15
GIF (Graphic Interchange Format)
    animated, 32
    background color index, 31
    color resolution, 31
    converting to MP4 files, 33
    data block composition of, 30
    header blocks, 30
    history of, 29
    interlacing feature, 34
    licensing issues surrounding, 34
    logical screen descriptors, 30
    LZW compression, 34
    optional blocks, 32
    pixel aspect ratio, 31
    vs. PNGs, 45
    sort flags, 31
    trailer blocks (3B), 32
    transparent, 33
    true color GIFs, 31
    utilities for, 309
GIF89a file format, 32
global color table flags (GIF format), 30
"good enough" approach, 237
GPU (graphics processing unit), 152
grayscale PNGs, 43
grid (SVG format), 86
GUI utilities, 309
Gulp tasks, 294

GZip, 102

H

Haystack, 264
header blocks (GIF format), 30
height attribute
    HTML, 112
    SVG, 87
hierarchical mode (JPEG format), 69
high-contrast settings, 115
high-resolution screens, 195
HTMLImageElement, 111
HTTP/1.1
    connection reuse in, 160
    content negotiation in, 245
    drawbacks of, 121
    vs. HTTP/2, 268
    lack of prioritization in, 121
HTTP/2 prioritization, 121, 128, 158, 264-270
Huffman encoding, 53-56, 68

I

I-frame encoding, 25
ICC (International Color Consortium), 20
icon fonts, 178-185
IDAT chunk (PNG format), 37
IDCT (Inverse Discrete-Cosine Transform), 56
identify command (ImageMagick), 283
IEND chunk (PNG format), 37
IHDR chunk (PNG format), 37
image breakpoints, 244
image build systems, 293-297
image consolidation
    challenges of small images, 157-165
    eligible content, 190
    vs. HTTP/2, 158
    overview of, 190
    raster images, 166-177
    technique selection, 190
    vector images, 178-189
image data representation
    additive vs. subtractive processes, 14-20
    bitmaps, 12
    color absence, 21
    color profiles, 20
    color spaces, 13
    encoders and decoders for, 20
    frequency domain conversion, 22, 56
    sampling rate and, 12

image delivery optimization
    cache offload, 256-260
    domain sharding, 264-270
    file storage and recovery, 261-264
    image dimensions, 241-244
    image format selection, 244-247
    image quality selection, 247-256
    overview of, 275
    performance budget and breakpoints, 243
    security and, 270-275
    single vs. multiple URLs, 260
image density, 204, 251
image pooling, 152
image processing
    decoding on lower-powered devices, 150
    decoding process, 143
    decoding time in Chrome, 144-149
    decoding time in Edge, 149
    GPU decoding, 152
    image memory pools, 150
    rasterization, 155
image rot, 170
image rotation, 289
    (see also art direction)
image spriting, 152, 166-172, 185-189
image workflow optimization
    business logic and watermarking, 280
    dynamic image servers, 297-300
    for e-commerce sites, 277
    for news sites, 279
    for social media sites, 278
    getting started with, 282
    image build systems, 293-297
    master and derivative images, 277
    using bash scripts, 290-293
    using ImageMagick, 282-289
image-related attacks, 272
ImageMagick
    benefits of, 77, 282
    download and installation, 282
    format conversions in, 283
    identify command, 283
    interlace field, 288
    JPEG 2000 support in, 82
    JPEG XR support, 79
    manual compilation, 283
    profiles field, 289
    project directory creation, 283
    properties field, 288

    quality field, 288
    resolution field, 288
images on demand, 130
"imagetragic", 272
<img defer> tag (HTML), 128
<img> tag (HTML), 112, 116, 128, 311-322
indexed PNGs, 43
inlining images, 172-177
interlacing feature
    GIF format, 34
    PNG vs. GIF formats, 39
IntersectionObserver, 131
intrinsic dimensions, 215
invisible (offscreen) images, 125
IPC (Inter-Process-Communication), 163
ITPC (International Press Telecommunications
    Council), 280
ITU T.81 standard, 47

J

Jailbreakme exploit, 272
JavaScript
    browsers lacking support for, 136
    delayed image display, 116
    device detection with Modernizr, 247
    image objects, 111
    lazy image loading with, 128-132
    task runners written in, 293
JFIF (JPEG File Interchange Format), 48
Joint Photographic Experts Group, 47
JPEG 2000 format, 79-82, 220, 244, 246
JPEG format
    color transformations, 50
    containers, 48
    DCT (Discrete-Cosine Transform), 56-66
    decoding process, 144
    encoding process, 143
    entropy encoding, 53
    file composition, 48
    hierarchical mode, 69
    history of, 47
    vs. JPEG XR format, 78
    lossless mode, 69
    lossless optimization, 70
    lossy optimization, 70
    malware attached to, 279
    markers, 48
    MozJPEG project, 71, 294
    progressive, 66-69, 219

quality loss with repeated quantization, 66
run-length-encoding, 65
subsampling, 51
ubiquitous nature of, 244
utilities for, 308
vs. WebP format, 75
JPEG XR format, 77-79, 244, 246
just-in-time images, 130
JxrEncApp/JxrDecApp, 79
jxrlib, 79

K

Kakadu Software, 82
Key response header (HTTP), 260

L

lazy image loading
  <img> tag and, 128
  "above the fold" first, 129
  browsers lacking JavaScript support, 136
  with data URIs, 173
  determining critical image status, 140
  digital fold and, 127
  event-driven image loading, 132
  IntersectionObserver, 131
  with JavaScript, 128-132
  low-quality image placeholders, 137
  on-demand images, 130
  overview of, 141
  point of, 140
  preloading images, 133
  wasteful image loading, 125, 127
lazyload attribute, 128
length field (PNG format), 35
libwebp, 77
ligatures, 179
loadImages function, 132
loading (see digital image loading)
local color tables (GIF format), 31
logical screen descriptors (GIF format), 30
logographic words, 164
look-ahead parsers, 117
lossless image formats
  GIF, 29-34, 45
  JPEG optimizations, 70
  vs. lossy, 23, 29
  PNG, 34-45
lossless mode (JPEG format), 69
lossy image formats

image quality comparisons, 25-27, 249
JPEG optimization, 70
vs. lossless, 23
quantization and, 66
LQIP (low-quality image placeholders), 137
LZV (Lempel-Ziv-Welch) compression, 34

M

malware, 273, 279
man-in-the-middle attacks, 258, 271
mapped characters, 181
markers (JPEG format), 48
master images, 277
MCUs (minimal coding units), 61, 66
memory pools, 150
meta-viewport element, 155
metadata
  copyright information, 280
  HTML5 data- prefix, 129
  impact on browser cache, 162
  impact on file size, 263
  retaining, 289
middle boxes, 257
mobile devices
  challenges of, 4
  Chrome Dev Tools and tracing for, 147
  client hints and, 233
  image optimization for, 302
  USB debugging, 148
  wasteful image loading on, 125
Modernizr, 247
MozJPEG project, 71, 294
MP4 files, 33, 45
MSE (Mean-Square-Error), 26
multithreaded browsers, 155

N

native apps, 4, 233
networking constraints, 119
new Image() constructor, 111
news sites, 279
Node packages, 294
non-Latin-based content, 178
<noscript> element, 137
NTFS filesystem, 262

O

onload event, 125, 128

OpenJPEG, 82
opj_compress, 82
opj_decompress, 82
optimization (see also image delivery optimization; image workflow optimization)
    creating consensus for, 304
    for different users, 302
    for mobile devices, 302
orientation data, 289

P

PageSpeed, 177
palette-based image formats, 30, 32, 37
parallel downloading, 119, 158, 264
<path> element (SVG format), 90
PCT (Photo Core Transform), 78
performance budgets, 243
photographic images, 11
Photoshop
    ancillary chunks placed by, 37
    Posterize filter, 44
    PSD format, 277
<picture> tag (HTML), 209-213, 244
pixels
    defined, 12
    pixel aspect ratio (GIFs), 31
    pixel density, 204, 251
placeholder images, 133, 137
PLTE chunk (PNG format), 37
PNG (Portable Network Graphics)
    alpha channel support, 213
    ancillary chunks, 37
    ancillary vs. critical chunks, 36
    components of, 35-43
    creation of, 34
    critical chunk types, 37
    delta encoding (filtering), 38
    vs. GIFs, 45
    image formats, 43
    interlacing feature, 39
    PNG signatures, 35
    private bits, 36
    reserved bits, 36
    safe-to-copy bits, 36
    transparent, 44
    utilities for, 307
posterization filters, 44
Precise Mode, 236
precompression filtering, 38

prediction, 24, 69
preload directive, 122
preloading images, 117, 133
preparsers, 117
primary colors, 13
prioritization, 119, 120, 128, 141, 158, 161
private bits (PNG format), 36
professional photography formats, 278
profiles, 20, 289
progressive JPEGs, 66-69, 219, 270
progressive loading, 80
PSD format, 277
PSNR (Peak Signal-to-Noise Ratio), 26

Q

quality
    balancing with user experience, 247
    best practices for, 255
    comparing, 25-27, 249
    gaining team consensus, 254
    image byte size and, 247
    loss with repeated quantization, 66
    quality graph, 248
    quality index, 249, 254
    quality index selection/application, 252
    use cases for, 253
quantization
    DCT matrix, 62
    lossy nature of, 66

R

raster image format
    benefits and drawbacks of, 83
    chart of, 305
    composition of, 83
    compression techniques, 23
    consolidation techniques, 166
    defined, 12
    rasterization, 155
    scaling, 84
RAW format, 277
<rect> element (SVG format), 90
referencing images
    <img> tag, 112
    available techniques, 111
    CSS background-image property, 113
reflow, 113
remote code execution, 272
render-blocking CSS, 121

reserved bits (PNG format), 36
resizing images, 150
resolution switching, 200, 203
Resource Priorities, 128
resource prioritization, 120, 128, 158
responsive images
    <picture> tag, 209-213
    benefits and drawbacks of, 221
    client hints, 217, 221
        (see also Client Hints Exchange)
    currentSrc property, 217
    feature detection and, 216, 236
    file formats, 219
    future of, 217-219
    history of, 194
    intrinsic dimensions and, 215
    polyfills for, 214
    responsive image containers, 220
    Responsive Web Design (RWD), 193
    selection algorithms, 215
    serving different image formats, 213
    srcset w descriptor, 204-209
    srcset x descriptor, 203-204
    syntax mechanisms for, 203
    use cases for, 195-203
retina screens
    image resolution requirements, 196
    progressive JPEGs and, 220
    retina-related blurriness, 194
    sizes value and, 209
    srcset x descriptor, 203
RGB (red, green, blue), 14
RGBA (red, green, blue, alpha), 143, 151
rods, 13
run-length-encoding, 65

S

safe-to-copy bits (PNG format), 36
sampling, 12
Save-Data Client Hint, 228
scrapers, 222
screen readers, 115, 178
<script> tags (HTML), 116
scroll bars, 125, 127
scroll events handling, 131
security, 270-275 (see also TLS (transport layer
    security))
    malware, 273
    man-in-the-middle attacks, 258, 271

    user-submitted images, 273, 279
sizes attribute (HTML), 205
small images
    blocking caused by, 161
    consolidation overview, 190
    CSS sprites and, 166-172
    delivery challenges, 157
    download frequency, 164
    impact on browser cache, 162
    impact on connection pool, 160
    implementing in vector format, 178-189
    logographic words, 164
    TCP latency, 160
social media sites, 278
SOF (Start of Frame) markers, 49
sort flags (GIF format), 31
spatial domain, 22, 56
spectral selection (JPEG format), 68
speculative parsers, 117
sprites (see image spriting)
spriting, 152, 166-172, 185-189
Sprity, 170
src attribute, 128
srcset w descriptor (HTML), 204-209
srcset x descriptor (HTML), 203-204
sRGB color space, 15, 20
SSIM (Structural Similarity), 26, 249
steganography, 272
storage and recovery, 261-264
subsampling (JPEG format), 51
subtractive color creation, 14
successive approximation (JPEG format), 68
SVG (Scalable Vector Graphics)
    <g> (group) element, 92
    <path> element, 90
    <rect> element, 90
    <text> element, 105
    automating optimization, 105-108
    basic shape creation, 90
    CSS stylesheet consolidation, 188
    in data URIs, 173
    defs element, 96
    filters, 97-101
    fundamentals of, 85-89
    grouping shapes together, 92-97
    optimizations for, 102-105
    reducing complexity, 103
    sprites, 185-189
    stack consolidation, 188

symbol element, 96
use element, 94
vector image composition, 84
web font creation, 180
SVGO (SVG Optimizer), 105-108
SW (service workers), 123
symbol element (SVG format), 96

T

T.81 standard, 47
task runners, 293
TCP (transmission control protocol)
    domain sharding and, 264
    efficient connection use, 161
    latency in, 159
    parallel downloading, 158
    preloaders and, 118
    small object delivery, 160
text
    character mapping, 181
    as embedded images, 164
    icon fonts, 178-185
    non-Latin-based content, 178
    typographic ligatures, 179
    web fonts, 180
TIFF (Tagged Image File Format), 277
TinySRGB, 289
TLS (transport layer security)
    handshakes, 118
    middle boxes and, 258
    secure image delivery with, 271
tokenization, 122
tools (see digital image tools)
traces, 145
trailer blocks (GIF format), 32
transformation engines, 271
transparency
    browser-specific formats, 73
    GIF format, 33
    PNG format, 44
true color GIFs, 31
truecolor PNGs, 43
256-color palette, 31
type attribute, 214
type field (PNG format), 36
typographic ligatures, 179

U

Unisys, 34
URLs, single vs. multiple, 260
USB debugging, 148
use element (SVG format), 94
user engagement
    challenges of mobile devices, 4
    enhanced by images, 1
    importance of speed, 5
    increased amount of, 2
User-Agent, 236
user-submitted images, 273, 279

V

variable-dimensions images, 196
Vary header (HTTP), 256-260
vector images (see also SVG (Scalable Vector
    Graphics))
    composition of, 84
    compression techniques for, 23
    consolidation techniques, 178-189
    scaling, 87
video formats, 25
viewBox attribute (SVG format), 87
Viewport-Width header, 224
visual comparison metrics, 25-27, 249
visually impaired users, 115, 178
voice-based actions, 115
VP8 video codec, 74

W

watermarking, 280
web fonts, 178
WebP format, 74-77, 244, 246, 294
width attribute
    HTML, 112
    SVG, 87
Width Client Hint, 226

X

x descriptor, 204

Y

YCbCr model, 16, 50, 66, 152
YCgCo model, 17, 78

About the Authors

Colin Bendell is part of Akamai's CTO Office, where he focuses on web performance. He speaks to global audiences about images, mobile, and web development while also trying to imagine six impossible things before breakfast. Colin has a Masters degree in Business and has worked in a variety of industries, including roles in software development for real estate to managing the Infrastructure and Operations for Cameco, the worlds largest uranium mining company. He is also an accomplished entrepreneur and former owner of KelvinsWheel, an automotive wheel repair shop. His musings and writings can be found at *http://bendell.ca*.

Tim Kadlec (@tkadlec) is a web technology advocate pushing for a faster web at Akamai. He speaks about all things web at conferences around the world, is the author of *Implementing Responsive Design: Building sites for an anywhere, everywhere web* (New Riders 2012), and is co-host of The Path to Performance podcast. You can find him writing about a variety of topics at *http://timkadlec.com*.

Yoav Weiss has been working on mobile web performance for longer than he cares to admit. He takes image bloat on the web as a personal insult, which is why he joined the Responsive Image Community Group and implemented the various responsive images features in Blink and WebKit.

Yoav is now working at Akamai as a Principal Architect, focused on making the web platform faster by adding performance-related features to browsers, as well as working on server-side optimizations.

When he's not writing code, Yoav is probably slapping his bass, mowing the lawn in the French countryside, or playing board games with his family.

Guy Podjarny (*@guypod*) is a web researcher and entrepreneur, constantly aiming to make the web faster and safer. Guy is currently cofounder at Snyk.io, focusing on securing open source code. He was previously CTO at Akamai and founder of Blaze.io (acquired by Akamai). Prior to that, Guy led dev and product for the first web app firewall and security code analyzer. Guy is a frequent conference speaker, the author of *Responsive & Fast* (O'Reilly 2014), and the creator of Mobitest, a mobile performance testing agent.

Nick Doyle is a software developer at Akamai on the Image Manager team, focusing on image transformations and optimizations. Previously, he worked on the Front End Optimization product with Blaze and Akamai, working on optimization development and web performance. Before Blaze, he worked with IBM on their Java Virtual Machine. When not optimizing the internet, Nick makes noise with modular synthesizers; sometimes it even sounds like music.

Mike McCall is a Product Architect at Akamai Technologies' Web Division, focusing on the development and management of image products. Mike has experience in in-depth performance analysis of a variety of environments, ranging from large-scale distributed systems to website end-user experience. He is well-versed in writing scripts or using SQL for data analysis, and more recently using technologies like Hadoop MapReduce and HBase to dig deep into data.

Mike has previous experience in large-scale systems administration on Linux and UNIX platforms and systems administration team management.

Colophon

The animal on the cover of *High Performance Images* is a brown hare (*Lepus europaeus*). It is part of the Leporidae family and can be found in Europe and parts of central and western Asia. It is also known as the European hare.

As with deer, male brown hares are known as bucks and females as does. Both males and females look alike, with body mass ranging between 5.5 and 15 pounds. They are larger than the rabbits they often get confused with, and have head and body lengths between 19 and 30 inches. Another giveaway that they're hares and not rabbits are the black tips on their ears and tails (the ears have an average length of about 4 inches). They are a rustic brown color on their backs and shoulders, with white undersides. In the winter, areas of the head and base of the ears develop white areas as well.

Brown hares are herbivores and eat various grasses and shrubs. With agriculture taking over much of their habitat, though, they are also known to eat farm crops in their foraging groups. In the winter season when grass and shrubs are bare, they will eat the bark of shrubs and buds of fruit trees. They also resort to eating their own pellet feces in order to retain protein and vitamins.

Breeding season for brown hares lasts for more than half the year, from January until August, but it isn't until March and April that females are able to carry more than one fetus to term. Once breeding is in full swing, females will carry around three or more fetuses, with gestation lasting up to 42 days. Females will give birth two to three times per year on average.

Many of the animals on O'Reilly covers are endangered; all of them are important to the world. To learn more about how you can help, go to *animals.oreilly.com*.

The cover image is from *British Quadrupeds*. The cover fonts are URW Typewriter and Guardian Sans. The text font is Adobe Minion Pro; the heading font is Adobe Myriad Condensed; and the code font is Dalton Maag's Ubuntu Mono.

Learn from experts.
Find the answers you need.

Sign up for a **10-day free trial** to get **unlimited access** to all of the content on Safari, including Learning Paths, interactive tutorials, and curated playlists that draw from thousands of ebooks and training videos on a wide range of topics, including data, design, DevOps, management, business—and much more.

Start your free trial at:

oreilly.com/safari

(No credit card required.)

31901060159029